PROPHETS OF A JUST SOCIETY

PROPHETS OF A JUST SOCIETY

JAKE C. MILLER

Novinka Books
New York

Library of Congress Cataloging-in-Publication Data

Miller, Jake C.
Prophets of a just society / Jake C. Miller.
p. cm.
Includes bibliographical references and index.
ISBN 1-59033-733-6.
1. Nonviolence—Case Studies. 2. Social reformers. 3. Social history—20th century. I. Title.

HM1281 .M54 2001
303.6'1—dc21

2001051325

Nova Science Publishers, Inc.
400 Oser Avenue, Suite 1600
Hauppauge, New York 11788
Tele. 631-231-7269 Fax 631-231-8175
E Mail: Novascience@earthlink.net

Printed in the United States of America

CONTENTS

PREFACE

This book was made possible by a grant from the United Negro College Fund Fellowship Program, and a leave of absence by Bethune-Cookman College. It was written for the purpose of enhancing knowledge of nonviolent resistance as a means of resolving social conflicts. Specifically, the book analyses the contributions of Mohandas K. Gandhi, Martin Luther King, Jr., Albert J. Luthuli and Desmond M. Tutu to the nonviolent effort.

The book is dedicated both to those who have sacrificed to advance the cause of peace through nonviolent resistance, and those who continue to advocate its use.

INDIAN TERMS*

Ashram	Religious community, institution or school, place of discipline and service.
Ba	Familiar title for mother in Gujarati. Used as a title of respect for Mrs. Gandhi.
Bapu	Familiar title for father in Gujarati, Used throughout India as a title of respect for Gandhi.
Bhagavad Gita	The Song of the Divine Lord.
Brahmacharya	Continence, sexual self-restraint; literally, conduct that leads one to God.
Gandhiji	A title of respect for Gandhi, the Ji a common suffix of respect corresponding to *sir* or *mister.*
Gujarati	Language spoken in the province of Gujarat, India, where Gandhi was born.
Harijans	A term given by Gandhi to the untouchables.
Hartal	Cessation of work; a form of non-violent demonstration in which all work ceases, shops are closed, etc.
Khaddar (Khadi)	Hand-spun or homespun cloth.
Khilafat	A Pan-Islamic movement in India in response to the deposal of the Sultan of Turkey (who was Caliph of Islam) as a result of Turkey's defeat in World War I.

---

* Terms are from Homer Jack, *The Gandian Reader* (New York: Grove Press, 1956.

Lathi	A long stick, usually made of bamboo, tipped with brass or iron.
Mahatma	Great Soul.
Mussulman	Follower of Islam: frequent Indian spelling of Moslem.
Satyagraha	Truth-force or soul-force; non-violent direct actions; passive resistance; civil disobedience; non-violent non-cooperation.
Satyagrahi	One who practices satyagraha.
Swadeshi	Belonging to, or made in, one's own country; applied to movement for boycott of foreign goods.
Swaraj	Self-government.
Untouchables	Castes or communities which, through ancestry, profession, or custom, are looked upon as impure by orthodox Hindus.

INTRODUCTION

Speak up for those who cannot speak for themselves,
for the rights of all who are destitute.
Speak up and judge fairly;
defend the rights of the poor and needy.
Proverbs 31:8-9

A *just society* is perceived as one that is free of discrimination based upon such arbitrary factors as race, religion, sex, residence, economic status and ethnic affiliation. Since a just society was not obtained during the last Century, its achievement must be a major priority for the current one. In undertaking this ambitious goal, we can profit by the work that was begun by past advocates of social justice. In particular, we can draw inspiration from four leaders who sought to achieve their goals by nonviolent means--Mohandas Gandhi of India, Martin Luther King, Jr. of the United States and Albert Luthuli, and Desmond Tutu of South Africa. In this book, we shall refer to them as *Prophets of a Just Society.*

Why prophets? To many of us the word is identified with great religious leaders of Biblical days, who offered predictions of what was to come, and advocated social change. *Webster Dictionary* suggests several definitions for the word, including "one gifted with more than ordinary spiritual and moral insight," and "an effective or leading spokesman for a cause, doctrine or group." Like the prophets before them, Gandhi, King, Luthuli and Tutu met the criteria associated with the above definitions.

Because prophets are "gifted with more than ordinary spiritual and moral insight," they are ordained for leadership. Isaiah recalled having responded to God's challenge of "whom shall I send as a messenger," by agreeing to go. Likewise, Amos related his experience as thus: "And the Lord took me as I followed the flock, and the Lord said to me, Go, prophesy unto my people Israel." Jeremiah apparently resisted God's call to serve as his spokesperson to the world, citing his youth as the reason for his lack of preparation for the assignment. He was advised, however, to go wherever he was sent, and God would instruct him what to say. Like the Biblical prophets, Gandhi, King, Luthuli, and Tutu could have obtained "success" in fields that were consistent with the status quo, but events of their times convinced them to respond to the call: "Whom shall I send?" In undertaking their campaigns, no doubt, they also had to be reminded constantly that although they were encountering danger, they had no need to fear. In this regard, they could always refer to God's instruction to Ezekiel following his call to prophesy, "Son of dust, don't be afraid of them; don't be frightened even though their threats are sharp and barbed and sting like scorpions. Don't be dismayed by their dark scowls. For remember, they are rebels!"

What were the messages of social justice delivered by the prophets during the Biblical days? Micah warned leaders of Israel that although they were supposed to know right from wrong they hated good and loved evil, they were responsible for leading the people astray, and because of their hatred for justice and love for unfairness, "Jerusalem will be plowed like a field and become a heap of rubble." Isaiah also prophesied against unjust judges who issued unfair laws that caused the poor, the orphans and widows to suffer. He warned them of their impending doom. Amos, taking note of how those in power had abused their authority by trampling the poor and stealing the smallest crumbs by their taxes, fines and usury, warned the leaders that "because they were enemies to everything good and had refused justice to the poor, they would never live in the beautiful stone houses which they were building and would not drink wine from the lush vineyard which they were planting." He advised them that they could be reformed by "hating evil, loving good and remodeling their courts into true halls of justice." According to Amos, God wanted to see "a mighty flood of justice...a torrent of doing good." Ezekiel also offered advice concerning reform. He defined a just man as one who "gives food to the hungry and clothes to those in need and grants loans without interest and stays away from sin and is honest and fair when judging others and obeys my [God's] laws."

Having studied the prophesies of the Old Testament prophets, the question arises as to how similar were they to those of the modern day. In their quest for a just society, Gandhi, King, Luthuli and Tutu sought, primarily, to eliminate racial and ethnic discrimination. Their struggles, however, were not limited to ending these forms of discriminations, but extended to the elimination of injustices of all types. Although there were many 20th Century prophets, we have selected for this analysis four advocates of social change who utilized nonviolent means to accomplish their goals. Gandhi was selected because of his pioneering efforts as a prophet of social justice, and the other three were chosen because of their having achieved international acclaim for their use of Gandhian methods in their struggles against racial discrimination. Except for Gandhi, all were Nobel Peace Laureates.

This book will assess the prophets' preparations for the tasks they assumed, the strategies they utilized, and their encounters with opponents of social change. A major assumption of this study is that the domestic reactions to the respective struggles were greatly influenced by international opinion. The success or failure of the various campaigns for a just society appeared to have been dependent upon the ability of the oppressed to raise the conscience of the international community. Indeed, the struggle to obtain a just society is global in scope.

PART ONE

INTRODUCING THE PROPHETS

Chapter 1

A TRIBUTE TO THE PROPHETS

In honor of his seventieth birthday, Mahatma Gandhi was presented a collection of essays and reflections on his life and work. While numerous tributes are included in the book, perhaps, none stands out as much as that of Dr. Jan C. Smuts, who headed the government of South Africa during Gandhi's stay in that country. The Mahatma was praised as "a great human, with deep sympathy for men of all classes and all races and especially for the underdog." According to his former adversary, Gandhi's "outlook has nothing sectional about it, but is distinguished by the universal and eternal human which is the hallmark of true greatness of spirit."[1]

On the same occasion, Pearl Buck, the distinguished writer, observed that "the name of Gandhi even in his lifetime has passed beyond the meaning of an individual to the meaning of a way of living in our troubled world."[2] While Winston Churchill and other supporters of the status quo condemned "Gandhism" as a form of rebellion, most of the world perceived the term in a more positive sense, defining it as the "doctrine of nonviolence as advocated by Gandhi." Although it was not the Mahatma who originated the idea, it was he who popularized it by utilizing it as an instrument in the resolving of conflicts on a mass scale. By the time of his death in 1948, both friends and foes, alike, were praising his contributions to the achievement of a just society.

---

[1] S. Radhakrishnan (ed.), *Mahatma Gandhi* (London: George Allen Unwin Ltd., 1939), 25.
[2] Radhakrishnan, 63.

Indeed, he was a man of peace. It was ironic, however, that because of politics, he was never presented the prestigious Nobel Peace Prize, which is given annually, as a recognition of effective work in pursuit of international peace. Slightly more than a decade after his death, however, the Nobel Prize Committee, recognized the cause for which he had devoted most of his life by presenting the award to Albert Luthuli for the use of nonviolent resistance in his effort to resolve social conflict. In later years, it also honored Dr. Martin Luther King, Jr. (1964), and Archbishop Desmond Tutu (1984) for similar endeavors.

In 1960, the Nobel Prize Committee, perceiving the danger which racial strife in South Africa posed, selected Albert J. Luthuli to be the recipient of the prestigious award. He was acclaimed for his firm and unswerving leadership of the African National Congress (ANC) during a critical period of South Africa's history. As a leader he allowed nothing to shake him "from the firm resolve, so firmly rooted in his conviction that violence and terror must not be employed" in the struggle to achieve social justice. Luthuli was regarded as a worthy recipient of the award since he was serving as a very appropriate role model for the nonwhites of the country, by not allowing the abuses that he had encountered to incite within him hatred for whites. Gunnar Jahn, chairman of the selection committee, suggested that if the oppressed people of South Africa are to rid themselves of "their humiliation without resorting to violence and terror...it will be above all because of the work of Luthuli, their fearless and incorruptible leader." By his high ethical standards he was perceived as rallying his fellow countrymen to the noble cause. The Chief, as he was affectionately called, was praised as one who had dedicated himself to the pursuit of racial justice, and had undergone suffering to accomplish it, "without bitterness and without allowing hatred and aggression to replace his abiding love of his fellowmen."[3]

The highly esteemed Nobel Peace Prize accorded international recognition to the struggle being led by Luthuli. Among those who supported his nomination were thirty-four members of the Parliament of Sweden, the *Manchester Guardian* and the Congregational Churches of America. Following the announcement of his selection, President Kennedy praised the decision as a "high recognition" of his "past and continuing efforts in the

[3] Frederick W. Haberman (ed.) *Nobel Lectures, Peace, 1951-1970*, (New York: Elsevier Publishing Co., 1979), 216.

cause of justice and the advancement through peaceful means of the brotherhood of man." While Luthuli was acclaimed abroad, such was not the case at home. The South African Government expressed resentment over the presentation of the award--considering it an attempt by the Nobel Committee to embarrass the country. Being aware of criticisms that the Committee was interfering in the internal affairs of a sovereign nation, Gunnar Jahn, its chairman, noted that although the struggle of Luthuli was being "waged within the borders of his country...the issues raised go far beyond them." The Chief was perceived as bringing "a message to all who work and strive to establish respect for human rights both within nations and between nations."[4]

With the presentation of the 1960 award to Luthuli, the Nobel Committee was belatedly recognizing the importance of nonviolent resistance as a legitimate means of resolving social conflict. Once this precedent had been established, it became easier for other human rights advocates to be awarded the distinguished prize in later years.

One of these recipients was Martin Luther King, Jr., who was honored in 1964 for the leadership which he was providing for the nonviolent civil rights movement in the United States. He was praised as "the first person in the Western World" to demonstrate that a campaign for justice could be conducted without violence. The civil rights leader was cited as a pioneer in making brotherly love an integral part of his struggle. According to the Nobel Committee, King never abandoned his faith in the unarmed struggle which he was waging, in spite of the suffering which he had undergone, including imprisonment, bomb attacks, and threats upon his life, and the lives of his family.[5]

In the presentation of the award, Jahn noted the international implication of a struggle being waged within a country. He suggested that King's nonviolent campaign might provide "a ray of hope to other parts of the world, a hope that conflicts between races, nations, and political systems can be resolved; not by fire and sword, but in a spirit of true brotherly love."[6]

In 1984, the Nobel Prize Committee turned, once again, to South Africa for the presentation of its annual peace award. Bishop Desmond M. Tutu, the general secretary of the South African Council of Churches (SACC) was presented the prize for his nonviolent struggle against racism in his homeland.

---

[4] Haberman, 216.
[5] Haberman, 332.
[6] Haberman, 331.

According to the Nobel Committee, the award to the Bishop should be viewed as "a renewed recognition of the courage and heroic patience shown by black South Africans in their use of peaceful means to oppose the apartheid system."[7] Anticipating the criticism that the presentation of the prize to Tutu was "a judgment on the South African apartheid system," Evil Aardvark, chairman of the Nobel Committee, insisted that "the system has judged itself." He contended that "racial discrimination can never be anything but an expression of shameful contempt for humankind," and that to defend its use as a political system is "totally incompatible with human civilization." According to Aarvik, the presentation of the award to Tutu was "an attempt to awaken conscience."[8]

As can be seen from the above, while the Nobel Committee acclaimed Luthuli, King, and Tutu for their personal contributions to peace, it also honored them as symbols of the movements which they led. Generously, the recipients of these awards recognized the important role played by the "unknowns" who participated in their nonviolent campaigns. In accepting the 1960 Nobel Prize, Albert Luthuli, president of the ANC, conceded that his humble contribution was not unique, inasmuch as he was not the initiator of the struggle for human freedom in his homeland. Indeed, Mohandas Gandhi, one of his predecessors in South Africa, had led the fight to secure rights for Indians in that country more than a half century earlier. Luthuli viewed the award as a "democratic declaration of solidarity with those who fight to widen the areas of liberty in Africa." He also considered the honor as "a welcome recognition" of the efforts of Africans during the last half century "to establish, peacefully, a society in which merit and not race, would fix the position of the individual in the life of the nation."[9]

King's acceptance of the award was in a spirit similar to that of Luthuli. He paid tribute to the numerous dedicated, but unheralded members of his "ground crew," whose labor and sacrifices had contributed to his effectiveness as the "pilot" of the civil rights movement in the United States. The Nobel Peace laureate accepted the honor as a trustee of all those who were involved in the struggle to achieve social justice.[10] Since King considered the ground

---

[7] Egil Aarvik, "Presentation of Nobel Peace Prize," Dec. 10, 1984 (New York: Norwegian Information Center).

[8] Aarvik.

[9] Albert J. Luthuli, "Africa and Freedom," *Vital Speeches*, 28: Feb. 15, 1962, 268.

[10] Martin Luther King, Jr., "Acceptance Statement of Nobel Peace Award," Dec.10, 1964, Martin Luther King, Jr. Center for Nonviolent Social Change (MLK/CNSC).

crew as being the rightful recipients of the award, he divided the $54,000 prize money among the Southern Christian Leadership Conference (SCLC), six other civil rights organizations which comprised the Unity Council, and a program designed to further education in the field of nonviolence.[11]

When the Nobel Peace Prize was awarded to Bishop Desmond Tutu in 1984, he accepted it as a representative of his family, the South African Council of Churches, and his fellow South Africans. He praised the efforts of all people who are "committed to the cause of justice, peace and reconciliation."[12]

While this study is designed to focus attention on the role of the individuals who led nonviolent campaigns, it is not intended to minimize the importance of others who participated in the movement. As indicated above, in accepting their awards, the Nobel Peace laureate paid tribute to the organizations and movements that constituted the backbone of their campaigns. The importance of the organizations varied, depending upon the nature of the campaign, and the charisma of the particular leader.

In India, the campaign was highly personalized, with the influence of Gandhi far exceeding that of the Indian National Congress and his supporting ashrams. According to Jawaharlal Nehru, a leading member of Congress, Gandhi "came to represent India to an amazing degree and to express the very spirit of the ancient and tortured land. Almost he was India, and his very failings were Indian failings." Nehru insisted that "a slight to him was hardly a personal matter, it was an insult to the nation."[13] When Gandhi decided to retire from the activities of Congress in 1934, he acknowledged the existence of a "growing and vital difference of outlook". Because of the Indians' exceptional loyalty to him as a person, he did not feel it fair to continue to put an undue strain upon them; thus, he selected to retire from the organization.[14] His withdrawal, however, did not alter the fact that in the eyes of most of his fellow countrymen, he was "India."

Like Gandhi, King's prestige was far greater than that of the Southern Christian Leadership Conference, which he founded. Whatever prestige that organization had, was due largely to the popularity of its charismatic leader.

---

[11] Martin Luther King, Jr., "Statement to the Press," Dec. 17, 1964 MLK/CNSC.

[12] Desmond Tutu, "Nobel Acceptance Remarks," Dec. 10, 1984 (New York: Norwegian Information Center).

[13] Jawaharlal Nehru, *Toward Freedom* (New York: John Day Co., 1942), 313.

[14] D. G. Tendulkar, *Mahatma* (New Delhi: Ministry of Information and Broad-casting, Government of India, 1951), 3: 295.

Indeed, the name of Martin Luther King, Jr. was synonymous with that of the American Civil Rights Movement. He became the one leader with whom the system had to come to terms. Likewise, it was he who usually was condemned by those who opposed the nonviolent efforts to achieve racial equality.

While the campaigns of Gandhi and King were conducted, in many instances, independent of the organizations in which they were associated, the same was not true with the efforts of Albert Luthuli. The latter usually is thought of, and analyzed in terms of his leadership of the African National Congress. In 1982, the editor of the *ANC South African Studies* wrote that in spite of the fact that Luthuli was "a great political personality and leader...his political greatness and organizational achievement cannot be divorced from his organisation and colleagues..." He considered it to be a wrong impression to view the Chief as a "pacifist, or some kind of an apostle of nonviolence." The editor insisted that the policy of nonviolence had been formulated and adopted by the ANC prior to the presidency of Luthuli, and as a man of "unquestionable integrity," he took care to implement them. When, however, "that policy was officially and constitutionally changed, he did not falter."[15]

As general secretary of the South African Council of Churches, and as a major religious leader in the Anglican Church, Archbishop Desmond Tutu has made his voice one of the most respected in the current South African nonviolent struggle. These organizations, however, were not created for the purpose of liberation, as were those associated with Gandhi, King, and Luthuli.

Although Gandhi, King, Luthuli and Tutu were all advocates of nonviolent resistance who built their campaigns around the appeal to the conscience, their strategies tended to differ, based upon the time and place in which each lived, and the nature of the injustice each faced. For Gandhi (1869-1948) his struggle in South Africa was one in which he sought to obtain justice for Indians, who constituted a minority of the population; but in his homeland, his nonviolent campaign was one of a majority seeking to liberate itself from a ruling foreign minority. Thus, in the latter, he had greater leverage than in the former. In the United States, King (1929-1968) led a peaceful revolution to enable African Americans, who constituted a minority, to enjoy rights which had been provided by the Constitution, but were being

[15] *Luthuli Speaks*, Published by Solidarity Committee of the German Democratic Republic in cooperation with United Nations Centre Against Apartheid, 1982, 6-7.

denied. In the case of South Africa, Luthuli (1898-1967) and Tutu (1931-) conducted campaigns to ensure that their fellow-Africans, who constituted the overwhelming majority of the population of South Africa, achieve their basic human rights. Unlike King's struggle in the United States, which had the backing of the Constitution, Luthuli and Tutu waged their campaigns in a country in which the Constitution did not recognize their claims to the rights they sought.

Who were these leaders, and how were they propelled into the struggle for social justice? Mohandas Karamchand Gandhi was born October 2, 1869 in Porbandar, India, the son of Karamchand and Putlibai. The family was "well-to-do," with his father and paternal grandfather having served as prime ministers of the region. While his father's education was rather limited, his rich practical experience enabled him to come to grip with most of the difficult problems that confronted him. Because Karamchand never had an ambition to accumulate wealth, he left little property for his family to inherit. Mohandas' most lasting impression of his mother was that of saintliness, being a woman of deep religious conviction, who took seriously such acts as fasting. Also, he admired her commonsense and her knowledge of public affairs.[16]

Although Mohandas showed an interest in medicine, he was encouraged by his brother to study law. It was suggested that since the prime ministership of Porbander was considered a family possession, a degree in law would better prepare him to assume that position. Likewise, he was advised that study in London would improve his credentials. His uncle, who at that time was the head of the family, objected, fearing that Mohandas might forsake important Indian traditions. Reluctantly, approval was given after the latter's mother had consented. While preparations were being made for the trip to London, Mohandas encountered the opposition of the head of the Modh Bania, the caste in which the Gandhis were members. When his plans were disapproved by him, Mohandas defied the order and sailed for England on September 4, 1888. As a consequence of his action he was ostracized by the caste.[17]

Consistent with his major purpose for going to England, Mohandas pursued the study of law--matriculating at Inner Temple and London University. His stay in the country also enabled him to obtain a better

[16] Mohandas Gandhi, *An Autobiography* (Boston: Beacon Press, 1957), 4-5.
[17] Gandhi, 240.

knowledge of Western culture, and a greater understanding of the Christian religion. After having completed his study of law, Mohandas began his return trip to India on June 12, 1891.

Once he was back in his homeland, Gandhi attempted to practice law, but regarding himself a failure, he sought employment opportunities abroad. Encouraging him in this endeavor was an incident which occurred at the office of a British political agent. Mohandas' elder brother, who had appeared to be next in line for the prime ministership of Porbander, was accused of insulting the agent; therefore, his appointment was placed in jeopardy. When Mohandas appeared to intervene for his brother, he was advised that the offender could seek redress through proper channel. When he persisted, he was told to leave, but he refused, and as a consequence was pushed out of the office by the agent's messenger. This incident, combined with Gandhi's having second thoughts about his career, motivated him to accept an offer by a firm of Porbander Moslems to serve as its representative in South Africa.[18]

During his stay in England and South Africa, Mohandas read many books, and discussed crucial issues with persons of various backgrounds. These experiences were important in later years when he sought ways to redress the evils of society. In the formation of his philosophy of nonviolent resistance, Gandhi borrowed from the *Bhagavad Gita*--the Holy Book of the Hindus--the teachings of Jesus, and the writings of such men as Leo Tolstoy, Henry D. Thoreau, and John Ruskin. The *Bhagavad Gita* was considered to have provided Gandhi with the foundation for his later beliefs. When in need of consolation as he experienced external tragedies, Mohandas often turned to the *Bhagavad Gita* for a ray of light. He read in this Holy Book important concepts relative to nonviolence and self-denial. While accepting most of what he read, he could not bring himself to agree with Hinduism in regard to untouchability. Gandhi challenged Hinduism to purge itself of untouchability, and to remove all distinctions of superiority and inferiority that too often were associated with it.[19]

Gandhi's first experience with Christianity was a very unpleasant one. He was very critical of Christian missionaries, who stood in strategic places in India, "pouring abuse on Hindus and their gods." Gandhi also recalled hearing of an incident in which a Hindu, after having been converted to Christianity

---

[18] Gandhi, 97-101.
[19] Gandhi, 393.

was baptized, and required to eat beef, drink liquor and change to European dress. He did not feel that a religion that perpetrated such acts was worthy of its name.[20] While in England and South Africa, Gandhi began to read the Bible, which for the most part, he found tedious and uninspiring. An exception, however, was the New Testament, which he found to be very impressive-- the "Sermon on the Mount," in particular. According to Vincent Sheean, "the Sermon on the Mount illumined his [Gandhi's] spirit through many decisive years, youthful years at that, and naturally left its imprint upon his character and external action to the end of his days."[21] While Gandhi admired the New Testament, and found the Sermon on the Mount appealing, he rejected "the schemes of salvation that his evangelistic Christian friends presented to him as essential Christianity." According to Horace Alexander, "it was the person of Jesus that caught his imagination, not any ecclesiastical dogma, so he saw no reason to stop calling himself a Hindu or to begin calling himself a Christian."[22]

Gandhi's search for the truth took him beyond the scriptures of major religions to the writings of noted advocates of social justice. Among those whose works were of great value was John Ruskin, a British essayist. The reading of his book, *Unto This Last*, was considered a turning point in the life of Gandhi. Insisting that "what is really desired, under the name of riches is essentially, power over men," Ruskin suggested that "the rich should abstain from luxuries until all, the poorest too, shall have enough." Gandhi was impressed with Ruskin's contention that "a laborer serves his country with his spade just as a man in the middle rank of life serves it with the sword, the pen, or the lancet." As a result of reading Ruskin's book, Gandhi concluded that "the life of labor, that is, the life of the tiller of the soil and the handicraftmen is the life worth living."[23]

Another author whose works contributed to the development of Gandhi's philosophy was Leo Tolstoy. Although born of wealth and ancient title, the latter gave up luxuries of life and adopted a simpler way of living. His book, *The Kingdom of God is Within You*, impressed Gandhi greatly. According to Tolstoy, "A Christian enters into no dispute with his neighbors, he neither

---

[20] Gandhi, 33-34.

[21] Vincent Sheean, *Lead Kindly Light* (New York: Random House, 1949), 45.

[22] Horace Alexander, *Gandhi Through Western Eyes* (Philadelphia: New Society Publishers, 1984), 95.

[23] Louis Fischer, *The Life of Mahatma Gandhi* (New York: Harper & Brothers, Publishers, 1950), 68.

attacks nor uses violence; on the contrary, he suffers himself, without resistance, and by his very attitude toward evil not only sets himself free, but helps to free the world at large from all outward authority."[24] Gandhi's acquaintance with Tolstoy extended beyond that of a familiarization of the writings of the Russian advocate of nonviolence. The two communicated on several occasions during the time Gandhi was waging his struggle against injustice in South Africa. In a letter to him, dated September 7, 1910, Tolstoy described passive resistance as "the teaching of love uncorrupted by false interpretations."[25]

During Gandhi's stay in jail in South Africa, he found Henry Thoreau's essay, "On Civil Disobedience," to be a perfect justification for being imprisoned for a righteous cause. The essayist, making a strong argument for disobeying unjust laws, contended that "under a government which imprisoned any unjustly, the true place for a just man is also a prison." While Gandhi studied Thoreau's essay carefully, he insisted that it was not the source of his development of the philosophy of *satyagraha.* He maintained that his campaign of resistance in South Africa had been launched prior to reading the essay. The title of Thoreau's essay, however, convinced Gandhi to use the term, "civil disobedience" to describe his struggle for English readers.[26]

Martin Luther King, Jr. was born in Atlanta, Georgia, January 15, 1929, the son of Martin Luther King, Sr. and Alberta William King. His father and maternal grandfather, Reverend Albert Daniel Williams were Baptist ministers, both of whom preceded Martin, Jr. as pastor of Ebenezar Baptist Church in Atlanta. His parents and maternal grandparents were instrumental in preparing the younger King for the segregated society in which he would have to live. They instilled within him a strong religious foundations, which aided him greatly in later years.

As his father before him, Martin, Jr. attended Morehouse College--having enrolled there as an early entrant at the age of fifteen. During his four year stay at the college, he became very impressed with President Benjamin Mays, whom he admired because of his commitment to the cause of racial justice. According to King, the " spiritually and intellectually stimulating sermons" of the president were instrumental in causing him to enter the ministry at the age

---

[24] Fischer, 96.
[25] Fischer, 100.
[26] Fischer, 88.

of seventeen. In Mays, King saw how "the ministry could become a respectable force of ideas, even for social protest."[27] While pursuing his degree in sociology, King sought to enhance his preparation for later life by participating in several extracurricular activities, including the Atlanta Intercollegiate Council--an inter-racial student group--which provided him with valuable insights into the thinking of young white Americans.[28]

Following his graduation from Morehouse in 1949, Martin enrolled as a student at Crozer Theological Seminary in Pennsylvania. Being aware of the need to "serve God and humanity from his pulpit," King sought to look beyond the walls of the classroom for his training. He explored means of eliminating social evils by reading various books on philosophy, and attending lectures by outstanding scholars. So impressed was he by a sermon on India by Dr. Mordecai Johnson, President of Howard University, that King read several books about the life and work of Gandhi. In June 1951, he graduated at the top of his class at Crozer with a bachelor of divinity degree, and received a scholarship to the graduate school of his choice--Boston University.

During his stay at Boston University, King continued his study on the role of non-violence in social change. In 1955, he was awarded the doctorate degree, after having completed his dissertation, "A Comparison of the Conception of God in the Thinking of Paul Tillich and Henry Nelson Wieman." By this time he was serving his first ministership as pastor of Dexter Avenue Baptist Church in Montgomery, Alabama--the pulpit from which he launched his civil rights crusade.

Through his formal education, Christian training and personal efforts, King became better acquainted with theories of nonviolence. His reading of Henry David Thoreau's essay, "On Civil Disobedience," better enlightened him on how one could undermine an evil system by refusing to cooperate with it.[29] As indicated earlier, Gandhian philosophy also had a profound effect upon King. He recalled that prior to his reading about Gandhi, he had virtually concluded that the ethics as taught by Jesus applied only to individual relations. He did not perceive the "turn the other cheek " and the "love your enemies" philosophies as being applicable to relationships between groups

---

[27] Stephen Oates, *Let the Trumpet Sound* (New York: Harper & Row Pub-lishers, 1982), 23.
[28] Oates, 21.
[29] Martin Luther King, Jr., *Stride Toward Freedom* (New York: Harper & RowPublishers, 1958), 91.

and nations. After reading Gandhi, he was convinced that they could apply to all relationships.[30]

King's study of Gandhian philosophy caused him to question Rienhold Niebuhr's assertion that pacifism was a sort of passive nonresistance to evil, expressing naive trust in the power of love. Considering this interpretation to be a serious distortion. King suggested that "true pacifism is not nonresistance to evil, but nonviolent resistance to evil." He noted that Gandhi "resisted evil with as much vigor and power as the violent resisters, but he resisted with love instead of hate." While King disagreed with Niebuhr's critique of pacifism, he was influenced in a positive way by certain aspects of his philosophy. King credited the philosopher with having an "extraordinary insight into human nature, especially the behavior of nations and social groups." After having read his works, King continued to believe in man's "potential for good," but he also realized his "potentials for evil."[31]

In his search for a technique to fight social injustice, King also explored the theory of Communism. Based upon his reading, he rejected the "materialistic interpretation of history," seeing no place in it for God. King maintained that "constructive ends can never give absolute moral justification to destructive means, because in the final analysis the end is preexistence in the means." In his rejection of the political totalitarianism identified with Communism, he contended that "man is an end because he is a child of God. Man is not made for the state; the state is made for man." King insisted that "to deprive man of freedom is to relegate him to the status of a thing, rather than elevate him to the status of a person." To him, Communism was an unacceptable means by which to rid the country of social injustice.[32]

King also familiarized himself with the works of Walter Rauschenbusch. His book, *Christianity and the Social Crisis,* provided King "a theological basis for the social concern" which had developed within him as a result of earlier experience. Although Rauschenbusch was perceived as having come close to identifying the kingdom of God with a particular social and economic system, his philosophy was considered very useful since it insisted that "the gospel deals with the whole man, not only his soul but his body; not only his spiritual well-being but his material well-being." King concluded that any religion that claims to be "concerned about the souls of men and is not

[30] King, 96-97.
[31] King, 98-99.
[32] King, 92-93.

concerned about the social and economic conditions that scar the souls of men is a spiritually moribund religion only waiting for the day to be buried."[33] With a philosophy well developed, King launched his campaign against inequality.

Albert J. Luthuli was born in 1898 of South African parents in Rhodesia. His father, John Luthuli, had moved there to serve in the Rhodesian forces during the Matabele Rebellion, and after the task was completed, he remained there as an evangelist and interpreter at the Seventh Day Adventist mission. Albert's mother, Mtonya, was a member of the royal house in Zululand. Following the death of his father, the family returned to South Africa and resided on the farm of a white adherent of the Seventh Day Adventist Church. Because his mother wanted him to secure an education, she sent him back to his home village to live with his uncle, who at that time was chief of Groutville. When his mother returned home, Albert welcomed the opportunity to become a part of her household, once again.

After having completed two years at Oblange Institute, Albert Luthuli transferred to a Methodist institution at Edendale. At the latter, he pursued a two year teacher-training course, and because of the high standards of his teachers, he developed a real love for teaching. Edendale, from which he was temporarily suspended for participation in a boycott over the manner of disciplining, placed heavy emphasis upon "personal responsibilities and the developing of active adult leadership." After he completed his training at that institution he became a principal of the one teacher school in Blaauwosch in the Natal Uplands.

As a teacher, Luthuli differed with those who emphasized the "manual work" concept, being more concerned with the "moulding of the pupil's mind." His philosophy of education led to an encounter with the chief inspector of native education, who was a strong advocate of manual work. The latter once admonished Luthuli that as a teacher he was supposed to be a leader in the community, yet he had failed to devote adequate time to the garden at the school.[34] Luthuli did not conceal his displeasure with the visit. About the same time, a higher teacher-training course was being established at Adams College, and he was recommended to receive funds to attend. Luthuli

---

[33] King, 91.
[34] Albert Luthuli, *Let My People Go* (New York: McGraw-Hill, 1962), 32.

regarded this as a "gift from the Almighty" since he had not applied for the scholarship.

After completing the program at Adams College, Luthuli remained at the institution as a teacher of Zulu and music, and in later years, he taught school organization. By the time he had completed his tour of duty at the college, he had become the supervisor of teachers-in-training of outlying schools, and the college choirmaster. Luthuli recalled that his stay at Adams College "contrived to insulate" them from the outside world of South Africa, not because of restraints placed upon them; instead, because of their busy schedules. In later years, when Luthuli assessed his educational training at Edendale and Adams, he expressed satisfaction with the programs, disagreeing with those who contended that such schools merely trained Blacks to be Englishmen. He insisted that "it was no more necessary for the pupils to become Black Englishmen than it was for the teachers to become White Africans." He envisioned Africans and European cultures as interacting, and each having an impact upon the others; thus, both were enriched. Luthuli noted that at the two institutions in which he attended, he was taught by European mentors, nevertheless, he did not cease to be an African in speech, thought, nor action.[35]

After having taught for seventeen years, Albert Luthuli left the teaching profession to accept the post from which he was to be launched into the struggle for human rights. It was not his dissatisfaction with teaching that caused him to leave his chosen field, but instead, the constant appeal by tribal elders in Groutville for him to return to the village as their chief. For two years they had sought to recruit him, and for two years he had rejected their offer, considering his comparative youth as not having provided him sufficient experience to rule effectively. Luthuli also was aware that the compensation for the job did not compare favorably with that of teaching, a field which he loved. Motivated, however, by the need to serve his community, he consented to the call and assumed office in 1936.

Desmond Mpilo Tutu was born October 7, 1931 in Klerksdorp in the Western Transvaal, the son of Zachariah Tutu, a school teacher and Aletta Tutu, a domestic worker. Although baptized a Methodist, Desmond and his family later converted to the Anglican Church. At the age of twelve, the family moved to Johannesburg, where his mother worked as a cook in a

[35] Luthuli, 31.

missionary school for the blind. It was his experiences there that impressed him of the need to serve the deprived.[36]

After having attended the Johannesburg Bantu High School, Desmond considered studying medicine, but because of the lack of financial means, he decided to prepare for a teaching career. He studied at the Pretoria Bantu Normal College, where he received a teacher's diploma, and in 1954 obtained a Bachelor of Arts degree through the University of South Africa. Following his graduation, he began a teaching career at the Musieville High School in Krugersdorp, but in 1959 he had second thought, therefore, he entered the ministry. He recalled that he was not "moved by very high ideals," but he thought that if the Church would accept him, it might be a very valuable means of performing service. According to Desmond, he was "grabbed by God by the scuff of the neck in order to spread his word, whether it is convenient or not."[37]

In 1959, Desmond pursued ordination training at St. Peter's Theological College in Rosettenville, Johannesburg, and in 1960, after having been ordained as a deacon, began his service in Benomi Location. A year later, he became Father Tutu. His next four years were spent in England where he served the Church while simultaneously furthering his education. He was awarded the Bachelor's degree in 1965 and the Master's degree one year later. Following his graduation, Father Tutu temporarily ended his stay in England and returned to South Africa where he served on the teaching staff of the Federal Theological Seminary in Alice, which is located in the tribal homeland of Ciskei. During the next two years, Tutu taught at the University of Botswana, Lesotho and Swaziland. He returned to England in 1972 and served as associate director of the Theological Education Fund of the World Council of Churches in Bromley, Kent (1972-75).

Back in South Africa, Tutu served as the Anglican Dean of Johannesburg before being consecrated Bishop of Lesotho in 1976. Two years later, he became the first black Secretary-General of the South African Council of Churches, an affiliate of the World Council of Churches, which represented about 13 million Christians--eighty percent of whom were blacks. It was in this role that the Bishop was accorded the necessary international credentials to wage a struggle against apartheid, without fear of receiving the maximum punishment.

[36] "Tutu, Desmond [Mpilo]," *Current Biography Yearbook, 1985,* 418.

As can be seen from the above, the four human rights advocates were prepared educationally to undertake their struggles. Also instilled within each was a strong religious commitment to aid the oppressed. As they launched their campaigns for a just society, they were aware of the pervasiveness of racial discrimination since each had personal encounters with it. Likewise, they were aware of obstacles that they would face in their struggles against injustice, but because they believed in the causes which they advocated they were willing to make the necessary sacrifices. Inspired by prophets who had gone before them, they developed philosophies that enabled them to develop strategies to achieve a just society. Because Gandhi, King, Luthuli, and Tutu were men of exceptional qualities they were able to respond to exceptional situations in an exceptional manner.

[37] *Current Biography,* 419.IIA Guiding Philosophy

Chapter 2

A GUIDING PHILOSOPHY

> Non-violence is a power which can be wielded equally by all--children, young men and women or grown up people, provided they have a living faith in the God of Love and have therefore equal love for all mankind.
>
> Mohandas Gandhi[1]

Being aware of the many ills of society, Gandhi, King, Luthuli, and Tutu developed philosophies that enabled them to wage vigorous campaigns for social change. In view of the strong religious beliefs which they held, it is not surprising that the lessons of the various Holy Books undergirded their philosophies, especially the teachings of Jesus Christ, which influenced all four--even Gandhi, who was not a Christian. Of special importance were lessons from the Sermon on the Mount, including the following passages, "But I say unto you that ye resist not evil, but whosoever shall smite thee on thy right cheek, turn to him the other also;" "Blessed are ye, when men shall revile you and persecute you and shall say all manner of evil against you falsely for my sake;" "...Love your enemies, bless them that curse you, do good to them that hate you, and pray for them which despitefully use you, and persecute you."

---

1 Nirmal K. Bose, *Selections from Gandhi* (Ahmedabad, India: Navajivan Publishing House, 1957), 154.

ACQUIESCENCE, VIOLENCE OR NONVIOLENCE

While the above is indicative of the behavior of a nonviolent person, such behavior, within itself, does not provide a prescription for a successful campaign against injustices of this world. Too often the above philosophy has been used by oppressed people to justify their refusal to act, positively, against those who oppress them. Gandhi rejected such a response, perceiving such persons as acting in a cowardly manner. To him, "meek submission to the will of the evildoers" is unacceptable. He contended that non-violence should be employed as an active force in the struggle to eliminate social injustice. Gandhi maintained that noncooperation with evil is as much a duty as cooperation with good. He suggested that instead of engaging in "passive spirituality," one should be active and "carry war into the enemy's camp."[2]

King also rejected acquiescence, contending that "to accept passively an unjust system is to cooperate with that system," one who does so is perceived as being as evil as the oppressor. King, like Gandhi, whom he admired greatly, and whose philosophy aided him in the formation of his, also considered noncooperation with evil as a moral obligation. He insisted that "to accept injustice or segregation passively is to say to the oppressor that his actions are morally right."[3] Realizing that noncooperation can serve as a destabilizing force in society, King contended that peace and stability which was built upon injustice could not be regarded as true peace and stability. In support of his position, he interpreted Jesus' warning that he had not "come to bring peace, but a sword," as meaning that Jesus had not come to bring a physical sword; instead, to build a positive peace, one of love and justice. True Christians, as he perceived them, precipitate conflict with the old, if the old is based upon injustice.[4]

Luthuli and Tutu also maintained that there could be no compromise between right and wrong. The former did not perceive Christians as standing by idly in a situation that debased "the God-factor in man or to set a limit beyond which the human being" might possibly go. Luthuli considered it unacceptable that Christians could "remain neutral in a situation where the laws of the land virtually criticized God for having created men of colour..."[5]

---

[2] Bose, 159.
[3] King, *Stride Toward Freedom*, 212.
[4] King, 40.
[5] Albert Luthuli, "Africa and Freedom," *Vital Speeches*, 28: Feb. 15, 1962, 268.

Likewise, Tutu rejected the contention that Christians or the Church could be neutral, suggesting that "in a situation of injustice and oppression...Not to choose to oppose, is in fact to have chosen to side with the powerful, with the exploiter, with the oppressor."[6]

It has been suggested that because of the abhorrent nature of racial oppression, one has the obligation to oppose it in any manner which appears to be appropriate. The violent approach was perceived by some as the most practical way in which to wage the struggle against this evil. This approach was rejected by Gandhi, King, Luthuli, and Tutu. In his South African and Indian campaigns, Gandhi resisted efforts of some Indians to turn to guns rather than turning the other cheek. He concluded that "violent non-cooperation only multiplies evil and that can only be sustained by violence."[7]

King also rejected violence as a means of overcoming oppression. He conceded that it may bring about a temporary victory, but he maintained that it will not insure a permanent peace. King credited violence with solving no social problems; instead, creating additional ones and making them more complicated. He insisted that as a means of achieving racial justice, the use of violence was both impractical and immoral. According to King, because of its emphasis upon hatred rather than love, it "destroys community and makes brotherhood impossible." He warned the downtrodden that if they make violence their weapon to fight oppression, they would create for generations to follow "a desolate night of bitterness," and their main legacy will be "an endless reign of meaningless chaos."[8]

Both Luthuli and Tutu were advocates of nonviolence, nevertheless, they were aware of the growing impatience of many of their followers with this approach. The former perceived nonviolent resistance as the only "nonrevolutionary legitimate and humane way" in which an oppressed people could overcome. Luthuli noted that historically, the ANC has pursued such a course in spite of the obstinate stand of the racists of South Africa. As he neared the end of his career, he continued to advocate nonviolence, nevertheless, he expressed an understanding of those "brave just men" who had become disillusioned over the South African response to the quest for

---

6 Desmond Tutu, *Crying in the Wilderness* (Grand Rapids, MI: Eerdmans Publishing Co., 1982), 34.

7 K.P.K. Menon, "The Great Trial," in Homer Jack, *The Gandhi Reader* (NewYork: Grove Press, 1956), 205.

8 King, 213.

racial justice; thus, had turned to violence. Luthuli questioned whether others should condemn them for trying 'to create an organized force to ultimately establish peace and racial harmony."[9] Likewise, Bishop Tutu deplored all forms of violence--both structural and legalized. Nevertheless, he observed that "a people made desperate by despair, injustice and oppression will use desperate means." The Bishop expressed fear that "we may soon reach a point of no return, when events will generate a momentum of their own, when nothing will stop their reaching a bloody denouement which is 'too ghastly to contemplate..."[10]

Having rejected acquiescence and violence, Gandhi, King, Luthuli, and Tutu suggested nonviolent resistance as an acceptable alternative. Although popularized by Gandhi, the doctrine was very consistent with the teaching of Jesus, and the writings of Henry Thoreau. When the Indians became enraged over the injustices, Gandhi suggested the waging of a passive resistance campaign to force the government to relinquish its efforts. Passive resistance, as practiced in South Africa during the campaign and later advocated in Gandhi's "Indian Home Rule," was defined as a means of securing rights thorough personal suffering, rather than through arm resistance. He suggested that by following the first approach, one utilizes "soul force," but in pursuing the latter, he/she makes use of "body-force."[11]

Because the term was often interpreted to mean "a weapon for the weak," and an implied hatred which could be manifested by violence, Gandhi sought a new name for his nonviolent campaign. The name that emerged was that of *Satyagraha*, which is defined as "Truth-force or Soul-force." In the meantime, Gandhi read Henry Thoreau's essay, "On Civil Government," which impressed him; therefore, he chose for an English description of his campaign, the term, "Civil Disobedience." This name did not convey the full meaning of the struggle; therefore, it was later changed to "Civil Resistance."[12]

According to Gandhi, nonviolence is "the most harmless and yet effective way of dealing with the political and economic wrongs of the downtrodden portion of humanity." The following conclusions can be drawn in regard to nonviolence as he perceived it:

---

[9] Albert Luthuli, "Statement following the Rivonia Verdict," June 12, 1964, inThomas Karris and Gwendolen Carter, *From Protest to Challenge, III* (Stanford, CA:Hoover Institution Press, 1977), 799.

[10] Desmond Tutu, *Hope and Suffering* Grand Rapids, MI: Eerdmans Publishing Co., 1983), 32.

[11] M.K. Gandhi, *Indian Home Rule* (Navajivan Publishing House, 1962) Reprint, 79.

[12] M. K. Gandhi, "The Advent of Satyagraha," in Jack, 59-65.

- Non-violence is the law of the human race and is infinitely greater than and superior to brute force.
- In the last resort it does not avail to those who do not possess a living faith in the God of Love.
- Non-violence affords the fullest protection to one's self respect and sense of honour, but not always to possession of land or movable property...Non-violence in the very nature of things is of no assistance in the defence of ill-gotten gains and immoral acts.
- Individuals and nations who would practice non-violence must be prepared to sacrifice their all except honour.
- Non-violence is a power which can be wielded equally by all--children, young men and women or grown up people, provided they have a living faith in the God of Love and have therefore equal love for all mankind.[13]

King also perceived nonviolent resistance as bringing together the best qualities of acquiescence and violence. He suggested that like those who acquiesce, the nonviolent resisters believe that no individual or group need submit to any wrong, nor need anyone resort to violence in order to right a wrong." In preferring this approach, King envisioned a means by which African-Americans could "rise to the noble height of opposing the unjust system while loving the perpetrators of the system."[14] When applied to the American race problem, nonviolent resistance was perceived as enabling African-Americans to remain in the South and struggle to make it a better place in which to live, rather than runaway from the problem by migrating to other sections of the country. By using the non-violent method of fighting injustices in the South, King envisioned African-Americans as making a "lasting contribution to the moral strength of the nation." While simultaneously setting a "sublime example of courage for generations yet unborn."[15]

Nonviolent resistance denotes the opposing of evil, without the use of violence. Jesus instructed us to resist evil and to ally ourselves with right and just causes. We can do this by helping to alleviate suffering, both by refusing

[13] Bose, 154.
[14] King, 213-214.
[15] King, 214.

to join those who are oppressors, and by waging an active battle against unjust situations. Jesus was aware of our inability to cope with evil forces that in physical strength were stronger than we; therefore, he suggested a method by which a struggle could be waged successfully. We were advised that "whosoever shall smite thee on thy right cheek, turn to him the other also."

ANALYSIS OF NONVIOLENT RESISTANCE

Martin Luther King, Jr. identified the following characteristics of nonviolent resistance:

- It is not a method utilized by cowards.
- It does not seek to defeat or humiliate the opponents, but to win his friendship and understanding.
- Its attack is directed against forces of evil rather than against persons who happen to be doing evil.
- Its adherents are willing to accept suffering without retaliation.
- It avoids not only external physical violence but also internal violence of spirit.
- It is based on the conviction that the universe is on the side of justice.[16]

By pursuing the "turn the other cheek" approach as suggested by Jesus, one has to be courageous. King contended that "if one uses this method because he is afraid or merely because he lacks the instruments of violence, he is not truly nonviolent."[17] Smith and Zepp interpreted King as meaning that "moral merit and power may be attributed only to one who has the strength and desire to be violent but who nevertheless demonstrates free choice by electing to be nonviolent."[18]

Earlier, Gandhi, while maintaining that "nonviolence is infinitely superior to violence," insisted that if a choice had to be made between cowardice and violence," he would recommend the latter. He expressed a preference for India

[16] King, 102-107.
[17] King, 102.
[18] Kenneth L. Smith and Ira G. Zepp, Jr., *Search for the Beloved Community* (Valley Forge, PA: Judson Press, 1974), 58.

resorting to arms in defense of her honour rather than act in a cowardly manner, and "become or remain a helpless witness to her own dishonour."[19]

In imploring his fellow countrymen to be courageous and to continue their struggle for the realization of a glorious and democratic South Africa, Luthuli paraphrased a Biblical statement which advised that "all those who are cowards, all those who run away from the struggle...they shall not be able to reach that Glorious place." To him, cowards and evildoers were linked together.[20]

In later years, Tutu emphasized a similar theme, suggesting that the struggle for liberation can be won only if good people take a stand. He challenged his followers not to be apathetic and lacking in courage, contending that the government is abusive only because good people refused to stand up and be counted. To him, being a Christian meant having the courage to identify oneself with the cause of the oppressed, realizing that being a servant of God requires suffering.[21]

As suggested, a nonviolent resister was perceived as one who seeks not to destroy or humiliate the opponent, instead, to win his/her friendship and understanding. Gandhi viewed such persons not as braggers or bluffers; but as individuals seeking to convert others to their ways through humility rather than acts of violence. According to the Mahatma, a non-cooperationist "allows his solid action to speak for his creed. His strength lies in his reliance upon the correctness of his position. And the conviction of it grows most in his opponent when he least interposes his speech between his action and his opponent."[22] As Gandhi perceived it, it was the accomplishment of the deed that was important, and not the victor or the loser. He believed that the less one boasted about his "victory", the more likely it was to achieve reconciliation in the end.

For King, nonviolence was "a way of humility and self restraint." He contended that in the effort to obtain freedom, we should not "try to leap from a position of disadvantage to one of advantage; thus subverting justice." The civil rights leader suggested that "our aim must never be to defeat or humiliate the white man." and we should not "become victimized with a philosophy of

---

[19] Bose, 162.
[20] Albert Luthuli, "Freedom is the Apex," in Karis and Carter, 463.
[21] Tutu, *Hope and Suffering*, 32-33.
[22] M.K. Gandhi, "The Need for Humility," *Young India*, Dec, 1, 1921.

black supremacy."[23] He did not envision a society in which democracy would be substituted by tyranny. Consistent with his belief, King insisted that the major objective in his various campaigns was not to win victory, but to achieve justice and reconciliation; therefore, he displayed humility after having achieved significant goals.

In waging his liberation struggle in South Africa, Luthuli expressed a similar opinion, suggesting that "what we have aimed to do in South Africa is to bring the white man to his senses, not slaughter him." According to Luthuli, "our desire has been that he should cooperate with us, and we with him."[24] In speech after speech, he contended that they were not seeking to drive whites out of Africa, but to bring about a system where all races could share in the political and economic life of the nation.

Approximately two decades later, Archbishop Tutu repeated Luthuli's assurance to whites of South Africa that blacks were not seeking to drive them into the sea; instead, to bring about political powersharing "in an orderly fashion, rather than seeing this come about through bloodshed and chaos where you [whites] will stand to lose everything." Tutu appealed to white political leaders to understand the plight of blacks and to seek reconciliation before it was too late.[25]

Advocates of nonviolent resistance also insisted upon making a distinction between evil and those who are the doers of evil. According to Gandhi "A *satyagrahi* must never forget the distinction between evil and the evil-doer. He must not harbor ill will or bitterness against the latter." Even the use of needless offensive language against a perceived evil person was not permitted.[26] Gandhi's contention was that all evil could be transformed into goodness; thus the *Satyagrahi* should seek to destroy the evil system, but the major goal should be to convert the evil-doers to ways of righteousness. In his various civil disobedience campaigns, Gandhi found it possible to maintain good relations with the government, while opposing evil measures undertaken by it. Such was the case in South Africa where he led demonstrations against anti-Indian policies, but terminated them when the government was threatened with other crisis situations. Likewise, in India, his various actions indicated that he drew a distinction between the British viceroy and other officials, on

---

[23] King, *Stride Toward Freedom*, 220-221.
[24] Luthuli, *Let My People Go*, 113.
[25] Tutu, *Crying in the Wilderness*, 44-45.
[26] Bose, 156.

the one hand, and the "evil system", on the other. In a letter to Lord Irwin in 1930, Gandhi expressed the view that although the British rule was a curse to India, he did not intend to harm any Englishman or his/her legitimate interest. He acknowledged that many Englishmen were among his best friends. Gandhi attributed his knowledge of the evil of British rule "to the writings of frank and courageous Englishmen who have not hesitated to tell the unpalatable truth about that rule."[27]

Like Gandhi, King frequently warned his followers that it was the evil, not "the person victimized by evil, that nonviolent resisters seek to defeat. In the struggle against racial oppression, he maintained, one should not view the basic tension as existing between races, but "between justice and injustice, between the forces of light and the forces of darkness. In such a conflict, he contended, there could be no victory of blacks over whites; instead, "a victory for justice and the forces of light." According to King, the goal should always be to "defeat injustice and not white persons who may be unjust."[28]

Albert Luthuli's views were similar to those of Gandhi and King. While he did not consider the South African political system, within itself to be evil, he did perceive it as having been converted into a Fascist state by the ruling Nationalist Party. He regarded the existing government as being both "undemocratic and unSouth African."[29] Luthuli sought to remove the evils which had been perpetrated by the Nationalist Party, and to build "a democracy which shall provide for a partnership in the Government of the Union of South Africa within the present framework of the Union." It was not his objective to exclude the white ruling minority from the political system, but since the process would be democratic, their racist views would not be translated into governmental policies. Considering that there were many good and decent Afrikaners who had been "brainwashed" by the advocates of apartheid, Luthuli condemned the policies of the latter, which he regarded as being evil, and not those who had adhered to the policies.

As a minister of the Gospel, Archbishop Tutu constantly preached that it was the evil rather than the doer of evil that had to be destroyed. Even in the worst people, he believed that there was some good; therefore, his campaign, like those of other advocates of nonviolence, was designed to convert the misinformed to rightful thinking. Although Tutu condemned apartheid as one

---

[27] *Collective Works of Mahatma Gandhi*, XLIII, 2-3.
[28] King, 102-103.
[29] Albert Luthuli, "Presidential Address," Dec. 18, 1953, in Karis and Carter, 119

of the most evil systems of the world, he did not hold a similar hatred for John Vorster, who as prime minister, was the major enforcer of the despised racist policy. In a letter, dated May 6, 1976, Tutu viewed him as possessing characteristics similar to his--being “a loving and caring father and husband,” a human person, gloriously created in the image of the self-same God, as a Christian, and as “a member of a race that has known what it has meant in frustration and hurt, in agony and humiliation, to be a subject people.” Tutu also recognized that he and the Prime Minister were both committed to “real reconciliation with justice for all, and to peaceful change to a more just and open society...”[30]

Another characteristic of a nonviolent resister is his/her willingness to accept suffering without retaliation. According to Gandhi, in order to accomplish an important feat, not only is it necessary to “satisfy the reason, you must move the heart also.” He suggested that “the appeal of reason is more to the head but the penetration of the heart comes from suffering.” The Mahatma concluded that “suffering is the badge of the human race, not the sword;”[31] thus, throughout his career, unearned suffering was his most important weapon in his fight against injustice. Constantly, he warned his follower of the difficulty that they would encounter in their efforts to pursue nonviolence, and urged only those who were fully prepared to embark upon such a course. On several occasions, it became necessary for Gandhi to terminate civil disobedient campaigns because of the resort to violence by some Indians who preferred to endure no more suffering. His personal suffering included fasting and imprisonment, and typical of the extreme suffering which his followers endured were the mass slaughter at Jallianwala Bagh (See p. 64), and the unmerciful beating and slaughtering at the salt depots at Dharsana (See p. 71).

King maintained a belief similar to that of Gandhi, insisting that “the nonviolent resister is willing to accept violence, if necessary, but never inflict it.” He advised that “the way to nonviolence means a willingness to suffer and sacrifice.” According to King if the suffering results in death, that is “the price that a man must pay to free his children and his white brethren from a permanent death of the spirit, then nothing could be more redemptive.”[32]

---

[30] Tutu, *Hope and Suffering*, 28-30.
[31] Bose, 154.
[32] King, 216.

James P. Hanigan, in his assessment of King's view on suffering, interpreted him as saying that: the suffering servant suffers because of his or her service, because of fidelity to a personal calling and freely accepted responsibility; the servant is not of service simply by suffering. The suffering is a consequence of a steadfast loyalty to the work God has summoned the servant to do.[33]

In pursuit of racial justice in South Africa, Luthuli warned that "it is inevitable that in working for Freedom some individuals and some families must take the lead and suffer." He suggested that "the road to freedom is via the cross." Luthuli realized that his future was an uncertain one, and he might be faced with "ridicule, imprisonment, concentration camp, flogging, banishment and even death." His prayer was that God would give him the strength to endure such suffering; therefore, contribute to making his beloved country " a true democracy and a true union in form and spirit of all the communities in the land."[34]

Archbishop Tutu warned his followers that liberation is a costly process, and that before reaching the promised land, many will be banned, detained without trial, die in detention, and sent into exile. These hardships, however, should not prevent nonviolent resisters from striving to achieve social justice, he challenged. The Archbishop reminded them of the example of Jesus, who suffered and died for a cause, and who advised others that "if the world hates you, it hated me first..." He expressed a determination to continue the struggle to achieve a just society, in spite of the efforts of the government and perpetrators of oppression to inflict undue suffering upon him and his followers.[35]

The fifth characteristic of nonviolent resisters was the avoiding of both external and internal violence. To Gandhi, nonviolence could not be a "potent force" if only used in outward relations. He insisted that it must be accompanied by an inward peace that comes with love. According to the Mahatma: "If we bear malice and hatred in our bosoms and pretend not to retaliate, it must recoil upon us and lead to our destruction. For abstention from mere bodily violence not to be injurious, it is at least necessary not to

[33] James P. Hanigan, *Martin Luther King, Jr. and the Foundation of Non-violence* (Latham, MD: University Press of America), 270.

[34] Luthuli, *Let My People Go*, 238.

[35] Tutu, 188-189.

entertain hatred if we cannot generate active love."[36] "Love" was regarded by Gandhi as the major ingredient in any effective nonviolent resistance campaign. He perceived it as being a very attractive force, which in turn, could generate more love. Gandhi suggested that in the fight against injustice, "having flung aside the sword, there is nothing except the cup of love" which he can offer to his opponent, and by offering that cup they can be drawn closer to him.[37]

A similar view was expressed by King, who maintained that a resister must not only refrain from the use of physical violence against his opponents, but must also bear whatever suffering he is forced to endure without hate. He recalled the Biblical admonition of "Love your enemies, bless them that curse you." In advising his followers to love their enemies, King made a distinction between types of love. He considered it nonsense," to urge men to love their oppressors in an affectionate sense," but he advised them to show an understanding of their plight and to demonstrate a "redeeming good will" toward them. King perceived this love as meaning "a willingness to forgive, not seven times, but seventy times seven." The civil rights leader suggested that "since the white man's personality is greatly distorted by segregation, and his soul is greatly scarred, he needs the love of the Negro." King suggested "the Negro must love the white man, because the white man needs his love to remove his tensions, insecurities, and fears."[38]

Being deeply committed to Christian principles, Luthuli and Tutu placed heavy emphasis on "love" as a component of nonviolent resistance. Like Gandhi, and King, they were willing to forgive their oppressors, since they regarded hatred as imposing upon them an additional burden. In the new South Africa, Luthuli and Tutu did not envision the emancipated blacks as seeking revenge from their former white oppressors. In contrast, they perceived them as working cooperatively with their former enemies to build a just society based upon reconciliation.

Advocates of nonviolent resistance also perceived it as being based on the belief that the universe is on the side of justice. It was their conviction that the world was inhabited, basically, by good people, who in the end, would recognize the struggle against injustice as being a worthy cause; thus, would side with the oppressed. From the outset, Gandhi was very certain of the

---

[36] Bose, 161.
[37] Bose, 157-158.
[38] King, 105.

triumph of his campaign, since he considered it to be divinely inspired. To him, nonviolence, which he considered as the logical response to the world's weariness of hatred, was based on a "living faith in the God of love." Having rejected brute force, which had been used for thousands of years, and which had only caused misery to humankind, he envisioned India as making a valuable contribution to the world by delivering to it the "message of nonviolence."[39] Gandhi was confident that in the end, love, as exemplified in nonviolence, will triumph over hatred, and the violence associated with it.

King, also, contended that because of the belief that the universe was on the side of justice, "nonviolent resisters can accept suffering without retaliation," since they perceived themselves as having "cosmic companionship." He expressed the belief that "there is a creative force in the universe that works to bring the disconnected aspect of reality into a harmonious whole."[40] As a strong believer in God, King was convinced that because God was on the side of the oppressed, they would be victorious in the end. By the use of such weapons as love, understanding, goodwill, and nonviolence, Black Americans were perceived as conveying to the world, God's warning that "all who take the sword will perish by the sword."[41]

Similarly, Luthuli considered his struggle against injustice in South Africa as having been ordained by God. He contended that "a man is not whole if he is deprived of participating in some aspects of life." He did not believe it to be the intent that blacks of South Africa should be lopsided.[42] Luthuli expressed the belief that an increasing number of South Africans regardless of color will consider the cause of the blacks to be just. He viewed the plight of blacks as being a "human cause...a divine cause." According to Luthuli, South Africa cannot continue to be isolated from the rest of the world, which generally favor democracy. Because this is what blacks seek, eventually the world would say, "we stand for this cause."[43]

According to Desmond Tutu, "it is part of God's mission and purpose for his world to bring about wholeness, justice, good health, righteousness, peace, and harmony and reconciliation. These are what belong to the Kingdom of God, and we are his agents to work with him as His partners to bring to pass

---

[39] M. K. Gandhi, *Non-Violence in Peace and War* (Ahmedabad: Navajivan Publishing House, 1962), Reprint, I, 119.
[40] King, 107.
[41] King, 224.
[42] Albert Luthuli, "Freedom is the Apex," in Karis and Carter, 459-460.
[43] Luthuli, 460.

all that God wants for His universe." He felt that injustice, exploitation and oppression will eventually be uprooted by God. Tutu perceived the people as being "involved with God in His activity to set us all free from all that enslaves us, from all that makes us less than what he intended us to be."[44]

Nonviolent resistance as interpreted by Gandhi, King, Luthuli, and Tutu can best be summarized as an attempt by courageous fighters to obtain social justice by use of non-violent means to convince opponents of the rightness of their cause, not by defeat and humiliation, but by an appeal to their conscience. In this endeavor, prophets of social justice willingly accepted suffering without retaliation since they believed that, in the end, the cause of justice would triumph.

The Civil Disobedience Component

A major instrument of nonviolent resistance is civil disobedience--the breaking of unjust laws, and the willingness to suffer the consequence of such action. In his essay, "Civil Disobedience," Henry David Thoreau suggested that "under a government that imprisons any unjustly, the true place for a just man is also a prison." In later years, advocates of social justice, finding inspiration in the essay, sought to follow his advice. Gandhi, King, Luthuli, and Tutu--all have been arrested for their struggles in behalf of those who were unjustly treated in society.

In rejecting the contention that laws should be obeyed because they were adopted by the government, Gandhi maintained that, historically, "people disregarded those laws they did not like and suffered the penalties for their breach." The mahatma did not consider it to be a characteristic of humanity for one to obey laws that he/she regarded as repugnant to his/her conscience. He suggested that such teaching is opposed to religion and means slavery. Gandhi contended that man-made laws are not binding on us, and since the government realizes this, it instituted penalties for those who fail to obey them. He observed that too often we feel that it is our duty both to the government and to our religion to obey laws even though they are unjust, but he advised that "if man will only realize that it is unmanly to obey laws that are unjust, no man's tyranny will enslave him." He rejected the contention that an act of a majority binds a minority, suggesting that there have been

[44] Tutu, 178.

numerous occasions in which the minority has been found to be right. According to Gandhi, those who do not feel obligated to obey laws that are repugnant to their conscience, there is only "the remedy of passive resistance, since any other course would be disastrous."[45]

King's best known defense of civil disobedience was presented in his "Letter From Birmingham Jail." In reply to the question as to how could he advocate breaking some laws and obeying others, he pointed out that "just laws" should be obeyed, while "unjust laws" should be disobeyed. King defined a just law as "a man-made code that squares with the moral law or the law of God," and an unjust law as "a code that is out of harmony with the moral law." He further characterized a just law as one that "uplifts human personality," while an unjust law, "degrades human personality. According to King, "all segregation statutes are unjust because segregation distorts the soul and damages the personality." He perceived it as giving to the segregator "a false sense of superiority and the segregated a false sense of inferiority." In response to the original question as to how could he advise the obeying of some laws and the disobeying of others, he suggested that he could urge others to "obey the 1954 decision of the Supreme Court, for it is morally right," while urging them "to disobey segregation ordinances for they are morally wrong." For one who participates in civil disobedience campaigns, much is expected; thus, King cautioned his followers that "one who breaks an unjust law must do so openly, lovingly, and with a willingness to accept the penalty." According to the civil rights leader, "...an individual who breaks a law that conscience tells him is unjust and who willingly accepts the penalty of imprisonment in order to arouse the conscience of the community over its injustice, is in reality expressing the highest respect for law."[46]

Noting that "contrary to the plan and purpose of God," the South African Government had acted arrogantly in its attempt to assign blacks to "positions of permanent inferiority" in their own country, Luthuli insisted that they have "all the human and moral rights to resist laws and policies which create a climate inimical to the full development of our human personalities as individuals, and our development as a people." Because the apartheid laws were inconsistent with the full development of blacks, he called upon them and South Africans of all walks of life to use civil disobedience to oppose the

---

[45] Mohandas Gandhi, *An Autobiography* (Boston: Beacon Press, 1957), 80-81.

[46] Martin Luther King, *Why We Can't Wait* (New York: Harper and Row Publishers, 1967), Ch. V.

attempt to deprive blacks of their human dignity.[47] According to Luthuli, "the target of the campaign was unjust, oppressive laws," which he recommended that Africans disobey, and suffer the consequences without resorting to violence. He admitted that he was engaged in activities designed to enhance the policies of the ANC since it was the only way available to show opposition to laws without a moral basis. Luthuli described the motives of his followers as being political, and designed to highlight the African plight and their "refusal to consent to being governed by criminal laws." Luthuli contended that "our hope is that white people will look into our grievances, take us seriously, realize that we are serious about this." He insisted that the Defiance Campaign that he organized was "a political demonstration against discriminatory laws."[48]

Archbishop Tutu also rejected the contention that because something is legally right, it is automatically morally right. He challenged the assumption that because laws were adopted by the government, Christians were obligated to obey them, suggesting, instead, that it is God, whom we should obey and not man. Apartheid laws were regarded by the Archbishop as being "not only unjust, but totally immoral and totally unChristian," therefore, he advised against compliance with them. According to Tutu, when the state acts in a proper manner, it deserves to be obeyed, but he insisted that "when it exceeds its bounds, when it wants to claim what belongs to God for itself, then it is a religious duty to condemn this abuse of power..."[49] Consistent with the words of Jesus that one should "render unto Caesar the things that are Caesar's and to God the things that are God's," Tutu maintained that laws that have been passed by the people in a democratic manner, and are just should be obeyed. Tutu rejected the notion that apartheid would ever be acceptable, noting that "it is an evil system and it is at variance with the gospel of Jesus Christ." He cited this as his reason for opposing it and refusing to compromise with it.[50]

In India, the United States, and South Africa, there were opponents of racial injustice who sought to participate in campaigns of civil disobedience, but because of their violent-oriented attitudes, were not ready for such peaceful pursuits. One of the prerequisites for civil disobedience that was laid down by Gandhi was that participants must be persons who previously had

---

[47] Albert Luthuli, "Resist Apartheid," address delivered July 11, 1954, in Karisand Carter, 132.
[48] Luthuli, *Let My People Go*, 121.
[49] Tutu, *Crying in the Wilderness*, 54.
[50] Tutu, 54-55.

"rendered a willing and respectful obedience to the state laws." He insisted that only after a person had been obedient to the general laws of society that he was able "to judge as to which particular rules are good and just."[51]

While there were many who gave lip-service to the doctrine of nonviolence, fewer were willing to undergo the suffering that was involved in its implementation. Although it was easy to talk about replacing hatred with love, some protesters were not able to meet the challenge when they came face to face with grave provocation. Thus, in order to ensure the success of civil disobedience as a weapon, it was necessary to prepare would-be-protesters for the difficult role in which they were expected to play. Self purification was regarded as very essential in this process.

Fasting, praying, and meditating were vital components of Gandhi's campaign for nonviolent resistance. He perceived fasting and similar acts of discipline as means of self-restraint, but he insisted that "if physical fasting is not accompanied by mental fasting it is bound to end in hypocrisy and disaster."[52] While Gandhi viewed the fast as playing a major role in the process of self purification, he was aware that it could be misused or misinterpreted. Thus, he cautioned his followers that it was not to be utilized as a weapon against their enemies, but rather as a means of strengthening their own resolve. During his campaign for social justice, the term, "Gandhian method" was perceived by many as meaning fasting for a just cause.

As Gandhi viewed it, once a would-be-protester had undergone the process of self purification, then--and only then--is he prepared to take a pledge to engage in civil disobedience. He warned, however, that the act of pledging should not be taken lightly. According to Gandhi, when a person takes an oath "in the name of that God or with Him as witness is not something to be trifled with," When one violates such a pledge he becomes guilty before God and man. Gandhi maintained that a man, "who deliberately and intelligently takes a pledge and then breaks it, forfeits his manhood."[53]

King also considered self purification as a necessary prerequisite for civil disobedience and other nonviolent resistance campaigns. Would-be-participants were expected to meditate and pray in order that they could obtain the necessary strength to encounter the abuse that would be inflicted upon them without resorting to retaliation. They were advised to search their hearts

[51] M.K. Gandhi, "A Himalayan Miscalculation," in Jack, 187.
[52] Gandhi, *An Autobiography*, 332.
[53] M. K. Gandhi, "The Advent of Satyagraha," in Jack, 62.

for answers to such questions as: are we able "to accept blows without retaliating?" and are we able to "endure the ordeal of jail?" Workshops were perceived as necessary to facilitate the preparation for civil disobedience. Likewise, mass meetings were regarded as essential since they provided opportunities for singing and praying together; thus, binding protesters and giving them collective courage.[54]

Luthuli and Tutu also regarded spiritual preparations as essential in conducting successful campaigns against unjust situations.

CONSTRUCTIVE PURSUITS

In his campaign for a better India, Gandhi insisted that the people had a right and obligation to refuse cooperation with a government that was immoral and unjust. He expressed the belief that non-cooperation could be implemented more effectively, if Indians, simultaneously, developed alternatives to the evil system; therefore, he suggested a broad range of constructive pursuits, including: the achievement of communal unity, the removal of untouchability, the prohibition of the use of intoxicants, the introduction of village industries, the implementation of the Khadi program (See below), the improvement of health standards, the revision of the educational system, and the achievement of economic equalities.

In order to achieve the unity that would bring about the true independence of India, Gandhi suggested the cultivation of "personal friendship with persons representing faiths other than his own" as essential. Likewise, he believed that "every Hindu had to make common cause" with the untouchables, and "befriend them in their awful isolation." Not only was religious hostility viewed as an obstacle to a free India, but also the curse of intoxicants and narcotics. According to Gandhi, the elimination of such habits as the drinking of alcohol and the use of drugs could not await the actions of the new government: instead, the issue had to be resolved during the struggle for independence. The Mahatma also urged Indians to improve their health standards.[55]

---

[54] King, 80.

[55] M.K. Gandhi, *Constructive Programme* (Ahmedabad: Navajivan Publishing House, 1961), Reprint, 8 -12.

In Gandhi's constructive program, education was perceived as a vital instrument in the reforming of the society. He considered the British-imported system of education inadequate for Indians, since it was "based upon foreign culture to the almost entire exclusion of indigenous culture." It was also criticized because "it ignores the culture of the heart and hand and confines itself simply to the head."[56] The education which Gandhi proposed was designed to "develop both the body and the mind, and keep the child rooted to the soil with a glorious vision of the future in the realization of which he or she begins to take his or her share from the very commencement of his or her career in school." He envisioned basic education, as linking "the children whether of the cities or the villages to all that is best and lasting in India."[57]

Gandhi's most controversial blueprint for the development of a free India, appeared to be that of the Khadi program, which he perceived as bringing about "a revolutionary change in the mentality and taste" of many Indians. The program emphasized the reliance of Indians upon goods produced in their country by their own intellect and labor, rather than the use of foreign imports to satisfy their needs. To Gandhi, Khadi was the "symbol of unity of Indian humanity, of its economic freedom and equality..."[58] The centerpiece of the Khadi program was "hand spinning," which he suggested was the only solution to the problem of mass starvation which resulted from "the enforced idleness for nearly six months in the year of an overwhelming majority of India's population," due to the "lack of a suitable occupation supplementary to agriculture."[59]

Economic inequality was a major concern of Gandhi since it posed a threat to the nonviolent system that he proposed. As long as the gap between the rich and poor existed, he considered such a government as being impossible. Gandhi contended that "a violent and bloody revolution is a certainty one day unless there is a voluntary abdication of riches and the power that riches give, and sharing them for the common good." It was not his conviction that independence for India would "drop from heaven all of a sudden one fine morning." Instead, he insisted that it had to be "built up brick by brick by corporate self-effort."[60] For Gandhi, the constructive program was

---

[56] M. K. Gandhi, "National Education," *Young India*, Sept. 1, 1921, Reprinted in *Young India* (Ahmedabad: Navajivan Publishing House), 386-387.

[57] Gandhi, *Constructive Programme*, 18.

[58] Gandhi, 12-13.

[59] C. F. Andrews, *Mahatma Gandhi's Ideas* (New York: MacMillan Co., 1930), 147-148.

[60] Gandhi, 24-25.

essential to the obtaining of freedom, and he considered its effective use as limiting the need for nonviolent protest.

Although King's emphasis on constructive pursuits was not as great as that of Gandhi, he did consider such efforts as essential. Nonviolence as he perceived it, did not only require "noncooperation with evil," but also "cooperation with the constructive force of good." According to King, "without this constructive aspect noncooperation ends where its begins," therefore, blacks must institute a program of positive goals, including the improvement of their economic plight, the increasing of their political participation, and the modification of personal standards. Perceiving the struggle of blacks as a dual one, King suggested that while we must "continue to resist the system of segregation which is the basic cause of our lagging standards; on the other hand we must work constructively to improve the standards themselves."[61]

According to Tutu, apartheid is the cause of many of the problems of Africans, but that all problems cannot be attributed to it. Perceiving the need to look inwardly, he suggested that we examine what is going wrong in the black community. Tutu warned that "we in the black community have lost our sense of ubuntu--our humaneness, caring, hospitality, our sense of connectedness..." He cited as evidence of losing our self-respect "the horrible extent of dumping and littering in our townships."[62] The archbishop insisted that while we live in "squalor and in slum ghettos, we are not rubbish." He challenged Africans to better treat their environment. To accomplish this, he solicited the assistance of local governments, churches, community organizations and political groupings in cleaning up the townships. Through efforts of this type, Tutu envisaged the people, as perhaps, regaining "a self-esteem, self-respect and pride that they are loosing." He also insisted that the people develop "the culture of tolerance: live and let live."[63]

Archbishop Tutu pleaded with his fellow Africans to have pride and not be ashamed of being black. He admonished them, "Let us come together and be one, let us be people of peace, let us be people of harmony." Realizing the

---

[61] King, *Stride Toward Freedom*, 224.

[62] Tutu, *The Rainbow People of God: The Making of a Revolution* (New York: Doubleday, 1994), 229-230.

[63] Tutu, 230-231.

needs of the new South Africa for doctors, nurses, teachers pilots and engineers, he challenged them to obtain education.[64]

In pursuit of a just society, true advocates have to work to achieve equality among the oppressed while they seek to achieve equality for the oppressed in the broader society. Gandhi, King, Luthuli and Tutu, all advocated this approach.

[64] Tutu, 212.III Mahatma Gandhi: His Agenda for Action

PART TWO

CAMPAIGNS OF THE PROPHETS

Chapter 3

MAHATMA GANDHI: HIS AGENDA FOR ACTION

> The accumulated experience of the past thirty years, fills me with the greatest hope that in the adoption of non-violence lies the future of India and the world. It is the most harmless and yet equally effective way of dealing with the political and economic wrongs of the downtrodden portion of humanity.[1]
>
> Monhandas Gandhi

As a result of his study, travel, and other personal experiences, Gandhi perceived many social ills that were in need of elimination. In response, he devoted most of his life to the effort of bringing about changes that would result in a just society. Among his major objectives were:

1. Obtaining racial justice in South Africa for the Indians.
2. Gaining independence for India.
3. Relieving the plight of the untouchables.
4. Harmonizing relations between the Hindus and Moslems.

RACIAL JUSTICE IN SOUTH AFRICA

As a barrister in South Africa during the period, 1893-1914, Gandhi, like other Indians, was a victim of racial injustice. He reacted to his dehumanizing

---

[1] Nirmal Kumar Bose. *Selection From Gandhi*, (Ahmedabad, India: Navajivan Publishing House, 1957), 150.

experiences, and those of his countrymen, by organizing Indians--both Hindus and Moslems--into a movement to fight such abuse. In this initial effort, Gandhi perceived racial justice as being easier to achieve if Indians in South Africa approached it by making self-improvement, reducing friction among themselves, and becoming more competitive. Specifically, he urged them to be honest in their various relations, adopt more sanitary habits, set aside religious and caste differences, and become more competent in the use of English. To Gandhi, it was more important to improve human means than to obtain political goals.[2]

In the achieving of racial justice in South Africa, an important facet of Gandhi's strategy was the portraying of Indians as loyal subjects. This he did, by volunteering to recruit a corps of Indian stretcher bearers and medical orderlies to support the British efforts in the Boers War of 1899-1902. According to Gandhi, if he "demanded rights as a British citizen," it was his duty to "participate in the defense of the British Empire." He acknowledged that as a result of their war efforts, their "humble work was at the moment much applauded, and the Indians' prestige was enhanced."[3]

Several years later, Gandhi, once again, found himself volunteering for service to the British Commonwealth--this time to form an Indian ambulance corps to aid the British efforts in quelling the "Zulu uprising." The task assigned to the Indian Ambulance Corps was that of attending to the medical needs of the Zulus. Once he had reached the scene of the so-called rebellion, he became convinced that "the disturbance had been magnified into a rebellion," and that the incident had occurred, in the first place, because a Zulu chief had advised his people not to pay a new tax which had been imposed on them and had assaulted a sergeant who had attempted to collect it. After having learned this, Gandhi's sympathy was with the Zulus, but he considered his work as having been worthwhile since the arrival of the Ambulance Corps was hailed as a "Godsend for these innocent people."[4]

One of the major battles waged by Gandhi in South Africa was the campaign against the Asiatic Registration Act of July 31, 1907, which required all Indians over the age of eight to register and be fingerprinted. Failure to obey the law could result in a fine, imprisonment, or deportation from the province of Natal. In reacting to the despised act, Gandhi challenged

[2] Fischer, 23
[3] Gandhi, *An Autobiography*, 216.
[4] Gandhi, 216.

his followers: "If we are conscious of the mark of slavery the act will put on us, we will meet it and refuse to submit to it." To oppose the "Black Act", as it was called, he organized the Passive Resistance Association, which undertook a campaign to picket the permit office, and to pass out anti-registration material to those who went to register. Gandhi's efforts appeared to have achieved success, with only about 100 of the1,500 Indians registering. The Government was quick to respond to the activities of the Passive Resistance Association, warning that "if resistance of Indians leads to unpleasant results, they will have only themselves and their leaders to blame." Gandhi was informed that Indians who refused to register by the required date would be put across the border. Also the Government threatened to withhold trade licenses to persons who had refused to comply with the law. According to Smuts, the Government was prepared to make South Africa a white man's country, and it was determined to achieve that objective regardless of the difficulty involved.[5]

Shortly after the arrest of Gandhi, the South African Government sent an emissary to propose that if the Indians would register voluntarily, the Act would be repealed. Following this overture, Gandhi was released from jail to consult with General Smuts. The former applauded the agreement, noting that the well-being of the community was greatly enhanced by the settlement. Gandhi suggested that "we must register voluntarily to show that we do not intend to bring a single Indian into the Transvaal surreptitiously or by fraud." In spite of strong opposition from some Indians, who contended that the Act should be repealed prior to voluntary registration, Gandhi insisted upon leading the way in giving his fingerprints and registering. To his embarrassment, General Smuts refused to honor the agreement.[6]

The *Satyagrahi*s sought to persuade Smuts to fulfill his part of the agreement, while simultaneously, attempting to educate the Indian community. Certificates were collected for burning, in case the Act was not repealed. In a letter to Smuts, the *Satyagrahis* warned that consistent with the agreement, if the Asiatic Act was not repealed, and a decision to that effect communicated to the Indians by a designated date, the certificates which had been collected by the Indians would be burnt, and "they would humbly but

[5] Tendulkar, *Mahatma*, 1: 83-84.
[6] Tendulkar, 90-91.

firmly take the consequences."[7] When the Government refused to honor its pledge, the *Satyagrahis* burned their registration certificates as an act of defiance. Gandhi observed that "by burning the certificate we declare our solemn resolution never to submit to the Black Act and divest ourselves of the power of even showing the certificate."[8] In defiance of the Act, Indians in Natal were arrested and deported after crossing the border into Transvaal where Indians were hawking their products without licenses, and were being arrested. In the meantime, Gandhi courted arrest by seeking to return from Natal to Transvaal without showing a certificate, or giving his thumb-print. Several times he was arrested for such offenses.[9]

By 1913, Indians were in a rebellious mood because of three acts of injustice, which they perceived as having been perpetrated against them by the South African Government. They expressed dissatisfaction because of: (1) the three pound annual tax which was placed upon indentured laborers, who sought to remain in the Natal Province, (2) the immigration law, which banned Indians from entering into Transvaal, and (3) the court's ruling that only Christian marriages could be considered legal. Through various civil disobedience campaigns, the Indians expressed their disapproval of these actions in various ways, including waging a strike at the Newcastle Coal Mines. The owners reacted by turning off the water and lights, causing Gandhi to suggest to the miners, camping under the open sky.[10]

Confronted with a decision as to the accommodation of the approximately 5,000 Indians, who had gone on strike, Gandhi considered taking them to the Transvaal and having them placed in jail for crossing the border. In order to pursue this objective, he would have had to provide railway fare for them, or to have marched them. Not having the money, and wanting to test their morale, he decided to march his "army of peace" to the border town of Charlestown in a two-day pilgrimage. Prior to undertaking the march, however, Gandhi conferred with mine owners, and urged them to exert their influence in order to secure the repeal of the three pound tax. He perceived the tax as having been imposed to benefit the owners, who sought to prevent the

---

[7] Gandhi, *Satyagraha in South Africa* (Ahmedabad, India: Navajivan Publishing House, 1928), 199.

[8] Tendulkar, 1:96.

[9] Tendulkar, 1:99.

[10] Gandhi, "Preparing for the March," in Jack's *The Gandhi Reader*, 85.

Indians from working as free men.[11] When his efforts proved futile, he proceeded with his plans for the march.

Because Gandhi was very devoted to the cause of the strikers, he promised to live and have meals with them until they had secured the victory. Warning them of the hard days ahead, he called upon them to remain steadfast in their determination. In order to sustain them during the journey, he could only assure them that bread and an ounce of sugar would be provided. Once the marchers arrived in Charlestown, Gandhi contacted the Government before crossing the border, and informed it that the pilgrims did not intend "to enter the Transvaal with a view of domicile, but as an effective protest against the minister's breach of pledge and as a pure demonstration of distress at the loss of our self-respect.[12] He notified the Government that the marchers would be greatly relieved if they were arrested while there in Charlestown, but if the Government did not accommodate them with arrest, the "army of peace" would march 20 to 24 miles per day in order to arrive at their destination, Tolstoy Farm, in eight days. Gandhi assured the Government that if the three pound tax was repealed, the strikers would return to work, and they would not be asked to join the *Satyagrahis* in seeking the redress of other grievances.[13]

Prior to launching the campaign, Gandhi, again, appealed to Smuts to consider the repeal of the three pound tax, but to no avail. Having failed to persuade the Government, he led the marchers into Transvaal, and was arrested several times on charges related to the march. Consistent with the wishes of Gandhi, the entourage continued in his absence for a while, but later, the miners were transported back to the mines. Once there, they refused to work, and violence erupted.[14]

The Government reacted by establishing a commission to investigate the grievances of Indians in South Africa. Upon his release from jail in December 1913, Gandhi decried, publicly, the "packing" of the commission, and later informed Smuts of his displeasure with the selection of anti-Asiatic commission members, but his criticism was disregarded. The Indian leader reacted by announcing that on January 1, 1914, a march would be held to seek to regain lost rights, but later canceled it, when the Government found itself

---

[11] Gandhi, *Satyagraha in South Africa*, 291-292.
[12] Gandhi, 298.
[13] Gandhi.
[14] Fischer, *The Life of Mahatma Gandhi* (New York: Harper and Row Publishers, 1950), 112-113.

faced with a strike by white employees of the South African railroad, simultaneously. Gandhi insisted that *Satyagraha* "never take advantage of the Government's difficulty or form unnatural alliances." As a result of his action, messages of congratulations poured in from England, India, and various cities in South Africa. Smuts reacted to this gesture by summoning Gandhi for talks, in spite of the fact that the former had broken his pledge in 1908--a fact that Indians did not allow Gandhi to forget.[15]

Gandhi's hands in the negotiation, however, were strengthened by his "knightly forbearance in canceling the march," and in the arrival of an extraordinary envoy of the viceroy, who was worried about hostile reactions in India to South African persecutions. After weeks of negotiations, the two reached an accord, which later became the Indian Relief Act. According to its terms:

1. Hindu, Moslem, and Parsi marriages were made valid.
2. The three pound annual tax on indentured laborers who sought to remain in Natal was abolished, and the arrears were canceled.
3. Indentured labor was to cease coming from India by 1920.
4. Indians could not move freely from one province of the Union to another, but Indians born in South Africa might enter the Cape Colony.[16]

Smuts promised to administer laws justly, respecting the rights of Indians. Both sides appeared to be satisfied with the compromise. Gandhi acknowledged that under the Act, Blacks would continue to be severely restricted, nevertheless, he regarded the agreement as the South African Indians' "Magna Charta." He did not consider intrinsic gains to be the important element; instead, "the vindication of the abstract principles of racial equality and the removal of the "racial taints." Writing in the *Indian Opinion*, Gandhi viewed the victory as "a vindication of civil resistance," which, "if it became universal, would revolutionize social ideals and do away with despotism and the ever-growing militarism under which the nations of the West are groaning and are being almost crushed to death, and which fairly promises to overwhelm even the nations of the East."[17]

---

[15] Fischer, 114-115.
[16] Fischer, 117.
[17] Fischer, 117.

In spite of the fact that Gandhi and Smuts were adversaries, the two men had high regards for each other. Just prior to his leaving for India, Gandhi sent a gift to General Smuts, a pair of sandals that he had made while in prison. Smuts wore them every summer before returning them on the 70th birthday of Gandhi, noting, "I have worn these sandals for many a summer since then, even though I may feel that I am not worthy to stand in the shoes of so great a man."[18] On that occasion, Smuts praised his former adversary as one who had helped to "redeem us from a sense of commonplace and futility."[19]

When Gandhi first went to South Africa, he perceived his tour of duty as a short one, but because of the many inequalities in the society, he felt obligated to extend his stay. In 1914, he concluded that with some of the basic problems resolved, the Indian community was sufficiently organized to wage successful battles against the remaining injustices. In his farewell address before an audience in Johannesburg, Gandhi advised his fellow-countrymen that they need not have fear concerning the future, since with mutual cooperation, and mutual goodwill the Indian community needs never appear weak when facing the present or future government of South Africa. He expressed confidence that if Indians were treated with proper respect, they would always be supportive of the Government of the day when the need arose. He asked his European friends to understand that if Indians had insisted upon their rights, they also had discharged their responsibilities.[20] With his South African mission completed, Gandhi sailed for his homeland to engage in the struggle to liberate India.

LIBERATION OF INDIA

To Gandhi, liberation of the Indians meant the eradication of poverty and evils that it bred, and the freeing of India from foreign domination. Also regarded as essential to the liberation was the elimination of religious and caste hostilities, which will be analyzed later in this chapter.

Gandhi launched his first major campaign in 1917 on behalf of the peasants in Champaran. In this area, most of the arable land was divided into large estates owned by Englishmen but was worked by Indian tenants, who

---

[18] Radhakrishnan, 282.
[19] Radhakrishnan, 280.
[20] Gandhi, "Farewell Speech," in Jack, 102.

were forced to plant 15% of their land holdings in indigo, with the entire harvest relinquished as rent. When the landlords learned of the development of synthetic indigo in Germany, an attempt was made to make the sharecroppers pay them compensation for being released from the 15% arrangement. While many of the peasants paid, some resisted and hired lawyers, which provoked the landlords to bring in "thugs" to deal with the resisters.[21]

When Gandhi was informed, he went to the district and sought information concerning the arrangement from the British Landlords' Association, but was told that no information could be given to an outsider. Not considering himself an outsider, Gandhi consulted the British official commissioner of the district, who suggested that he leave the area. Refusing to comply, Gandhi became more actively involved in the investigation of the situation, causing officials to order him to leave the district, and when he failed to do so, he was summoned to appear in court. Once there, he entered a plea of guilty and proceeded to read a statement, which, in part, responded to the question of why, as an outsider, he had come to Champaran. Gandhi maintained that he had come in response to the invitation of the peasants, who were being treated unfairly by the indigo planters. Because he could not render aid to these victims until he understood the situation, he contended that he had come to study the problem, if possible, with the assistance of the administration and planters. Gandhi insisted that his visit should not be interpreted as meaning that he had come to cause disturbance and lost of life. The administration, viewing the matter differently, placed him under arrest. As a result, he felt obligated to offer an explanation as to why he disobeyed the order to leave the district. According to Gandhi, as one who was interested in abiding by the law, his first instinct was to obey the order, but he could not do so without doing an injustice to his sense of duty to those whom he had come to help. Since he decided that he could only serve them by remaining in the district, he concluded that he could not leave voluntarily. Because of his perceived conflict in duties, he suggested that it was the responsibility of the administration to remove him. Gandhi did not object to paying the penalty for disobedience of the law, since his failure to comply was not based upon his lack of "respect for lawful authority, but in obedience to the higher law of our being, the voice of conscience."[22] Later the case was dropped.

[21] Fischer, 149-150.
[22] Gandhi, *An Autobiography*, 414.

The scene, thus, was set for what Gandhi referred to as the "first direct object-lesson in Civil Disobedience in the country." Although he acknowledged the valuable role that could be played by the press in the campaign, he sought to discourage publicity, perceiving the situation as being of a delicate nature and that "over-energetic criticism or highly coloured reports might easily damage the cause." Gandhi wrote to editors requesting them to refrain from sending reporters to cover the story, and in return, he promised to supply them with necessary information. Likewise, he did not invite leaders from other provinces to participate, fearing that by doing so, the issue that he considered to be local in nature, would become politicized. It was in this setting that Gandhi and lawyers conducted an extensive investigation of the grievances of the peasants, with about 10,000 of them giving depositions.[23]

In June, the Lieutenant Governor summoned Gandhi for a discussion of the matter, and asked him to serve on the official commission of inquiry to review the indigo share-croppers situation. The Commission was composed of landlords, government officials, and Gandhi. After several meetings had been held, and extensive evidence had been compiled against the big planters, the Commission agreed, in principle, to make refunds to the peasants. Although Gandhi had suggested a 50% refund, he settled for 25% since, to him, the important thing was that the landlords had lost prestige. According to Louis Fischer, Gandhi's position appeared to have been justified, since shortly thereafter, the estates of the British planters were abandoned, and taken over by the peasants. Champaran was not designed as an act of defiance, instead, it grew out of the need to relieve the distress felt by many poor peasants. Gandhi's concern in the situation was not only with the broader issues of politics and economics, but also with the alleviation of the "cultural and social backwardness" of the people. In his efforts, he utilized the services of people who volunteered to be teachers, medical personnel, and lawyers.[24]

Prior to the completion of Gandhi's work in Champaran, labor unrest erupted in Ahmedabad; thus, he interrupted his current activities and went to the area, where he studied the conditions of the underpaid textile workers. After his investigation, the factory owners were called upon to arbitrate but they refused to do so; thus, Gandhi advised the workers to strike. Assuming the leadership, he extracted from the workers a pledge that they would resume

[23] Gandhi, 415.
[24] Fischer, 153.

work only after they had achieved their desired raise in wages, or until the dispute was referred to arbitration. The workers pledged that during the lockout, they would not "cause any disturbance or resort to violence or indulge in looting, nor damage any property of the employers or abuse anyone, but will remain peaceful."[25]

In order to keep the spirit of the strikers high, meetings were held daily under the shade of a babul tree by the river. Usually, Gandhi addressed the crowd, advising them to remain true to their pledge. On one evening he reminded them that even though they had no money, they had a wealth that was superior to money--"their hands, their courage and their fear of God." He used regularly published leaflets to reassure the employers that the workers did not hold any grudge against them. Likewise, from time to time, Gandhi met with the mill-owners to press the demands of the laborers.[26]

As time passed, and there was no victory in sight, some of the strikers appeared to weaken in their resolve. Gandhi appealed to them to remain true to their pledge, reminding them that if they had accepted defeat at the outset, he would not have involved himself in the strike, but because they had decided to fight, he and others had come to their aid. He reminded them that the world was taking note of what was happening at Ahmedabad, and that if they did not fulfill their pledge, posterity would question their failure to do so.[27]

Fearing the impact of an unsuccessful strike upon the larger community, Gandhi decided to undertake a fast to influence workers to honor the pledges, which they had taken. Gandhi believed that the failure of the strike would spell ruin for the nation since it would be impossible to ever raise labor-related issues again.[28] While the fast was designed to bring pressure upon the workers, it appeared to have accomplished a purpose far different from what had been intended--the settlement of the strike, itself. Apparently, the fast by Gandhi, constituted a pressure technique against the mill owners, some of whom were his good friends. Three days after he had begun the fast, the mill owners agreed to arbitration, and the strike, which had lasted for twenty-one days, was terminated.[29]

---

[25] *Collective Works of Mahatma Gandhi* (CWMG), 14: 215.
[26] *CWMG*, 14:217.
[27] *CWMG*, 14:22.
[28] *CWMG* 14:26-261.
[29] Fischer, 156.

With the civil disobedience campaign at Champaran and the strike at Ahmedabad behind him, the next focus of Gandhi's attention was the Rowlatt Bills, which became law on March 18, 1919. According to one of the bills, a person possessing a document regarded as seditious could be imprisoned if the intent was to publish or circulate it. In an effort to prevent the bills from becoming law, Gandhi waged a nonviolent campaign. Condemning them as unjust, subversive, and destructive he drafted a pledge which his followers took, affirming that:

> In the event of these bills becoming law and until they are withdrawn, we shall refuse civilly to obey these laws and such other laws as a committee, to be hereafter appointed, may think fit, and we further affirm that in this struggle, we will faithfully follow truth and refrain from violence to life, person or property.[30]

While admitting that persons engaged in secret violence posed a threat to society, Gandhi questioned why a bill should be drafted affecting the entire country and all of its people that would empower the government far beyond what it needed to cope with the situation.

When the second of the bills was published as a law on March 18, Gandhi reacted by suggesting a national *hartal*--a suspension of economic activities. Originally, it was scheduled to be launched on March 30, 1919, but was later delayed to April 6. Leaders in Delhi was informed of the change too late; thus, their observance was held on the 30th--an occasion which erupted in violence. When informed of this tragedy, Gandhi was enroute to Bombay to participate in the *hartal* in that city, which he had helped to organize. While he expressed regrets concerning the violence, he considered it praiseworthy that 40,000 well-disciplined persons were able to hold a mass meeting following the shooting incidents. He promised to go to Delhi following the *hartal* in Bombay.[31]

In the meantime, Gandhi suggested two practical ways in which civil disobedient campaigns could be waged in Bombay. Firstly, Indians could show their disapproval of the salt tax by using sea water to make salt in their homes, which would be a violation of the law, and secondly, to purchase literature, which had been proscribed by the Government. In order to

---

[30] Tendulkar, 1:241.
[31] Tendulkar, 1:248.

accomplish the latter, two of Gandhi's books, which were on the list, were reproduced and made available for sale. On the evening of the *hartal*, the books were sold rapidly. To the dismay of the protesters, however, the Government noted that no law had been violated since the books being sold were new editions, and not the ones that had been proscribed.[32]

Not to be outdone, Gandhi published an unregistered weekly, called *Satyagraha* and in its first edition on April 7, 1919, he encouraged others to do likewise. Gandhi suggested that once persons received copies they should "recopy till at last the process of multiplication is made to cover, if necessary, the whole of the masses of India." Since the aim of this action was to gain arrest, he advised those involved in the process to write their names and addresses as sellers, in order to make it easier for the Government to apprehend them for prosecution. *Satyagrahis* were advised to form small groups so as to facilitate the discussion of prohibited literature. According to Gandhi, the use of the prohibited literature was not only for the purpose of civil disobedience, but also to provide the people with "clean literature of a high moral value."[33]

Satisfied with the way the campaign was proceeding in Bombay, Gandhi turned his attention to Delhi, the scene of earlier violence. When he sought to go there to aid in the pacification, he was prevented from doing so by the British. While being returned to Bombay, he sent messages concerning his freedom and safety, nevertheless, the reports of his arrest had so enraged the people that rioting occurred in some Indian cities. Disturbed over the change of events, Gandhi warned his followers in Bombay that throwing stones, obstructing tram cars, and performing other acts of violence were inconsistent with *satyagraha*. He deplored, in particular, their efforts to secure the release of fifty men who had been arrested for violent acts. Gandhi informed his followers that it was a violation of their religious duty to seek the release of persons who had committed acts of violence. He threatened to abandon the campaign if it could not be conducted without violence.[34]

At Ahmedabad, he had similar words for his followers, noting that by their acts of violence, they had disgraced rather than honor him. He observed that in the name of *satyagraha*, the people of Ahmedabad had "burnt down buildings, forcibly captured weapons, extorted money, stopped trains, cut off

[32] Fischer, 177.
[33] Tendulkar, 1: 249.
[34] Tendulkar, 1:252.

telegraph wires, killed innocent people, and plundered shops and private houses." Gandhi advised them that if such acts were intended to gain his freedom from prison, he would have preferred not to be saved. He informed them that since the buildings that had been destroyed were public property, they would be rebuilt at their expense.[35] Regretting the outbreak of violence, Gandhi declared his call for the campaign a "Himalayan miscalculation," and proceeded to cancel the *Satyagraha* campaign. He confessed that he should have realized that "before a people could be fit for offering civil disobedience they should thoroughly understand its deeper implications." Gandhi concluded that as a prelude to resuming civil disobedience on a mass scale, an effort had to be made to recruit a band of volunteers who were well-tried and pure-hearted; thus, would understand the strict conditions of *Satyagraha*.[36]

Perceiving the need for penance, Gandhi announced that he would impose upon himself a fast of three days, and he requested his followers to submit themselves to a fast of one day. Likewise, he advised persons who had captured weapons to return them, and for all to show that they took the matter of penance, seriously, by contributing to a fund to aid families of those killed during the acts of violence.[37]

Although the *hartal* had been observed peacefully and successfully throughout the Punjab Province, the Government ordered the deportation and internment of the leaders of the Hindu and Moslem communities, whom it considered to be trouble makers. Indians of the city of Amritsar reacted by declaring another *hartal*, and marched in a procession to demand the release of the detained leaders. In order to break up the demonstration, shots were fired into the crowd of unarmed Indians, killing many of them. As a revenge, the protesters killed several Englishmen who were in their offices, and burned their banks. Other public buildings also were destroyed.[38]

In order to restore order to the city, the British sent General Reginald Dyer to Amritsar. Upon his arrival, he issued a proclamation that prohibited all public gatherings and even though the General was aware of a meeting scheduled to be held in Jallianwala Bagh on April 13, he took no steps to prevent it. Shortly after the meeting had begun, however, he arrived on the scene with armoured cars and troops, and without warning, ordered the troops

---

[35] Tendulkar, 1:253.
[36] Gandhi, "A Himalayan Miscalculation," In Jack, 186-187.
[37] Tendulkar, 1:254.
[38] Tendulkar, 1:257.

to begin firing. At the end of the tragic affair, more than 379 people had been killed--many of them trying desperately to escape.[39]

The Amritsar tragedy was not an isolated event; instead, part of a larger picture of repression that was taking place throughout the Punjab Province. Even though disappointed, Gandhi insisted that it was the duty of the *Satyagrahis* to restore order and to prevent further lawlessness. On May 11, 1919, he wrote a letter to the private secretary of the Viceroy, assuring him of his full support of efforts to restore peace. At the same time, he urged the Government to rescind the Rowlatt Act, which he perceived as the root of the unrest. The Government did not appear to be cooperative, declaring that it was prepared to use all available power to subdue the national movement. Gandhi also called for the appointment of an impartial committee to investigate the disturbances at Punjab, which the Government agreed to do. Noting this act as an indication of goodwill, he decided to delay further demonstrations, since he considered it to be a responsibility of civil resisters never to seek to humiliate the Government. In October 1919, Lord Justice Hunter was named chairman of the eight member commission of inquiry, which investigated the violence in the Punjab.[40]

In its report, the Hunter Commission criticized General Dyer for having opened fire upon the victims of Jallianwala Bagh, without having given adequate warning, and for having continued the firing after the crowd had begun to disperse. The Colonial Government of India agreed with the report, concluding that General Dyer "exceeded the reasonable requirements of the case, and showed a misconception of his duty which resulted in a lamentable and unnecessary loss of life."[41] The General was perceived as being sincere, feeling that his actions were consistent with the announced intentions of the Government to suppress disorder. According to the Government, "however injurious in its ultimate effect General Dyer's action may have been, it resulted in an immediate discouragement of the forces of disorder."[42]

After having analyzed the report of the Hunter Commission, the Government sought to link the disorders in the Punjab with the civil disobedience movement, noting that given the conditions in India at that time it should have been obvious that "the revolutionary effect of advising the

---

[39] Tendulkar, 1:258.
[40] Tendulkar, 1:264.
[41] *CWMG*, 17:555.
[42] *CWMG*, 17:555.

public to break selected laws was likely to encourage a situation which might lead to rebellion against all law and order. It suggested that a lesson should have been learned from the bitter experience of the previous year, but since it was not, it was hoped that "this lesson has been learnt once for all, and that in the future all right-thinking persons will set their faces firmly against the deliberate playing with fire which is involved in the promotion of such movements."[43]

While the Hunter Committee was investigating the Punjab disorders, a committee of the Indian National Congress (INC) was undertaking a similar assessment. In its report, which was believed to have been drafted by Gandhi, it was concluded that the Jallianwala Bagh massacre was a "calculated piece of inhumanity towards utterly innocent and unarmed men, including children, and unparalleled for its ferocity in the history of modern British administration." In order to redress wrongs which had been done to Indians, the INC Committee recommended the repeal of the Rowlatt Act, which it perceived as the root of the crisis. It also called for the relieving of General Dyer and others in responsible positions under the Crown.[44]

Gandhi suggested that the Jallianwala Baga be made into a national monument in memorial to the 500 Indians who were killed while doing nothing wrong. He considered it necessary to remind future generations that in efforts to achieve true freedom, they must be prepared for repetitions of such wrongs as the Jallianwala Bagh massacre. Recalling the spilling of the blood of people of various religions in the massacre, Gandhi perceived the memorial as serving as "a national emblem of an honest and sustained effort to achieve Hindu-Muslim unity."[45]

When Gandhi assumed the leadership of the National Congress in 1920, he made Indian self-government his major objective, and selected noncooperation as the best weapon to achieve it. According to Fischer, this concept was "negative enough to be peaceful but positive enough to be effective." Gandhi was viewed as personalizing the struggle, making those who did not support the effort feel that they were obstacles to the achievement of home rule. To dramatize his willingness to set an example for others, he

[43] *CWMG*, 17:575.
[44] *CWMG*, 17:291-292.
[45] *CWMG*, 17:36-38.

returned his two South African war medals and his gold medal for humanitarian work in South Africa.[46]

Realizing that his action might result in his arrest, Gandhi advised his followers to remain calm, since resorting to violence would only play into the hands of the Government. In pursuing the campaign of noncooperation, he suggested the closing of governmental schools, and the opening of numerous national schools and colleges; the withdrawal of lawyers from regular practice; the settlement of disputes by private arbitration, rather than through the use of the law courts; the refusal to enlist in the army and other forms of governmental service; and the contribution of funds toward national projects. Gandhi urged the "renunciation of all foreign cloth in favor of the exclusive use of hand spun and hand woven garments..." Maintaining that we "get what Government we deserve," he suggested the achievement of a better government by the use of noncooperation.[47]

Considering a civil disobedience campaign as instrumental in persuading the British to grant India a greater degree of independence than they apparently thought it merited, Gandhi announced his intention of launching a massive civil disobedience campaign in Bardoli. As a prelude to the start of the campaign, he informed the Viceroy of his intentions. The plans, however, were not implemented, due to the outbreak of violence at Chauri Chaura, which was eight hundred miles away.[48] Saddened and disturbed over the turn of events, Gandhi suspended the proposed Bardoli campaign, maintaining that "suspension of mass civil disobedience and subsidence of excitement are necessary for further progress, indeed, indispensable to prevent further retrogression." He did not regard the suspension of the civil disobedience campaign, however, as sufficient penance to atone for having been an involuntary instrument of the "brutal violence of the people at Chauri Chaura." He announced that he would undergo a process of personal cleansing through a fast.[49]

Being aware of criticisms of his suspension of the campaign by some leaders of Congress, Gandhi suggested that many of the adherents of nonviolence seemed to have accepted such a course only because of their helplessness. He maintained that many civil resisters appeared to have been

---

[46] Fischer, 187.
[47] Gandhi, *Young India,* 1028-1031.
[48] Fischer, 198.
[49] Tendulkar, 2:85.

awaiting the opportunity to get revenge for their mistreatment by the British. To the faint-hearted, Gandhi challenged: "The patriotic spirit demands loyal and strict adherence to non-violence and truth. Those who do not believe in them should retire from the Congress organization."[50]

Six years after the Bardoli campaign had been originally scheduled, it finally took place. On February 12, 1928, Gandhi called for a peaceful protest against a 22% increase in taxes that had been decreed by the British Government. The refusal of the residents of Bardoli to pay the tax had resulted in their personal belongings being confiscated, including their water buffaloes and other farm equipment. In challenging them to be strong, Gandhi advised them that even though they might have lost their possessions, they would have kept what must be "dearest of all to good men and women--their honor."[51] As the protest continued, voluntary contributions arrived to aid the indigenous people in their struggle.

In the meantime, the Government became more repressive, undertaking efforts to strip the entire village of property that could be moved, and to sell some of the land which it had seized. Likewise, it threatened to auction off the farms in Bardoli, if the tenants refused to pay the tax. In response to the harsh governmental action, Gandhi called for the celebration of a *hartal* on June 12. The response was magnificent, both in terms of moral and physical support. Two months later, the British capitulated by canceling the tax increase and returning confiscated property.[52]

In December 1929, at the urging of Gandhi, Congress passed a resolution, which demanded total independence from the British, and secession from the empire. The organization requested him to lead a civil disobedience campaign in order to implement the resolution. As he had done on previous occasions, Gandhi informed the Viceroy of his intentions, pointing out the evils of British rule in India, and justifying the need for a civil disobedience campaign. In his letter, he criticized the British use of the salt tax "to crush the very life" out of the Indians. The tax was perceived as especially burdensome on the peasants, who were required to use more of its because of their constant perspiration as a result of having to work under the sun. Because Great Britain was envisioned as being so preoccupied with its Indian commerce and interests that she would utilize all the forces it possessed to maintain its dominance,

[50] Tendulkar, 2:92.
[51] Fischer, 254.
[52] Fischer, 254-255.

Gandhi suggested that India must respond in such a manner to "free herself from the embrace of death." He advised the Viceroy that the purification of greed from British commerce would open the doors to opportunities for cooperation between the British and Indians as equals. Gandhi warned that if the evils, which he described in his letter, had not been dealt with prior to March 11, 1930, he would lead a demonstration against the salt tax.[53]

On March 11, Gandhi advised those who desired to participate in the civil disobedience campaign against the salt monopoly to do so by violating one of the following: carrying away the natural salt deposits from the seashore, manufacturing of salt, or possessing and selling contraband salt.[54] On the following day, after having prayer, Gandhi and 78 members of the *ashram* began their 200 mile march to the sea, which required 24 days. Although he was 61 at the time, he insisted upon walking rather than making use of the horse that had been provided for him. In his description of the march, Fischer noted that the roads were sprinkled with leaves, and that "every settlement in the line of march was festooned and decorated with India's national colors. All along the way peasants gathered and kneeled as the pilgrims passed."[55] By the time the marchers reached their destination on April 5, the procession that had begun with 78 participants had reached several thousands.

The night of April 5, 1930 was one of prayer, as the ashramites anticipated the events to follow. At the appointed time, Gandhi "dipped into the water, returned to the beach, and then picked up some salt left by the waves." With this significant act done, he had broken British law. Having given a signal to the nation, Gandhi withdrew from the scene, leaving it to his followers to pursue the effort. Following this act of defiance, thousands of villagers, along India's long seacoast, went to the beaches and gathered salt. The police responded by making arrests, using violence in these efforts.[56]

Later that month, Gandhi announced his intention of leading a raid on the salt depots at Dharsana, but such a raid, however, did not take place under his leadership since he was arrested during the late hour of May 4. His arrest, under an obscure hundred-year-old British regulation, served to focus world attention on the salt demonstration. In the absence of Gandhi, his son, Manilal and Mrs. Sarajini Naidu, a noted poet, led the 200 *Satyagrahis* in a

[53] *CWMG*, 43:2-8.
[54] Tendulkar, 3:23.
[55] Fischer, 268.
[56] Fischer, 268.

confrontation with 400 policemen under six British commanders as they attempted to raid the Dharsana Salt Works on May 21, 1930.[57]

Illustrative of the world-wide coverage which the tragedy of Dharsana received, was a report filed by Webb Miller, a foreign correspondent of the United Press. He described the courageous manner in which Indian protesters endured blows against their unprotected skulls, without raising a hand to fend off the blows. According to the account, as one column of innocent men were beaten unconsciously and left on the ground with fractured skulls and broken shoulders, the next column would move forward to encounter its share of unearned suffering. Miller praised the courage of the Indians, noting that "they marched steadily with heads up, without the encouragement of music or cheering or any possibility that they might escape serious injury or death. The police reacted by rushing in and attacking them." According to Miller, "there was no fight, no struggle; the marchers simply walked forward until struck down. There were no outcries, only groans after they fell."[58]

In the wake of the Dharsana Salt Raid, nonviolent campaigns were waged throughout the country, with more than a hundred thousand jailed. Calvin Kytle noted that Indians were quitting their government jobs, and an increasing number of civil resisters were refusing to pay taxes. Likewise, they were boycotting foreign cloth. Generally, the salt protest, with its related campaigns could be regarded as a success, with the country almost brought to economic stagnation. Also it caused a great outcry from the international community. Kytle observed that "though it was to be seventeen years before India became formally independent, freedom for India was inevitable from the moment Gandhi stooped on the beach at Dandi for a handful of salt."[59]

Although Gandhi was now confined to Yeravda Jail, the British were greatly concerned over the manner in which to deal with him. While Prime Minister Ramsay MacDonald had appeared willing to display a more conciliatory attitude toward him, it was not true with Winston Churchill, who sought to crush what he referred to as "Gandhism." After having served for eight months in prison, Gandhi was released, and on March 5, 1931, he and the Viceroy, Lord Irwin, signed a pact, in which the Government "agreed to release all nonviolent prisoners, to recognize the boycott of foreign cloth as a

---

[57] Calvin Kytle, *Gandhi: Soldier of Nonviolence*, Rev. (Washington: Seven Lock Press, 1982), 145.

[58] Webb Miller, *I Found No Peace* (New York: Literary Guild, Inc., 1936), 194

[59] Kytle, 148-149.

legitimate right, to restore all confiscated property, and--most significantly--to withdraw the ban on making salt at home." In return, Gandhi agreed to suspend his campaign of civil disobedience and to participate in the second Round Table Conference in London in the fall. A disappointing feature of the pact was the absence of a commitment to grant India independence or dominion status.[60]

While Gandhi was in England during the fall of 1931, he was preoccupied with two major objectives: presenting the Indian cause to the British people, and conferring with British officials concerning independence for India. While he appeared to have achieved success in regard to the first goal, he obtained very few concessions in regard to the second. During his stay in London, he was granted an audience with the King and Queen at Buckingham Palace, and was received as a guest of Prime Minister David Lloyd George. Among others whom he consulted were Lord Irwin and Jan Christian Smuts, both former adversaries. He also held conversations with actors, writers, governmental officials, religious leaders, educators, and students. According to Fischer, Gandhi was able to win friends because of "his charm, frankness, humanity, and accessibility." Christians in England, who regarded him as a brother and ally, were especially impressed with him. On the other hand, Gandhi's participation in the Round Table discussions was ineffective, with the British Government using the Hindu-Moslem issue to frustrate his efforts to achieve a free and united India. Considering the conference a failure, Gandhi returned home to continue his campaign for independence.[61]

Shortly after his return from London, the Government began to challenge India's "new sense of freedom," arresting many of the major leaders of Congress, and declaring a state of emergency in many parts of the country. The military was authorized to seize buildings, impound bank deposits, and confiscate wealth. During this governmental "crackdown", suspects were arrested without warrants, and they were denied basic due process rights. Likewise, political organizations were disbanded, newspapers were deprived of their mailing privileges, and picketing and boycotting were prohibited. Gandhi reacted to the acts of repression by sending a telegraph to the Viceroy, which denounced the ordinances and arrests, and suggested an interview. Replying for the Viceroy, his secretary sought to justify the ordinances on the

[60] Kytle, 150.
[61] Fischer, 286.

basis of what the Government perceived to be seditious activities of the Congress. While the letter expressed a willingness on the part of the Viceroy to confer with Gandhi concerning the ways in which he could best exert his influence, the Government did not anticipate engaging in a dialogue with him relative to the measures which had been taken to preserve the well-being of the country.[62]

Gandhi defended the actions of the Congress, and suggested that it might be necessary for him to initiate, once again, a civil disobedience campaign. Upon hearing this, the Viceroy expressed disbelief that Gandhi or the working committee of the Congress would anticipate that he would confer with him under the threat of the resumption of civil disobedience. While denying that his remarks were intended as a threat, Gandhi noted that the previous viceroy consulted with him prior to the adoption of the Delhi Pact. The Mahatma considered it prudent for "any popular and constitutional government" to "welcome and consider sympathetically suggestions made by public bodies and their representatives."[63] Early in January 1932, the Government closed the dialogue by, once again, placing Gandhi under arrest. During the campaign to destroy the Congress, the police conducted many raids, and made numerous arrests, with more than 17,000 being apprehended during the month of February. Governmental persecution, however, did not prevent Indians from continuing their march to freedom.[64]

In years that followed, Gandhi continued his struggle for the liberation of India--conducting nonviolent campaigns, undertaking fasts, and courting arrest. While the drafting of a new Indian constitution was important to him, at times, the objective appeared to be secondary to two issues which he felt compelled to devote much of his attention. As a prelude to a new India, he sought to eliminate Hindu-Moslem hostility, and to remove the stain of untouchability. We will now focus attention upon these critical issues.

HINDU-MOSLEM HOSTILITY

During Gandhi's campaign to better the conditions of Indians in South Africa, he realized that Hindu-Moslem hostility posed a major obstacle to the

[62] Fischer, 299.
[63] Fischer, 300.
[64] Fischer.

achievement of that goal; therefore, he sought to eliminate it. When he returned to his homeland in 1915, he found the existence of similar religious friction. Being aware that without unity there could be no independence for the country, he devoted a lifetime effort to bringing about "one India" rather than a divided country.

Following the close of the First World War, a major effort was made to achieve religious harmony. At that time, a primary concern of the Moslems of India was the future status of the *Khalifat*--a major religious leader. They had sought to use Indian influence to moderate terms of the peace treaty that the Allies were seeking to impose upon Turkey, a defeated nation. In November 1919 when a conference was called for that purpose, a strategy was developed to consider the problem of cow protection simultaneously, in order to secure the cooperation of Hindus. Gandhi disagreed with the linking of the two issues, complaining that each should be treated separately, and decided on its own merit. He contended that if the *Khalifat* question had a just and legitimate basis-- which he believed it did--then he suggested the Hindus should support the demands of their Moslem neighbors. According to Gandhi, it would not be appropriate, however, to use the issue of cow protection as a condition for their support. Likewise, he maintained that the Moslems should not offer to support cow protection as the price for having obtained Hindu backing on the *Khalifat* question. On the other hand, he contended that it would be a graceful gesture, if on their own free will, the Moslems would stop the slaughtering of cows because of respect for the religious beliefs of the Hindus. When the conference convened, the *Khalifat* issue was considered separately, but Moslem leaders suggested that out of respect for the Hindus, the Moslems should voluntarily cease the killing of cows. The conference produced a Hindu-Moslem honeymoon, which later resulted in the birth of the Congress, the leading nationalists organization of India.[65]

In 1924, when relations between the Hindus and Moslems deteriorated sharply, and the noncooperation movement was faltering, Gandhi wrote an article in *Young India,* which examined the causes of Hindu-Moslem tensions, and suggested ways in which to resolve them. He considered the two major causes of the friction to be cowslaughtering, and music, and perceived the key to the problem as residing with the Hindus. According to Gandhi, while the Hindus condemned the Moslems for the slaughtering of cows, they were relatively quiet about similar action by the British. He questioned the effectiveness of the Hindu protest concerning the killing of cows, noting that "all the riots that have taken place in the name of the cow have been an insane waste of effort. They have not saved a single cow, but they have, on the contrary, stiffened the backs of the Mussulmans [Moslems] and resulted in more slaughter."[66] Gandhi contended that more cows were saved voluntarily during 1921 than through all of the Hindu efforts of the previous twenty years. He suggested that the protection of cows should begin with the Hindus, noting that in no other part of the world are cattle treated worse than in India. He observed that the half-starved cattle of India was a disgrace to the Hindus, and he placed the blame upon them for selling cattle to butchers. Gandhi challenged cow protection societies to devote their efforts to "the feeding of cattle, prevention of cruelty, preservation of the fast disappearing pasture land, improving the breed of cattle," and similar activities.[67]

The second source of Hindu-Moslem conflict was the playing of music in Hindu processions as they passed mosques during prayer services. Hindus were believed to have deliberately timed their processions to irritate the Moslems. Gandhi, while considering such acts to be unfriendly and insensitive, suggested that Moslems not attempt to use force to seek to halt the music, just as the Hindus should not attempt to use force to prevent the killing of cows. As a Hindu, however, he advised his co-religionists to be more mindful of the feelings of their Moslem neighbors, and to seek to accommodate them.[68]

In order to bring about greater unity in the country, in September 1924, Gandhi began a twenty-one day fast at the home of his Moslem friend, Mohammed Ali. On the second day of the fast, he advised Indians that their greatest need was "not one religion, but instead a greater respect and tolerance of the worshippers of the various religions." On the twelfth day, Gandhi noted that in the past, the struggle had been to change the attitudes of the Englishmen who formed the government of India, but currently, the struggle was to change the hearts of Hindus and Moslems. He challenged Indians that "before they dare think of freedom they must be brave enough to love one

[65] R. K. Prabhu, ed., *India of My Dream* (Ahmedabad: Navajivan Publishing House, 1947), 244-247.
[66] Prabhu, 245.
[67] Prabhu, 245-246.
[68] Prabhu, 246.

another, to tolerate one another." Having brought attention to the problem, he broke the fast on the twenty-first day.[69]

As Indians intensified their campaign for freedom from Great Britain, the relationship between the Hindus and Moslems became more strained. By 1937, Mohammed Ali Jinnah, head of the Muslim League, had begun to envision a two India solution. While Congress continued to make the achievement of independence its top priority, Jinnah and his followers were beginning to insist that as a prelude to freedom a settlement had to be reached regarding the religious question. Addressing the annual session of the Moslem League in Lahore on March 22, 1940, he expressed serious doubts concerning the coexistence of the two religious groups. The following day the conference adopted a resolution calling for the division of the country.[70] Gandhi challenged the Moslem's description of India as two distinct nations with different cultures, languages, and outlooks. He contended that it was impossible to separate India into two nations, noting that "every Muslim will have a Hindu name if he goes back far enough in his family history." According to Gandhi, "every Muslim is merely a Hindu who has accepted Islam."[71] In the meantime, Indians continued to negotiate with the British Government concerning the future of their country.

Being dissatisfied with the new Indian constitution, the Moslems refused to participate in the provisional government headed by Nehru. Instead, the Moslem League designated August 16, 1946 as "Direct Action Day," which was followed by four days of rioting in Calcutta, with approximately 5,000 killed and 15,000 wounded. In the weeks that followed, rioting broke out in other cities and rural areas. Fearing the consequences of the spread of community hatred to the countryside, Gandhi decided to go to the scene of the violence. After having visited Calcutta, he undertook a pilgrimage to Noakhali in the rural area of East Bengal.[72]

In Noakhali, the Moslem majority was accused of killing Hindus, using force to convert them to Islam, ravishing their women, and burning their homes and temples. In some cases, Moslems were said to have forced Hindus to slaughter their cows and eat meat. Violence was not confined to this area, however. The Hindu majority, in the neighboring province of Bihar, retaliated

---

[69] Fischer, 223.
[70] Allen H. Merrian, *Gandhi v. Jinnah* (Columbia, MO: South Asian Books, 1980), 66.
[71] Merrian, 78.
[72] Fischer, 443-445.

by declaring October 25, "Noakhali Day," and proceeding to kill more than 5,000 Moslems. Gandhi considered it necessary to make the pilgrimage to the latter, in order to convince frightened Hindus to cease fleeing their homes in response to Moslem violence. He rejected the advice of his associates that he suggest to the Hindus that they abandon the area and settle in provinces where they constituted a majority, Gandhi regarded the "exchanging of population" as a recognition of the inability of India to remain united. As a leader of the nonviolent campaign, he considered it his duty to teach the Noakhali Hindus the act of bravery, by being brave with them. Gandhi also sought to exert his influence upon the Moslems. He questioned, "if they were not accessible to the spirit of non-violence and non-retaliation and brotherhood, how could there be a free, united India."[73]

Gandhi considered his pilgrimage as one of penance, an act of self-purification for not having persuaded the people of Noakhali to pursue a course of nonviolence. As a part of his strategy, he selected a Moslem and a Hindu in each village to be responsible for guaranteeing "the safety of all the inhabitants, and die, if need be, in their protection." During his four month stay, Gandhi contributed to a less hostile environment, but because he had not established the type of Hindu-Moslem amity that he desired, he promised to return to the area at a later date, and then departed for the Bihar Province.[74]

In Bihar, Gandhi was warned that he should not condemn the Hindus for their action. His reply was that he would not be a true Hindu if he "bolstered the wrongdoing of fellow Hindus or to any other fellow being." Later, he angered some Hindus when he called upon them not to seek revenge for the killing of their fellow-religionists in Punjab. As Gandhi went from village to village, he toured ruined houses of Moslems, and visited families that had suffered deaths or physical injury. In addition to collecting money for Moslem relief, he insisted that Hindus welcome back Moslems who had fled, rebuild their huts, and reestablish them in business. Gandhi also requested Hindus to abandon their boycotts of Moslem firms. His attempt to befriend the Moslems brought hate mail from Hindus, while, at the same time, his insistence upon a unified India caused some Moslems to question his sincerity. In spite of his gallant effort, Gandhi was unable to prevent the creation of the state of Pakistan; thus, India's independence on August 15, 1947did not represent for

---

[73] Fischer, 448.
[74] Fischer, 449-457.

him the glorious occasion which he had anticipated. What disappointed him even more was the high level of violence which accompanied independence in both nations.[75]

One of the major centers of violence was Calcutta, which for a year had been engulfed in crisis. Still pursuing his nonviolent campaign, Gandhi came to the city on August9, 1947, and spent much of his time visiting refugee camps, and addressing many of the victims of violence. Even though what he witnessed in Calcutta dismayed him greatly, he was even more distressed over the reports he had received of millions of Hindus fleeing the newly created Pakistan in order to avoid persecution. Similarly, he was disturbed over the large number of Moslems, who were seeking to escape the violence which was being perpetrated against them by the Hindus. He urged the Hindus to be more tolerant of their Moslem neighbors in India, and he anticipated going to Pakistan to make a similar appeal to the Moslem majority. The Mahatma contended, however, that the Hindus should take the initiative in restoring peace to the two countries, insisting that "misdeeds of the Hindus in the Indian Union have to be proclaimed by the Hindus from the housetop if those of the Moslems in Pakistan are to be arrested or stopped."[76] It was a major goal of Gandhi to see every Moslem who sought to live in India guaranteed that opportunity, and likewise, to see that Hindus who lived in Pakistan were unmolested. Even though he undertook a fast, he still did not achieve the Hindu-Moslem unity that he sought.

On January 13, 1948, in his last great effort to harmonize relations between Moslems and Hindus, Gandhi undertook a fast that was intended to last until death, if necessary. As announced, the fast was directed at the conscience of all--the Hindus and Moslems in the Indian Union, and to the Moslems in Pakistan. Even though Gandhi realized that death was a possibility, he envisioned it as a "glorious deliverance," inasmuch as he would be spared being a "helpless witness to the destruction of India, Hinduism, Sikhism, and Islam," He was quite disturbed over the behavior of the Hindus and Sikhs in regard to the Moslems, and considered their attempts to drive them out as a betrayal of India and its religious beliefs. During the fast, Gandhi took time to write a letter to the Government of India, requesting it to pay the 180,000,000 rupees due to Pakistan as its pre-independence portion of the national treasury. He had hoped that the Indian gesture of friendship might

[75] Fischer, 461-462.

be followed by a counter gesture by Pakistan; thus, bringing about a settlement of their many disputes, including the disagreement over Kashmir.[77]

On the third day of the fast, Gandhi appealed to his followers not to be concerned with the actions of others, but instead, to "turn the searchlight inward and purify his or her heart as much as possible." He urged them to consider how they might improve themselves and work for the advancement of the country. As Gandhi became weaker, influential Hindus, Moslems and others began to reflect concern, and they reacted on January 18 by signing a pledge to "protect the life, property and faith of the Moslems," and to assure that the incidents of violence would not be repeated. Among the other pledges was one that the Hindus and Sikhs would return the Mosques left by the Moslems, which they had occupied. After careful consideration, Gandhi accepted the pledge and agreed to break the fast in a ceremonial manner--with the reading of scriptures from Parsi, Moslem, and Japanese; the reading of verses from Hindu; and the singing of a Hindu song before the singing of the Christian hymn; "When I Survey the Wondros Cross."[78] Slightly more than a week later, the life of Gandhi was brought to an end, not because of a fast, but by an assassin bullet.

THE PLIGHT OF THE UNTOUCHABLES

To the outside world, Gandhi is best known for his campaign to achieve the independence of India, but he also made valuable contributions to the establishment of a just society within the country. Throughout his nonviolent campaign, the Mahatma emphasized that without improving the lives of the untouchables, India could never hope to be truly free. Gandhi recalled that as a child, he was forbidden to touch the man who came to clean their latrines, but if he did, he would be required to cleanse himself. He admitted that he would do as his mother demanded, but not without making known to her his feeling that in viewing physical contact with an untouchable a sin, she was entirely wrong. Gandhi also recalled that he was advised by his mother that when he touched untouchables at school, that his "shortest cut to purification after the

[76] Fischer, 486.
[77] Fischer, 495.
[78] Fischer, 499-502.

unholy touch was to cancel the touch by touching any Mussulman [Moslem] passing by."[79]

As Gandhi grew older, and began to read more from the *Bhagavad Gita*, he began to question how could untouchability be consistent with Hinduism. He maintained that "the fact that we addressed God as the 'purifier of the polluted' and by similar appellation, shows that it is a sin to regard anyone born in Hinduism as polluted or untouchable."[80] According to Gandhi, while it might have been difficult to make his point by quoting from the *Bhagavad Gita*, he insisted that his understanding of the spirit of Hinduism led him to conclude that in sanctioning untouchability, Hinduism has committed a sin. He reminded his fellow-Hindus of their guilt in having suppressed their brethren and making them "crawl on their bellies." Gandhi maintained, "we have made them rub their noses on the ground; with eyes red with rage, we push them out of railway compartments." He asked, "what more than this had British Rule done?"[81]

Addressing untouchables, Gandhi advised them that their emancipation was in their own hands. He suggested that they make the Hindus ashamed by their purity and cleanliness. They were told that this could be achieved by using soap to clean themselves, and by refraining from such habits as drinking and gambling. They also were encouraged to learn to spin and weave in order to keep themselves out of the doors of poverty. Gandhi admonished them to cease accepting leavings from plates, regardless of how clean they appear to be, and to accept only good sound grain. He advised them that if they can meet the challenge which he had laid down, their emancipation can be secured within days.[82]

Gandhi was very sympathetic with the plight of the untouchables, observing that if he were reborn, he would want to reappear as an untouchable in order to know "their sorrows, sufferings, and the affronts" which they face, and therefore be able to do something to free himself and them from their plight.[83] His fight for their dignity was not limited to words, but included action as well. He adopted their lifestyle.

---

[79] Gandhi, "Mr. Gandhi and the Suppressed Classes," *Young India*, 472.
[80] Gandhi, "The Untouchables," in Jack, 163.
[81] Gandhi, *Young India* 471.
[82] Gandhi, *The Removal of Untouchability* (Ahmedabad: Navajivan Publishing House, 1954), 175.
[83] Jack, 164-165.

Shortly after he established his *ashram*, Gandhi admitted an untouchable family. Although the current members agreed to accept them if the family abided by the rules, objections were raised by friends who had been supporting the *ashram*, financially. This support was curtailed to the extent that Gandhi entertained the idea of abandoning the *ashram,* if necessary, and moving into the untouchable quarters. Just as the *ashram* was about to deplete its funds, however, a wealthy gentleman, who made few inquiries, contributed, substantially, to the effort. Gandhi considered the admission of the untouchable family as playing a valuable role--giving notice to the world that the *ashram* would not tolerate untouchability. He noted that, "the fact that it is mostly the real orthodox Hindus who have met the daily growing expenses of the *ashram* is perhaps a clear indication that untouchability is shaken to its foundation."[84]

So concerned was Gandhi with the problem of untouchability that in 1922 he conducted a fast to death to assure that the British Government did not create for them a separate electorate. Reacting to an article that he had read in the newspaper, Gandhi complained that a separate electorate for the depressed classes (untouchables) would be harmful both for them and the Hindus. He suggested that if the policy was pursued, he would undertake a fast to death. According to Gandhi, the fast was designed to appeal to the conscience of the Hindus, since the British Government already had stated that it would accept any plan which the Hindus and Harijans had mutually agreed upon. As Gandhi lost strength, a major effort was made to find a solution to the problem. On the fifth day of the fast, a compromise was reached, which while eliminating the separate electorate, called for reserved seats to be set aside within the Hindu allotment for the Harijans. The way of nominating the candidates, however, would assure the Harijans of being able to elect its "bravest and best champions in the legislature," while retaining the system of joint electorate."[85]

Following the signing of the Yeravda Pact and its acceptance by the British Government, a series of accommodations were made throughout India to relieve the plight of the untouchables. Included among the terms were: the admission of them to temples where they previously had been banned, the permitting of them to drink water from wells in towns and villages where they were previously prohibited, and the walking on roads and streets once

[84] Gandhi, *An Autobiography*, 399.
[85] Fischer, 313.

forbidden. Fischer viewed the pact as marking a "religious reformation," and a "psychological revolution." He perceived Hinduism as "purging itself as a millennial sickness."[86]

By the time of his death in 1948, Gandhi had not obtained his major goal of a liberated society within a united India; nevertheless, his unrelenting efforts had won for him universal acclaim as a champion of peace and justice. His use of nonviolent resistance, as an instrument to resolve social conflict, was praised highly, and served later as a model for civil rights advocates in the United States, and anti-apartheid forces in South Africa. Indeed, he was a prophet of a just society.

[86] Fischer, 320.IV The Drum Major for Justice.

Chapter 4

The Drum Major for Justice

> Every minister of the gospel has a mandate to stand up courageously for righteousness, to proclaim the eternal verities of the gospel, and to lead men from the darkness of falsehood and fear to the light of truth and love.[1]
>
> Martin Luther King, Jr.

The society which Martin Luther King, Jr. confronted in 1955 was one that was characterized by injustices perpetrated both by the government and individuals. While most of the legal segregation was found in the South, other parts of the country were not totally free of such practices. The Federal Government also could be implicated since it could not claim to have acted in good faith in eliminating segregation in situations under its control. For years, African-Americans had been showing their resentment of this dual society, but their efforts had been limited to the search for improvement through legal means. In 1955, when Rosa Parks refused to give her seat on a bus to a white passenger, the incident ignited a crisis, which had been smoldering for years. Fortunately for African-Americans, and the nation at large, Martin Luther King, Jr. was on the scene when the crisis erupted, and was able to launch a struggle for racial justice, which continued until his death in Memphis in 1968. During this campaign, he devoted his efforts to the achievement of (1) equal accommodations, (2) political rights for African-Americans, (3) elimination of poverty, and (4) a peaceful world.

---

[1] King, *Stride Toward Freedom*, 208.

EQUAL ACCOMMODATIONS

While King's struggle to secure equal accommodations for African-Americans was waged throughout the South, the major battlefields were Montgomery, and Birmingham Alabama, and Albany, Georgia. The campaign was further nationalized in 1963 with the successful March on Washington, which dramatized the plight of African-Americans.

The Montgomery Bus Protest

Montgomery, that often has been referred to as the "Cradle of the Confederacy," also has been called the "Cradle of the Civil Rights Movement." It was in that city that the bus protest of 1955 launched the civil rights campaign of Martin Luther King, Jr. The protest was pursued in order to achieve three basic goals: (1) courteous treatment of African Americans by bus operators, (2) the seating of passengers on a first-come, first-served basis, with African-Americans seating from the back to the front, and whites from the front to the back, and (3) the employment of African-American operators on predominantly black routes.[2] In order to achieve these goals, the Montgomery Improvement Association (MIA) was formed, with Martin Luther King, Jr. as its leader. In pursuit of its goals, the Organization sought to withdraw economic support from the bus company. King insisted that because the goal of the Movement was to "put justice into the business of the company rather than put the bus company out of business," the use of the term "bus boycott" would be inappropriate in describing the action.[3] Through mass meetings and other means, the MIA was able to persuade the majority of the African-Americans to refuse to ride the bus and to choose, instead, to walk, ride bicycles, or utilize car pools which had been established to lessen the burden of transportation.

Frustrated by the success of the protest, the City sought to end the crisis by arresting leaders of the MIA for violating the state's anti-boycott law, and by prosecuting those who operated the car pool. It claimed that this "illegal operation" had cost the city more than $15,000. Similarly, insurance companies were persuaded to cancel coverage for cars used in the motor pool,

[2] King, 63-64.
[3] King, 51.

forcing the MIA to negotiate an arrangement with Lloyds of London.[4] Others who resented the protest took such action as the firing of African-American workers, and the cancelling of loans and mortgage notes. Anti-black organizations, like the Ku Klux Klan and the White Citizen Council, also sought to intimidate African-Americans by perpetrating acts of violence. During the course of the protest, both the home of Martin Luther King, Jr. and the church that was pastored by the Reverend Ralph Abernathy were bombed. In spite of the insults, inconveniences, and acts of violence, however, the protesters persisted in their efforts to bring justice to the bus system. Their campaign yielded tangible results on November 13, 1966, when the Supreme Court upheld the decisions of lower courts, declaring the operation of segregated buses in Montgomery illegal. Upon learning of the decision, King advised the protesters to regard the victory not merely as one for African-American protesters, but for Montgomery and the South, as well. He admonished them to return to the buses in a quiet, friendly and dignified manner, displaying courteous and good behavior. They were told that since all white people were not opposed to integrated buses they should not reject the goodwill on the part of those who offered it. Likewise, they were advised to pray for guidance as they committed themselves to continued nonviolence.[5]

The success of the Montgomery Bus Protest encouraged similar undertakings in other cities, including Mobile, Birmingham, and Tallahassee. Likewise, it propelled King on to the national scene as a recognized spokesperson for the cause of African-Americans. When he attended the Prayer Pilgrimage in Washington on May 17, 1957, he was warmly applauded by the estimated 25,000 who had gathered there from across the nation. Having achieved success as the head of the Montgomery Improvement Association, King proceeded to organize and provide leadership for the Southern Christian Leadership Conference (SCLC), which came into existence in 1957. In later years, he characterized the organization as a "major civil and human rights organization, structured under a loose federation of nearly 300 nationwide affiliates that adhere to the moral imperatives of a philosophy of nonviolence deeply rooted in the thinking of Jesus, Henry Thoreau, and Mahatma Gandhi." According to King, the Organization was "designed to launch coordinated non-violent attacks against the ignoble walls

[4] King, 158.
[5] King, 164.

of ignorance, misunderstanding and hatred which exist between individuals, ethnic and local groups."[6]

Having been encouraged by student sit-ins, King attended a conference of students that convened at Shaw University during the spring of 1960, and urged them to establish an organization to facilitate the struggle for equal accommodations. This conference inspired the formation of the Student Nonviolent Coordinating Committee (SNCC) several months later. Having been instrumental in the establishment of the organization, King sought to encourage the students by participating with them in a "sit-in" at Rich Department Store in Atlanta, GA in October 1960. Like the students, he was arrested and served for a short period in jail. During the following year, King and the SCLC offered moral and financial support to participants of the Freedom Riders, who were seeking to integrate transportation facilities. In response to this protest, on November 1, 1961, the Interstate Commerce Commission handed down a decision calling for the desegregation of interstate bus and train facilities. Albany, GA was selected as one of the target cities in which to test the implementation of the decree.

The Albany Campaign

King did not organize the protest in Albany, nevertheless, once it was underway, he played a crucial role in the campaign. In December 1961, he and the SCLC were urged to come to the city and give support to the faltering efforts of the Albany Movement--a collection of African-American organizations which were interested in securing racial justice in the city. Not all of the participating organizations approved the invitation to King. The SNCC, in particular, objected because it preferred a local-oriented campaign, rather than a well publicized King-led protest that would attract national attention.[7]

Unlike the Montgomery Bus Protest in that African-Americans sought to obtain their goals by withdrawing their economic support from the bus company, the Albany campaign was characterized by sit-ins and marches which yielded numerous arrests; thus, necessitating money for bail. In waging

---

[6] King, "Statement to SCLC Convention," Miami, FL, April 14, 1966, King's Papers, MLK/CNSC.

[7] David L. Lewis, *King: A Biography*, 2nd ed. (Urbana, IL: University of Illinois Press, 1978), 147.

the battle, King and his strategists had several obstacles to overcome, including: the lack of unity within the Movement, the lack of enthusiasm among average African-American citizens, the determination of the city and downtown merchants to outmaneuver him, and the inability of King to devote adequate time to the campaign.

Because operating within the framework of the Albany Movement were both the militant students of the SNCC, and the older and more conservative members of the NAACP, it was sometimes difficult for participants of the broader organization to achieve common ground. Once King's team began its operation in the city, members of the SNCC expressed dissatisfaction with the strategy pursued by it. He was perceived as being too conservative in his approach--too willing to accept a half-loaf, rather than pursue the matter to its logical conclusion.[8]

Initially, the average African-American in Albany appeared to lack enthusiasm for the demonstrations. David Lewis observed that "it was one thing to chant hallelujahs in the electric but secure atmosphere of a militant prayer meeting, but those who were not students, who had jobs to protect were hesitant about joining the march."[9] King decried those who for selfish gains were willing to cooperate with the oppressors. He perceived the city as having too many African-Americans, who dared to oppose segregation for fear of losing their "favored status," and endangering their standing with the white establishment.[10]

In the Albany campaign, King's strategy had been anticipated; thus, city officials were able to counteract it effectively. His effort to fill the jail with protesters failed because the police chief had made preparation for such a move by having secured additional jail space in nearby counties. Stephen Oates observed that "as fast as his (king's) non-violent columns reached their targets, Chief Pritchett put them in paddy wagons and dispatched them to jails in other counties." Leaders of the Movement were unable to solicit enough recruits to fill all the jails at the city's disposal.[11] Reacting to the acclaim which Pritchett was receiving in the press for his efficient manner of maintaining peace in the racially torn city, Howard Zinn, compared the city

---

[8] Lewis, 163.

[9] Lewis, 148.

[10] Stephen B. Oates, *Let The Trumpet Sound* (New York: Harper and Row Publishers, 1982), 195.

[11] Oates, 191.

with an "efficient police state," where no attempt was made to balance "the right of free speech and assembly and the police powers." He noted that "the police kept a peace which had not been broken, by putting into prison over 700 men, women and children who were exercising basic American rights to assemble peacefully and to petition the government for a redress of grievance."[12] The city also frustrated King's plans to remain in jail by finding him guilty of violating the law, and ordering him released after having given him a suspended sentence. A "King" in jail might have galvanized support among the African-Americans of Albany, and simultaneously, focus international attention on the city, but the police counteracted this strategy.

Another reason cited for the failure in Albany was the inability of King to devote adequate time to the protest movement, because of church activities, family concern, and the need to raise money to support the civil rights effort. The result was an ineffective strategy on the part of the SCLC. Lewis concluded that " commuting between Atlanta and Albany, it was occasionally difficult for him to distinguish between the theoretical and the practical possibilities of the Albany situation." Lewis perceived him as "applying to it the lessons of Montgomery instead of revising his ideas in the light of the present circumstances."[13]

Howard Zinn saw still another reason for the failure of the Albany campaign--the refusal of the Federal Government to take an active role in upholding the Constitution. Because of this failure, African-Americans and their allies were forced to engage in protest activities in order to obtain their rights. Zinn, not only was critical of the "general silence" of the President and the "feebleness" of the Justice Department in regard to the rights of African-Americans, but the FBI, as well. He observed that "with all the clear violations by local police of constitutional rights, with undisputed evidence of beatings by sheriffs and deputy sheriffs, the FBI did not make a single arrest on behalf of Negro citizens."[14]

Generally, the Albany campaign was regarded as a failure, but fortunately for King, he was able to analyze the weaknesses and remedy them before launching the next great effort in Birmingham. There were also strengths, including the apparent effective appeal to the conscious of the religious

[12] Howard Zinn, *The Southern Mystique* (New York: Simon and Schuster Publishers, 1972), 193.
[13] Lewis, 156.
[14] Zinn, 197-203.

community, which was manifested by the support of ministers, rabbis, nuns, and others who came to Albany. Labor unions, also, responded to the call, by contributing their efforts to such tasks as the rebuilding of churches, which had been destroyed or damaged during the protest. Both the Church and labor unions were called upon to play vital roles in later campaigns.

The Birmingham Confrontation

While the battle for equal accommodations was being fought in Albany, similar ones were being conducted elsewhere. One of these was waged in Birmingham, Alabama, which King described as the most segregated city in the United States. Having been inspired by the successful Montgomery Bus Protest, Rev. Fred Shuttleworth organized the Alabama Christian Movement for Human Rights (ACMHR) to lead an assault against segregation in Birmingham. Later, the organization became an affiliate of the SCLC. Consistent with the techniques of Gandhi, King was willing to respond to the call of a local organization to assist in its campaign for racial justice. Remembering, however, the errors of Albany, an extensive assessment of the situation was undertaken prior to the SCLC consenting to join the campaign.

One of the first concerns to be explored was the impact which demonstrations would have upon the upcoming city elections. Would Police Commissioner "Bull" Conner, a racist, receive a sizable backlash vote for mayor as a result of the demonstrations? In order to prevent such a disaster, the campaign was scheduled to be launched after the elections. When Conner received enough votes to enter the run-off, however, it became necessary to postpone the campaign for a second time. This posed a serious problem, since a major strategy was to focus attention on a boycott of downtown merchants during the Easter season, which was rapidly approaching.

Another matter that needed to be resolved prior to the beginning of the campaign was that of participation. Contact was established with civil rights organizations, including the NAACP, CORE, SNCC, and the Southern Regional Conference, and likewise, appeals for aid were sent to religious leaders and others who had participated in the Albany protest. Similarly, because funds were needed to assure the success of the campaign, a mechanism had to be established for that purpose. As in the case of the previous campaign, Harry Belafonte, the noted entertainer, assumed a major role in fund-raising efforts. In order to coordinate the arrangements for the demonstrations, the SCLC dispatched Wyatt Walker, its executive director, to Birmingham to assess the situation. Among the tasks which he performed were: conferring with lawyers concerning city codes on picketing, demonstrations, etc.; securing information relative to bail-bonds; surveying the downtown section; studying the lay-out of stores; and conducting workshops on direct-action techniques for recruits.[15]

As in the case of Albany, King found African-Americans of Birmingham to be divided regarding their attitudes toward demonstrations. There were those who thought that the new city government represented a major change; thus, should be given an opportunity to resolve some of the racial problems before the beginning of demonstrations. Similar views were held by some members of the Kennedy Administration and some of the leading newspapers. There were other African-Americans who had resigned themselves to their status; thus, not interested in protest activities. In spite of this opposition, King was determined that the time was right for the campaign; therefore, he launched it in March 1963.

Unlike Pritchett in Albany, Police Commissioner Bull Conner had not familiarized himself with Gandhian strategy; thus, he attempted to contain nonviolent protest with excessive force. His use of police dogs and fire hoses to prevent marches by protesters, many of whom were children, attracted international attention. Likewise, the arrest, and abusive treatment of King during his detention, enhanced the cause of civil rights. Among the results produced by Conner's inhumane tactics were: more sympathetic news coverage of the campaign, an increased number of volunteers who came to Birmingham to aid the cause, a greater financial contribution for civil rights efforts, and a growing concern by the President and Congress. By arresting and detaining King, officials provided him with a platform from which he could appeal to the conscience of the world. His historic "Letter from Birmingham Jail," which was written during his detention, is viewed as a brilliant defense of civil disobedience.[16]

Reacting to the violence which was characterizing the city, the Kennedy Administration sought to use its influence with Northern industrialists to bring pressure to bear upon their Southern subsidiaries to negotiate, meaningfully, with the demonstrators. Simultaneously, white citizens of Birmingham,

---

[15] King, *Why We Can't Wait* (New York: Harper and Row Publishers, 1964), 49, 52.

[16] King, 63, 64.

including the Senior Citizen Committee, used their influence to bring peace to the city.[17] Finally, on May 10, 1963, a tentative accord was achieved, which provided the following:

1. The desegregation of lunch counters, rest rooms, fitting rooms, and drinking fountains, in planned stages within ninety days after signing.
2. The upgrading and hiring of Negroes on a nondiscriminatory basis throughout the industrial community of Birmingham.
3. Official cooperation with the movement's legal representatives in working out the release of all jailed persons on bond or on their personal recognizance.
4. The establishment of a mechanism, either through the Senior Citizens Committee or Chamber of Commerce, by which communications between whites and blacks can be better maintained.[18]

King considered the signing of the agreement a "climax of a long struggle for justice, freedom and human dignity." Although he did not perceive this as being the millennium, he did feel that "Birmingham had made a fresh, bold step toward equality."[19] Ten days after the signing of the accord, another victory was achieved when the Supreme Court handed down a decision which legalized "sit-in" demonstrations in cities which sought to enforce segregation.

As was the case in the Albany protest, there were critics of King's performance in Birmingham, but generally, he was credited with having conducted an effective campaign "thanks" to the excessive force used by the police, and the violence perpetrated by anticivil rights demonstrators. Not only did the protest achieve better conditions for African-Americans in Birmingham, but it also served to awake the conscience of the nation--making it aware of the need for greater federal action in defense of civil rights. The Birmingham campaign and the March on Washington, held later that summer, were major contributing factors to the enactment of the Civil Rights Act of 1964.

[17] Lewis, 198.
[18] King. 112-113.
[19] King, 116.

The March on Washington

The March on Washington represented a high point in the civil rights career of Martin Luther King, Jr. His "I Have a Dream" address, which was delivered on that occasion, is regarded as the most famous of all his speeches. The event was not one that was organized by King; instead, it was a major effort of civil rights, religious, and labor organizations from various parts of the United States.

In mid-1963, A Philip Randolph, the former president of the Brotherhood of Sleeping Car Porters, revived an idea that he had advanced in November 1962 relative to a march on Washington and sought to implement it. In order to pursue the idea, approximately 200 civil rights leaders and representatives of sympathetic national organizations convened in New York on July 2, 1963. After agreeing to pursue the project, the next task was to determine how to finance it. Stephen Currier, the president of the Taconic Foundation, and Whitney Young, head of the National Urban League, co-chaired the Council for United Civil Rights Leadership (CUCRL), which sought to raise $1.5 million in emergency funds for the major civil rights organizations, including the NAACP, CORE, SCLC, SNCC, the National Urban League, and the National Council of Negro Women (NCNW).[20]

The initial reaction of the Kennedy Administration was less than enthusiastic. According to the President, he was not interested in "just a big show at the Capitol;" instead, he wanted positive results. He perceived the March as giving the impression of an "atmosphere of intimidation" at a crucial stage in the legislative history of the Civil Rights Bill. Kennedy expressed fear that the March would give senators an excuse for opposing the bill and other important legislation of the Administration. King insisted, however, that it was necessary to go ahead with the March, noting that he had never "engaged in any direct action movement which did not seem ill-timed."[21] Once the Kennedy Administration realized that the civil rights leaders were determined to proceed with the March, it sought to make it successful, since it had a vested interest in the outcome. The Justice Department analyzed the plans for the March, and gave consideration to all of the things which could possibly go wrong. Perceiving the negative impact which demonstrations at the Capitol

---

[20] Lewis, 219.

[21] Arthur Schlessinger, Jr., *Robert Kennedy and His Times* (Boston: Houghton-Mifflin Co., 1978), 342-350.

would have on legislators, it used its influence to persuade planners to forego the original plan, and settle for a march from the Washington Monument to the Lincoln Memorial. Other major concerns of the Kennedy Administration were the composition, and the size of the March. Fearing that an all-black march would have an unfavorable impact, the President conferred with Walter Reuther, president of the United Auto Workers, who later was instrumental in bringing into the movement whites from labor unions and churches. Likewise, it was believed that if less than 100,000 persons participated, it might convince members of Congress that the demand for civil rights legislation was overstated. In the end, however, the concern was not justified, since more than 250,000 participated in the March.[22] The Justice Department also exerted its influence in bringing about a revision of the intended remarks of John Lewis, chairman of SNCC. A moment of tension had developed earlier, when certain religious leaders threatened to withdraw from participation if he insisted upon making a "tough speech" criticizing the Kennedy Administration.[23]

Among the participants in the March were blacks and whites, Jews and Christians, and poor and rich. There were entertainers, athletes, politicians, civil rights activists and the rank and file. Generally, speakers representing various sponsoring organizations, reviewed the plight of African-Americans, and challenged the American Government to take necessary steps to relieve the centuries of oppression. As noted above, the most memorable address was that of Martin Luther King, Jr., who envisioned the advent of a just society.

While the March was generally applauded, there were critics who accused the civil rights leaders of allowing the Kennedy Administration and liberal whites to co-opt the March for their vested interest. In his analysis, David Lewis rejected the criticism that "black leaders of the March betrayed their followers by accepting the financial support and political endorsement of liberal whites." He contended that such an argument could be made only if "initially, the men and goals behind the March were revolutionary," which he considered to be untrue.[24]

The nonviolent manner in which the March was conducted did much to awaken the conscience of people throughout the world, which, in turn, generated the necessary support to secure the passage of the Civil Rights Act of 1964. With the passage of this historic act, which included a provision

---

[22] Schlessinger, 350-351.
[23] Schlessinger, 351.
[24] Lewis, 220.

concerning equal accommodation of public facilities, King and other civil rights advocates turned their attention to the task of securing political rights.

POLITICAL RIGHTS OF AFRICAN-AMERICANS

Although constitutional restrictions on the voting rights of African-Americans were removed by the 15th Amendment in 1870, nearly a century later such had not become a reality in too many states of the Union. Opponents of that amendment utilized such devices as the poll tax, white primary, literacy test, grandfather's clause, and intimidation to prevent African-Americans from voting. Even though court decisions had erased some of these barriers, too many African-Americans continued to be denied their right to vote. King was aware of this when, at the Prayer Pilgrimage in Washington, DC in 1957, he issued the challenge that if African-Americans were given the right to vote, it would no longer be necessary to plea for federal protection of basic rights. He perceived the gaining of political power as enabling them to determine who would sit in Congress, state legislatures, and the federal judiciary, and who would occupy the governorships.[25]

In order to increase voting registration of African-Americans, the SCLC initiated its "Crusade for Citizenship" project, on Lincoln Birthday in 1958. Although the securing of political rights for African-Americans had been a priority for King throughout his campaign for racial justice, it was not until the Selma campaign of 1965 that the effort received true national attention. Selma was a logical choice for the launching of the campaign since only about one percent of its predominantly African-American population was registered voters.

The selection of Selma disturbed Wilson Baker, its director of city police, who went immediately to Washington to seek the aid of Assistant Attorney General Burke Marshall in the cancellation or delay of the demonstrations. Marshall conferred with King, but was told that too much time and effort had been invested in the project to make a change.[26] On January 18, the registration drive was launched, when approximately 400 protesters marched to the Courthouse. Among those who confronted the demonstrators were

---

[25] King, "Give Us the Ballot - We Will Transform the South," an address delivered at the Pilgrimage to Washington, May 17, 1957, King's Papers, MLK/CNSC.

[26] David J. Garrow, *Protest at Selma* (New Haven: Yale University Press, 1978), 35.

members of the States Rights, and Nazi parties. King interrupted his campaign in order to attend a banquet in honor of his having been presented the Nobel Peace Award, but he returned to Selma shortly thereafter and resumed his protest activities. On February 1, 1965, he was among the 770 persons arrested as they conducted a massive voting registration march, and on the following day, an additional 550 were arrested. After his release on February 5, King announced that he was requesting the President to prepare a new and stronger voting rights law, and simultaneously, he demanded that the federal court instruct Selma voting registrars to maintain daily hours to facilitate a rapid enrollment of African-American voters.[27]

The response of Washington to the situation in Dallas County was encouraging, with Congressman Charles Diggs of Michigan leading a Congressional delegation of fifteen to inspect the situation in Selma. On February 9, King conferred with Vice President Hubert Humphrey and Attorney General-designate Nicholas Katsenbach, and was assured by them that a strong voting rights proposal would be sent to Congress. While King was optimistic about what was taking place in Washington, the events in Selma did not suggest an improvement of the situation. Sheriff Clark, acting as if he had received his indoctrination from Bull Connor of Birmingham, used excessive force; thus, bringing about a violent confrontation with demonstrators. In the aftermath of the incident, seventy white ministers marched to the Dallas County Courthouse to protest the violence.[28]

On February 15, the crisis deepened when King led a march of 2,800 in Selma, and followed it with visits to neighboring Wilcox and Perry Counties. While participating in a voter registration drive in the latter, Jimmie Lee Jackson was shot, and later died. With news of the tragedy reaching a national audience, an effort was made by "the progressives" of Selma to improve the racial climate. In the meantime, King suggested a march from Selma to Montgomery to lay the voting registration problem at the feet of Governor Wallace. As plans were being made for the march, the attorney general and others became greatly concerned about the safety of King; thus, suggested that he not participate, personally. Heeding the advice, and needing to be present at his church in Atlanta--after having been absent for several Sundays--King designated Hosea Williams of the SCLC to join with John Lewis of SNCC in

---

[27] Lewis, 265-269.
[28] Lewis, 269.

leading the march. On March 7, more than 500 marchers set out for Montgomery in a very jovial mood, but trouble beset them after they crossed the Pettus Bridge, which led out of town. After having been told to disperse, which they refused to do, the police used gas and other violent means to terminate the march.[29]

Speaking from Atlanta, King expressed regrets over the violence, and then proceeded to announce his intentions of returning to Selma to lead a second march. Simultaneously, he requested a federal injunction to prevent state interference with the marchers. Contrary to his expectation, the Federal Judge ordered him to postpone the march until after a proper judicial determination had been made concerning the case. The decision presented King with a dilemma as to whether to honor, or to defy the order and proceed with the march. Charles Fager noted that King had taken into consideration the fact that in the past, "the federal courts had almost always been a refuge for him and his movements in the South, and that Judge Johnson's record was one of the best."[30] Initially, King decided to yield to the injunction, but "the magnitude and intensity of the response to the plea for support" caused him to have second thoughts about the matter. Attorney General Nicholas Katsenbach and former Florida Governor Leroy Collins, who was head of the Community Relations Service, sought to convince him that he should obey the injunction, and later, the White House announced that the President had requested a postponement of the march.[31]

Insisting that African-Americans had a right to walk the highways, King proceeded with the protest march, which apparently had been modified after he had held conferences with Governor Collins. With hundreds of priests, rabbis, and ministers at the front of the procession, thousands marched from Brown's Chapel, singing freedom songs. When they reached the Pettus Bridge, a US Marshall read the restraining order, then King asked if the protesters could pray. After permission was granted, the demonstrators prayed, then returned to the church. Ironically, before their return, the state troopers had been instructed to "fall back" from the highway, leaving the road to Montgomery open in case King chose to disobey the injunction. Fager suggested that "apparently Wallace had either wanted to entice him into a clear violation of the federal court order, or to make him look timid in the eyes

---

[29] Lewis, 270-274.
[30] Charles E. Fager, *Selma 1965* (New York: Charles Scribner's Publisher, 1974), 101-102.
[31] Fager, 102.

of the more militant marchers."[32] At the mass meeting, following the march, King suggested that "by marching to the site of the Sunday assault in such massive and distinguished numbers, they had communicated to the country the magnitude of the oppression in the Black Belt."[33] His critics disagreed.

While events were unfurling in Selma, people throughout the United States and Canada were mobilizing in protest against the violence in Alabama. Demonstrations were held in such cities as New York, Chicago, Boston, Cleveland, Oakland, Syracuse, New Haven, Detroit, and Toronto. In Washington, more than seven hundred people picketed the White House, and protestors conducted a "sit in" at the Justice Department. The President deplored the violence, and announced his intentions of submitting a proposal for a new voting rights act to the Congress.[34]

In a special message to Congress on March 15, 1965, President Johnson referred to the struggle in Selma as characteristic of "a larger movement which reaches every section and State of America," one in which African-Americans are engaged in an effort "to secure for themselves the full blessings of American life." Johnson challenged other Americans that "their cause must be our cause too. Because it is not just Negroes but really it is all of us, who must overcome the crippling legacy of bigotry and injustice."[35] King expressed pleasure over the support of the President, noting that he had made one of the most "passionate pleas for human rights" ever made by a president. He praised Johnson's pledge to employ "the might of the Federal Government to cast off the centuries-old blight" of racial discrimination.[36]

On March 17, Judge Johnson authorized the Selma-Montgomery March, and enjoined state and county officials from interfering. With the legal roadblock removed, four days later, the March commenced with a cast of notable from throughout the country. The Federal Judge limited the number of participants in the highway march to 300. Federal troops were dispatched along the road to prevent violence. After traveling through hostile areas, and

---

[32] Fager, 104.

[33] Fager, 105.

[34] Fager, 106.

[35] U.S. Presidents, *Public Papers of the Presidents of the United States* (Washington, DC: Office of the *Federal Register*, National Archives and Records Service, 1965) Lyndon B. Johnson.1965, I, 107.

[36] King, "Conclusion of Selma to Montgomery March," March 25, 1965, MLK/CNSC.

encountering numerous insults, the marchers reached Montgomery, where more than 50,000 gathered for the climatic event.[37]

In his address, King praised the courage of African-Americans in "awakening the conscience of the nation," and paid respect to the white Americans who "cherished their democratic traditions over the ugly customs and privileges of generations." He challenged the audience to:

> ...march on ballots until race haters disappear from the political arena ... until the Wallaces of our nation tremble away in silence--until we send to our city councils, state legislatures and U.S. Congress, men who will not fear to do justly, love mercy and walk humbly, with their God...until brotherhood becomes more than a meaningless word in an opening prayer, but the order of the day on every legislative agenda."[38]

The Selma campaign, at times, represented Americans at their best, while at other times, it showed them at their worst. While the participation of whites from across the country was applauded as a movement in the right direction, the several tragedies that characterized the campaign, indicated the extent to which some whites were willing to go in order to preserve their segregated ways of life. In addition to the murdering of Jimmy Lee Jackson in nearby Perry County, race haters also beat to death the Reverend James Reeb, a white Unitarian minister on the street of Selma. A similar tragedy befell Viola Liuzzo, a white housewife from Detroit, Michigan, on the Selma-Montgomery highway following the completion of the historic march. King expressed regret over the high price by which the voting rights of African-Americans had to be purchased.

In the aftermath of the Selma campaign, Congress passed the Voting Rights Act, which provided for the suspension of the literacy test in cases where it was being used in a discriminatory manner, and authorized the use of federal registrars in states where the literacy test was being used, and less than 50% of the eligible voters were registered. King concluded that "with Selma and the Voting Rights Act, one phase of development in the revolution came to an end." As he reflected on the campaign, he recalled that in Selma the major goal of the demonstration was "to dramatize the existence of injustice and to bring about the presence of justice by methods of nonviolence."

[37] King,
[38] King.

According to King, as a pre-requisite for victory in Selma, four things occurred:

1. Nonviolent demonstrators went into the streets to exercise their constitutional rights.
2. Racists resisted these efforts by unleashing violence against them.
3. Americans of conscience in the name of decency demanded federal intervention and legislation.
4. The administration, under mass pressure, initiated measures of immediate intervention and remedial legislation.[39] With the voting rights of African-Americans guaranteed by new legislation, King now began to focus his attention on the elimination of poverty.

ELIMINATION OF POVERTY

Brown v. Board of Education (1954) declared null and void laws which required segregated school systems; the Civil Rights Act of 1964 provided for equal accommodations regardless of race; and the Voting Rights Act of 1965 made it easier for African Americans to exercise their right to vote. In spite of these legal accomplishments, African Americans in the United States continue to lag behind their white counterparts in regard to the enjoyment of the "good life." Bemoaning the fact that "of the good things in life he [the African American] has approximately one half those of whites; of the bad things in life he has twice those of whites,"[40] King decided to launch a campaign to liberate blacks from the state of poverty, in which too many found themselves trapped.

Much to the surprise of many, King found the plight of African Americans in the North to be worse than that of their counterpart in the South. He noted that in the South, the gains made by African Americans as a result of their nonviolent struggle were dramatic, cumulative, dynamic, and "moving constantly toward broad application." In the North, however, the "repellent slum life" of African-Americans "was altered not for the better but for the worse." He observed that the North should have made greater progress during the last decade in regard to the dissolution of ghettos, the disappearance of employment discrimination, the modification or eradication of tensions

[39] King, "Behind the Selma March," *Saturday Review*, 48, April 3, 1965, 16-17.
[40] King, *Where Do We Go From Here* (New York: Harper and Row Publishers, 1967), 6.

between blacks and the police and the overall improvement of interracial relations.[41] King concluded that instead of making profound progress "the North, at best, stood still as the South caught up." What he found to be very disturbing was that while African-Americans of the South made their progress through nonviolent means, their counterpart of the North rejected such an approach, contending that in "the complexities of urban life the tricks of sophisticated segregation cannot be defeated except by the power of violence." King concluded that "they are so close to white society but so alienated from it and consumed with revulsion toward its hypocrisies that they are disinterested in integration."[42]

The Chicago Campaign

Once King decided to launch a campaign in the North, Chicago appeared to be his logical choice of a target city. He referred to it as "an island of poverty in the midst of an ocean of plenty"--a city that claimed to have the highest per capita income of any city in the world, yet had confined most of its African-American population to poverty. King pointed to statistics which revealed that Chicago spent an average of $366 a year per pupil in predominantly white schools in the core city and from $450 to $900 per pupil in suburban white neighborhoods; contrasted with $266 per pupil in African-American neighborhoods. Similarly, the median rent in the predominantly African-American neighborhoods was ninety dollars per month contrasted with eighty for a larger apartment in a white suburban area. The situation was no better in regard to the purchase of goods, with consumer items ranging from five to twelve percent higher in black communities.[43] King referred to the plight of African-Americans as a vicious circle, giving this description:

> "You can't get a job because you are poorly educated, and you must depend on welfare to feed your children; but if you receive public aid in Chicago, you cannot own property, not even an automobile, so you are condemned to the jobs and shops which are closest to your home."[44]

---

[41] King, "Next Stop: The North," *Saturday Review*, 48, Nov 13, 1965, 33.
[42] King, 35.
[43] King, *Where Do We Go From Here*, 115.
[44] King, 116.

He noted that this confinement restricted their participation in a free economy and subjected them to outrageous prices by many of the merchants on whom they had to depend.

Perceiving a need to return the favor which Al Raby and others had performed during the campaigns in southern cities, King undertook an exploratory visit to Chicago in July 1965. He was responding to a request for aid from the Coordinating Council of Community Organization (CCCO)--a coalition of civil rights, religious and civil groups that were engaged in efforts to improve the educational system in Chicago. In an address on July 26, King noted that Chicago was far from being "the promised land." Insisting that the SNCC had come to the city to "issue a call to conscience," he pledged to return to the city at a later date and aid Chicagoans in their struggle.[45]

When King returned to Chicago in early 1966, in order to better identify with the poor, he moved into a flat in a section of the city called North Lawndale--generally referred to as Slumdale. Once he was settled in the community, he conducted hearings to determine the complaints of the tenants. Based upon what he had learned, he criticized the city for its high rate of unemployment, stores and landlords for their exploitation, and the police force for its indifference to ghetto crime. In his crusade against the evils of Chicago, King sought support of ministers of the city, and likewise, tried to convert youth gangs to the nonviolent cause. Although he found it difficult to convince them of the merits of his approach, he was able to recruit some of them to serve as marshals at demonstrations.[46]

King's campaign was launched with great anticipation, but by mid-March it had begun to lose momentum because of financial difficulties, apathy of African-Americans, and the perceived lack of a well-defined strategy. There also was dissatisfaction among members of CCCO because of a shift of emphasis by the movement away from its original goal. Another major problem was that of dealing with Mayor Richard Daley, who sought to discredit King's effort, by pointing to the success of his administration in the field of social justice. He produced fact sheets concerning his investigation of building code violations, the spraying of thousands of apartments for rats and insects, and the construction of 31,000 public housing units. The Mayor took his campaign to the ministers, where he and King engaged in a dialogue, in

---

[45] King, "Address Delivered at March on Chicago," July 26, 1965, MLK/CNSC.

[46] King, "Statement at Press Conference of Chicago Movement," Chicago, IL, July 7, 1965, MLK/CNSC.

which Daley pointed to the fact that Chicago's poverty had its origin elsewhere, namely, in the Southern states from which many Chicagoans had migrated. According to Stephen Oates, by mid-April, the Mayor had neutralized King, politically, by the strategic use of his own anti-poverty projects and promises," and the employment of "patronage to enlarge his potent outposts in the African-American community." Even some of the African-American political leaders had begun to suggest that King return to Atlanta.[47]

During the Chicago crusade, for the first time, King encountered boos by members of the Black Power Movement--a matter which troubled him, greatly. He questioned himself as to why one who was so closely identified with the struggle should be booed. Although he was very disturbed, he expressed an understanding as to why the young people had acted as they did. He recalled that for twelve years, he had held out to them, "radiant promises of progress, and as a result they, too, had become optimistic about the future."[48]

Perceiving his nonviolent campaign as losing ground nationally, King intensified his efforts--organizing a major Freedom Sunday rally, which was held July 10, 1966. Although 100,000 were anticipated, the weather and other factors held the crowd to approximately 30,000. In his address, King challenged his audience to use its economic power to bring about meaningful employment of African-Americans and other ethnic minorities in well-paying jobs, by withdrawing their funds from banks and financial houses. He, also, called upon them to withhold their votes from Mayor Daley if he did not respond to their demands.[49] Once the Soldier Field aspect of the program was completed, King and approximately 36,000 followers went to City Hall, where, in a manner similar to that of Martin Luther--his namesake, he posted his 95 theses on the door, and proclaimed the event as the "symbolic beginning of an American Revolution." Among the demands was a call for "an end to police brutality and discriminatory real-estate practices, increased Negro employment, and a civilian review board for the police department..." The following day, King attempted to present his demands to Daley, personally, but the Mayor rejected them, referring him to his massive anti-slum program. Perceiving Daley as inviting "social disaster" the civil rights

---

[47] Oates, 390.
[48] Oates, 394.
[49] King, *Where Do We Go From Here*, 45.

leader promised to "launch sit-ins, camp-ins, boycotts, and mass demonstrations in the streets."[50]

On July 12, the day following King's confrontation with the Mayor, the West Side erupted in a riot that left nine persons injured and twenty-four in jail. King sought to restore order by calling a mass meeting, but the effort was unsuccessful. He blamed the disorder on "police brutality", and renewed his demands for a civilian review board to oversee police activities. He also demanded the installing of swimming pools and parks on the West Side. A great deal of finger-pointing followed, with African-Americans who supported Daley blaming the disturbances on "outside interference," and the Mayor accusing anarchists and Communists. In the wake of the riots, King held a ninety minute meeting with Mayor Daley, and the latter made concessions, including the erecting of ten portable swimming pools on the West Side and the affixing of sprinkles to water hydrants for use by children. Daley later named a citizen committee to study the police department.[51] Perceiving the need for pursuing "creative tension" in Chicago, King, on July 30, 1966, called for a march against segregated housing in all-white neighborhoods that surrounded the ghettos. A major purpose of the campaign was to expose Chicago's housing discrimination to the nation, and to reveal its impact upon the human miseries of those forced to live in poverty. When the first march, which was conducted in King's absence, erupted into violence, he scheduled another one for August 6 to prove that peaceful demonstrations could be undertaken in the city. On that occasion, he led a contingent of 600 African-Americans and whites through an all-white area occupied by second generation Poles, Lithuanians, Italians, and Germans. As the marchers proceeded with the protection of 900 policemen, they were bombarded by rocks, bottles and other objects. With the march completed and demonstrators once again on their busses, counter-demonstrators pursued them as they returned to their Chicago base.[52]

In order to intensify his Chicago campaign, King announced plans for a march on the city of Cicero, which historically was associated with northern racism. The plan caused grave concern among former civil rights allies, who sought to convince him to reconsider his decision. After King's decision, and the reactions of members of "hate groups" which followed, Illinois' Governor

---

[50] Oates, 407.
[51] Oates, 407-408.
[52] Oates, 408-409.

Otto Kerner announced that he would use the National Guard to assist the Cicero Police Force in keeping order. King considered it tragic that an armed escort of guardsmen would be necessary for a peaceful march in a northern suburb, when African-Americans had marched in the "southern bastion of segregation" without such armed military protection.[53] The march, however, was deferred when King, Daley, and others reached an agreement relative to the housing crisis. The accord provided for the ending of segregated housing through the cooperative efforts of many groups and agencies, including the Chicago Real Estate Board, Chicago Housing Authority, Cook County Council of Insured Savings Association, Chicago Mortgage Bankers Association, Chicago Commission on Human Relations, and the Chicago Conference on Religion and Race. King praised the accord as "the most significant program ever conceived to make open housing a reality in the metropolitan area."[54] With the agreement achieved, he turned his priority to the task of pursuing jobs; thus, Operation Breadbasket was organized, with Jesse Jackson assigned the task of heading it. Once this program was in place, King closed his Chicago campaign, and returned to Atlanta.

The Memphis Campaign

King's concern for the economic plight of poor people was further reflected in his Memphis campaign. Most of the African-American workers of that city had organized themselves into a local chapter of the American Federation of State, County and Municipal Employees. The City, however, refused to recognize the union, or grant it a contract that would provide improved wages and better working conditions. On February 12, 1968, when 1,300 African-American sanitation workers went on strike, they were prevented from holding protest marches by policemen, using mace and night sticks. Such tactics provoked anger in the African-American community, which reacted by organizing the Community on the Move for Equality (COME) to support the union's efforts. Mayor Henry Loeb refused to negotiate and threatened to fire the workers if the strike continued. COME

---

[53] Lionel Lokos, *House Divided: The Life and Legacy of Martin Luther King* (New Rochelle, NY: Arlington House, Inc., 1968), 258.

[54] Lokos.

reacted to the intransigence of the City by inviting national civil rights leaders to come to Memphis to rally support for the strikers.[55]

King found the invitation appealing since the cause in Memphis was similar to that of his national campaign in behalf of poor people. At the time of the crisis, he was waging a "people to people tour" of Mississippi, which he interrupted to go to Memphis. On March 18, he addressed more than 17,000 people at the Mason Temple, and as he had done on previous occasions, King reminded them that too many African-Americans still live in houses that are dilapidated, and are "smothering in an air-tight cage of poverty." He challenged them that "if we are going to get adequate wages, we are going to have to struggle for it."[56]

King promised to return to the city for a massive march on March 22, and he appealed to students to leave their classes and employees to boycott their jobs in order to participate. A massive snow storm, however, forced the cancellation of the march, which then was rescheduled for March 28. As King and Jim Lawson of Memphis began the rescheduled march, they were not aware that more militant "Black Power" youths had penetrated their ranks. When violence erupted, King immediately terminated the march, and was then taken to a motel where, in dismay, he watched on television the violence which was then encompassing the city. One youth was dead, 60 persons were injured, and 155 stores were damaged. King was upset that violence had broken out in a demonstration which he had led, and he was even more disturbed that he had not been told of the Invaders, a militant group which had been accused of fomenting the violence.[57]

Early the next morning, three Invaders came by the motel to talk to King. They admitted inciting the violence, but sought to justify their behavior on the basis of having been ignored by the strike leaders, and not having been made "part of the action." King informed them that he would be coming back to Memphis and would see them at that time, but he advised them of his disapproval of violence. Later, King told a press conference that he would be returning to the city, no later than April 5 to lead a massive non-violent march.[58]

---

[55] Oates, 415.
[56] King, "Address at Mason Temple Mass Meeting," Memphis, TN, March 18, 1968.
[57] Oates.
[58] Oates.

When King returned to the city on April 3, he was escorted directly to the Lorraine Motel. Although he had made plans to challenge the temporary restraining order by the U.S. District Judge, King promised to lead the march, as scheduled. Plans had been made for him to deliver an address, but it was a dark rainy night with warnings of tornadoes and he was not in the mood for addressing what he thought would be a small crowd. In anticipation of the press' claim that the small crowd was an indication of the civil rights movement losing steam, King asked Abernathy to go in his place, which the latter consented to do. Because the large and enthusiastic audience appeared to be disappointed in not being able to hear King, Abernathy prevailed upon him to make a brief appearance at the rally. King, in his address, expressed the belief that even though he might not be able to enter the promised land, he had been able to see it from the mountain top and he could envision the day in which his people would finally be free.[59] As he had anticipated, he was not permitted to enter the earthly promised land--having been assassinated within twenty-four hours after his historic address. Among the task which remained for others to complete was the implementation of his "Poor People March," which at the time of his death, was still on the drawing board.

A National Campaign for the Poor

In Chicago, King's goal was to achieve better housing for African-Americans and in Memphis, he sought to aid sanitation workers obtain better working conditions. Even though these were local efforts they served to focus attention on the need for a national campaign to enhance the economic status of African-Americans. The Operation Bread-basket program, which by 1967 was being operated in twelve cities, was illustrative of the effort being made to address the problem, nationally. The major objective of this program was to secure more and better jobs for African-Americans, and in order to achieve that goal, they were urged "to support those businesses that will give a fair share of jobs to Negroes and to withdraw its support from those businesses that have discriminatory policies." Operation Breadbasket pursued its goals by investigating the practices of particular business firms, evaluating the findings, negotiating, and when feasible, applying pressure through such means as massive "economic withdrawal from the company's product and

[59] Oates, 486.

accompanying demonstrations if necessary."[60] Because of their awareness of the buying power of African-Americans, many companies did not force the issue to the final stage, however.

Concerned about the increased violence which was becoming rather commonplace in too many American cities, and the backlash in response to it, King sought to devise a program that would force the American Government to honor its commitment to the poor of this nation. Being especially disturbed by the response to the urban riots by the Johnson Administration, he called for a study of the problem and a day of prayer. King contended that "when a government commands more wealth and power than has ever been known in the history of the world and offers no more than this, it is worse than blind, it is provocative." While King maintained that he was not opposed to prayer, he insisted that he took it too seriously "to use it as an excuse for avoiding work and responsibility." With this thought in mind, he called upon the dispossessed of this nation to organize a revolution against the many injustices which had been inflicted upon them. He envisioned poor people--both black and white--as constituting a nonviolent army which, at the designated time, would descend upon Washington and remain there "until the legislative and executive branches of the government take serious and adequate action on jobs and income." To implement the plan, King suggested the recruitment of three thousand of the poorest people from ten different urban and rural areas who would spend three months in developing nonviolent action skills. Upon completion they would go to Washington and "lead a sustained, massive direct action movement."[61] During its second phase, the Poor People Army was envisioned as disrupting governmental operations with sit-ins and demonstrations. King gave the following illustration:

> "If you are, let's say, from rural Mississippi, and have never had medical attention, and your children are undernourished and unhealthy, you can take those little children into Washington hospitals and stay with them there until the medical workers cope with their needs..."[62]

In case the disruption of governmental activities did not bring about an adequate response by Congress, King suggested the use of nationwide

---

[60] King, *Where Do We Go From Here*, 143-144.
[61] King, *Trumpet of Conscience*, 60.
[62] King, 61.

boycotts of selected industries and shopping centers in targeted large cities to compel business leaders to exert their influence upon Congress to meet the demands of the poor.[63]

Why should Washington be the focus of the demonstration, critics asked? King's reply was "because only the federal Congress and administration can decide to use the billions of dollars we need for a real war on poverty." His suggestion of a "Poor People March" provoked an avalanche of criticisms--with some of the critics questioning its potentials for success and others viewing it as subversive. Bayard Rustin, one of the close advisers of King, opposed the idea, considering it to be untimely, especially in view of 1968 being an election year. He perceived the disruption of normal governmental activities as producing a great backlash and additional repression. Secondly, Rustin was concerned about attracting uncontrollable elements to the March, who might serve to disrupt the campaign. He feared that if the campaign erupted into violence there would be an immediate response by the Federal Government, which would have the effect of terminating the demonstration.[64]

According to the FBI, violence might well have been the goal of the organizers in planning the Poor People March. It attributed this strategy to black nationalists and Communists who it insisted were advising the civil rights leader. In a request for new wire-tapping of King's telephones, the FBI submitted a letter to the Attorney General, which noted the civil rights leader's warning that riots might result from the massive demonstrations, and suggested that the Bureau should "be in a position to obtain intelligence so that appropriate countermeasures can be taken to protect the internal security of the United State." Attorney General Ramsey Clark rejected the FBI's request for further wiretapping of King, however.[65]

King's assassination at Memphis made it impossible for him to pursue the project, but the Reverend David Abernathy, his successor, conducted a modified Poor People March in honor of the deceased.

---

[63] Oates, 461.
[64] Oates, 457.
[65] Garrow, 184.

A Peaceful World

Being aware that his struggle for integration would be in vain if there was no world to integrate, Martin Luther King, Jr. decided to become an active opponent of the War in Vietnam. He did not arrive at this decision easily, however. According to Mrs. King, prior to 1967 he was engaged in an inner conflict as to whether he should divide his limited time between the dual struggles for world peace and freedom for African-Americans, and thereby dilute the efforts of both, or to continue to pursue the latter with full vigor. During the preparations for the massive Thanksgiving week-end demonstration in 1965, efforts were made to recruit King to the anti-war cause. Not only did the sponsors seek to obtain him as one of their speakers, but they also sought to involve him almost totally in the peace campaign. Dr. Benjamin Spock tried to convince King to undertake a world tour in behalf of peace, and by so doing, obtain "world recognition as a symbol of peace," and as a result of this new status, return to this country and unify the peace movement.[66]

King declined the invitation, expressing the view that such involvement would be disruptive of the civil rights cause. He recalled the type of opposition, which had been engendered within the movement a year earlier when he had taken a strong position against the war. At that time, King issued a public appeal for immediate Vietnam negotiations, which was approved by the executive board of the SCLC. After having been criticized for the linkage of the civil rights and peace issues, he retreated, temporarily from the campaign against the Vietnamese War.[67]

By 1967, however, King had become sufficiently disturbed over the impact which the financing of the war was having on providing funds to fight poverty that he took an active role in opposing the war. In an address to the Nation Institute in Los Angeles, CA on February 25, 1967, King condemned the war as cruel and senseless. He cited estimates of $322,000 being spent on every enemy killed, contrasted with $53 spent for each person classified as "poor." King decried the American arrogance in "professing to be concerned about the freedom of foreign nations while not setting our own house in order." King suggested that "those of us who love peace must organize as

---

[66] Coretta Scott King, *My Life With Martin Luther King, Jr.* (New York: Holt, Rinchart and Winston, 1969), 291

[67] Coretta Scott King.

effectively as the war hawks... and spread the propaganda of peace." He urged a combination of the "fervor of the civil rights movement with the peace movement."[68]

Slightly more than a month later, King launched further into the deep, with his April 4 address at New York's Riverside Church, under the sponsorship of Clergy and Laymen Concerned about Vietnam. He advised the crowd that there comes a time when silence must be broken, and that the time in regard to Vietnam, was then. According to King, to break the silence was not easy. He noted that "even when pressed by the demands of inner truth, men do not easily assume the task of opposing their government's policy, especially in times of war."[69] Nevertheless, because of the consequences which the Amcrican involvement in Vietnam were causing, he felt compelled to take a stand.

In response to the question as to why he was speaking out against the war, King offered this justification. The increasing cost of waging the war in Vietnam was making it impossible for the United States to "invest the necessary funds or energies in rehabilitation of its poor." He insisted that he was therefore "compelled to see the war not only as a moral outrage but also as an enemy of the poor, and to attack it as such."[70] King considered it even more tragic that because of the war, sons, brothers, and husbands from the homes of the poor were being sent "to fight and to die in extraordinary high proportion relative to the rest of the population." He also was concerned with the extent to which the United States--by its actions--had become the "greatest purveyor of violence in the world today." With the United States bearing such a notorious title, King considered his job of preaching nonviolence to the oppressed in the ghettos as being impossible.[71]

Not only did King see his commitment to "the integrity and life of America" as forcing him to speak out, but he also saw his Nobel Prize for Peace as a "commission to work harder" than he had ever worked for the "brotherhood of man." He noted that this calling had taken him "beyond national allegiance," but even if this had not been the case, he insisted, he

---

[68] Coretta Scott King, 292.

[69] Martin Luther King, Jr., "The Casualities of the War in Vietnam," An Address Delivered at the National Institute. Los Angeles, CA, Feb. 25, 1967.

[70] King, "A Time to Break Silence," An Address Delivered at a Meeting Sponsored by Clergymen and Laymen Concerned about Vietnam," at Riverside Church, New York, April 4, 1967.

[71] King, *Trumpet of Conscience*, 22, 23.

would have had to live with the meaning of his "commitment to the ministry of Jesus Christ." King viewed the tie between this ministry and the maintenance of peace as being so obvious that no one should have ever inquired as to why he was speaking out against the war.[72]

After having presented a detailed analysis of how the Vietnamese were affected by the war, King recommended the following: the ending of the bombing in North and South Vietnam, the declaring of a unilateral ceasefire in order to produce an atmosphere of negotiation, the curtailing of our military buildup and interference in other countries of South East Asia, the reassessing of our attitude concerning the National Liberation Front, and the setting of a date for the removal of all foreign troops from Vietnam.[73]

One of those who rejoiced when Martin came out in support of the anti-war effort was his wife, who for years had been active as a peace advocate. After he had won the Nobel Prize for Peace, she challenged him to play a more active role in the achievement of world peace, and now that the time had arrived when he had become a spokesperson for the cause, she was jubilant. Coretta viewed this as "the beginning of a larger work for him, which would develop into something greater than we could conceive at the time." By "defining the debasing national deficiencies and in offering constructive solutions," King was perceived as "supporting the best in the American traditions."[74]

King rejected the contention that his activities should be limited to civil rights, maintaining that the issues of racial discrimination, poverty, and war were interrelated, and that the first could not be resolved until solutions could be found for the others. Likewise, King viewed the American racial problem as being a part of the global problem of racial discrimination; therefore, his concerns transcended national boundaries.

[72] King, 23, 24.
[73] King, 25.
[74] King, "A Time to Break Silence".

Chapter 5

THE CHIEF: HIS SOUTH AFRICAN CAMPAIGN

> What the future has in store for me I do not know. It might be ridicule, imprisonment, concentration camp, flogging, banishment and even death. I only pray to the Almighty to strengthen my resolve so that none of these grim possibilities may deter me from striving for the sake of the good name of our beloved country, the Union of South Africa to make it a true democracy and a true union in form and spirit of all the communities in the land.[1]
>
> Albert Luthuli

As a young teacher at Adams College, Albert Luthuli, although involved in a segregated society, anticipated a South Africa that would one day be truly a home for all of its sons and daughters. By 1936, however, he was living in a country which was in the process of "turning back the hands of time." The Hertzog Bills of that year made clear the intentions of the white minority to make the blacks a homeless people in a country in which they were indigenous. Under the Representation of Native Acts, Africans of the Cape Province were disenfranchised, and the Native Representative Council was established, supposedly, for the purpose of providing representation of their interest. Within ten years, however, that body had become defunct. Another reflection of the reactionary mood of the white minority could be seen in the adoption of the Native Land and Trust Act, which limited the land that could be owned by the 12 million blacks to 12.5% of the total acreage of South Africa, contrasted with 87.5% reserved for the less than three million whites.

---

[1] Chief Albert Luthuli, "If I Were Prime Minister," *The Atlantic Monthly*, 209, Mar. 1962, 63.

Confronted with such a South Africa, Luthuli tried to advance the interest of the blacks through his chieftaincy, and his participation in such organizations as the Christian Council of South Africa, and the Joint Council of Europeans and Africans. More and more he realized that his efforts were proving to be fruitless, as the government reacted to his moderation by adopting even more restrictive laws. Considering the oppressive nature of the South African Government, and perceiving the need to oppose these injustices in an organized and nonviolent manner, Luthuli became a member of the African National Congress.

EARLY YEARS WITH THE AFRICAN NATIONAL CONGRESS

The African National Congress (ANC) was organized in 1912 as a response to the adoption of the Act of Union, which in essence, made the whites the exclusive owners of South Africa and virtually relegated members of other races to a status similar to that of livestock which went with the estate. Luthuli first began to play an active role in the ANC in 1945, and almost immediately was named to the executive council of the Natal branch. In 1949, he participated in the "Programme of Action" campaign, which was perceived as a milestone in the history of the ANC. Through this campaign, the anti-apartheid forces undertook demonstrations, strikes, and civil disobedience on a national scale--launching the effort with a major nonviolent observance on June 26, 1950. According to Luthuli, the campaign was directed against the various discriminatory laws which the South African Government had adopted, which were not based on morality. Of immediate concern were the proposed Group Area and Suppression of Communist Acts. As a result of the passage of the former, the Government was empowered to remove people residing in an area which had been zoned for another. Under the provisions of the latter, one could be considered a Communist; thus, arrested and detained for such acts as advocating the elimination of apartheid.[2] The one-day stay-at-home demonstration against the acts was perceived as being very successful in Johannesburg, Port Elizabeth, and Durban. Not only did Africans participate in the protest, but Indians and Coloured, as well.

---

[2] Leonard M. Thompson, *Politics in the Republic of South Africa* (Boston: Little, Brown and Company, 1966), 185.

The ANC noted that while it did not achieve its desired goals, it was satisfied that it had wide scale support. In the official report, however, some of the difficulties of the organization were cited, including a lack of faith in the struggle by many, a lack of sufficient funds, a lack of propaganda organs such as the press, failure of some of the officials to perform their duties efficiently, and problems which resulted from restrictions placed upon freedom of assembly, speech, and movement.

With the rights of Coloured and Indians being rapidly eroded by new oppressive racial laws, an attempt was made to unite the efforts of the anti-apartheid forces. In May 1951, Africans and Indians joined the Coloured in Port Elizabeth and South Western Cape in protesting against the efforts of the Nationalist Government to remove the latter from the common electoral roll. Two months later, representatives of the three groups convened for the purpose of better coordinating their campaigns. The Conference agreed to establish a joint planning council "to coordinate the efforts of the National Organizations of the African, Indian and Coloured peoples" in their campaign against the Pass Laws, Stock Limitation, the Group Areas Act, Voters Representation Act, the Suppression of Communist Act, and the Bantu Authorities Act. Later, a joint planning council of the ANC and the South African Indian Congress recommended a campaign of defiance of unjust laws based upon noncooperation.[3]

When the National Conference of the ANC considered the Defiance Campaign, the Natal branch found itself at a disadvantage, inasmuch as Luthuli had recently assumed the leadership of the organization. At first, he had sought a postponement of the Campaign, but was satisfied when the Conference agreed to a provision that would have allowed the Natal Region to comply with the resolution at a later date. Much to the dismay of Luthuli, one female delegate accused him of acting in a cowardly manner. In reply, he reminded her that it was better to express his cowardice at the meeting, rather than remain silent and leave the gathering and act cowardly. While Luthuli perceived the need for immediate action, he considered inadequate preparation to be worse than not having taken any action at all. Recalling that historically, the ANC had not been an organization of violence and bloodshed, he insisted that the basic aim of the organization remains "the bringing of the white man to his senses, and not the slaughtering of him." Luthuli contended that

[3] Karris and Carter, II, 459.

violence and bloodshed, which he deplored, would not aid the ANC, or cause whites to change their ways.[4]

Prior to the launching of the Campaign in 1952, the Prime Minister of South Africa was made aware of the grievances of the Congresses, and was informed of the action which they would be taking. The President-General of the ANC advised Prime Minister D. F. Malan that the Campaign was not "directed against any race or national group but against the unjust laws which keep in perpetual subjection and misery vast sections of the population."[5] The ANC found the reply of the Prime Minister to be unsatisfactory; therefore, in a second letter, it expressed regrets over his rejection of their sincere offer of cooperation based upon full equality, and it informed him that inasmuch as the African people had no alternative, it would embark upon the Defiance Campaign in a peaceful manner.[6]

In preparation for the launching of the campaign on June 26, 1952, a "Day of the Volunteers" was proclaimed the preceding Sunday. After prayers were offered, volunteers took a solemn pledge to "participate fully and without reservations" to the best of their ability in the Campaign. With this done, the Campaign was launched. As it moved from city to city, and then to smaller towns, thousands were arrested--146 volunteers were taken into custody during the remaining days in June, 1,504 in July, 2,015 in August, and 2,058 in September. By mid-December a total of 8,057 had been arrested.[7]

In many cases, the Government reacted to the Campaign by giving out sentences of one or two months, and on occasion, even acquitting the arrested. However, to the dismay of some civil resisters who sought arrest, the police was not always willing to oblige them. Leo Kuper reported an incident in which twenty-three Africans sought arrest by defying the curfew law, but even though the police had been notified in advance, it refused to arrest them, insisting that it was "busy with more important matters." After several unsuccessful attempts, the civil resisters finally were arrested after they entered a railway waiting room that was reserved for Europeans. When tried, they entered pleas of guilty and chose to remain in jail rather than pay the fines. The lawyer for the defense sought to make a statement after the plea, but the magistrate denied the request, insisting that "the court was not a political

---

[4] Luthuli, *Let My People Go*, 113.
[5] Karris and Carter, 477.
[6] Karris and Carter, 482.
[7] Karris and Carter, 419.

arena." Rejecting the contention of the resisters that "it was the duty of the Court to refuse to administer unjust laws," the magistrate imposed heavy penalties, and advised them that "the laws of the country are there to be obeyed."[8]

In assessing the strategy of the protesters, Leo Kuper noted that even though the resisters did not have to "notify the authorities of their plans, nor to invite arrest" the *satyagraha* felt the need to court arrest and to submit to punishment willingly since these acts were "essential means for conversion of the rulers."[9]

Initially, the Campaign was waged in a very discipline and nonviolent manner. But later that year, riots erupted in Port Elizabeth, Johannesburg, Kimberley, and East London. About forty persons were killed and hundreds were injured during the melee, and governmental buildings and churches were damaged. While Luthuli expressed dismay over these incidents, he attributed the outbreak of violence to the policies pursued by the whites, and warned that, "every so often the yoke becomes unendurable, something explodes, and for a while blind resentment takes control." According to Luthuli, the conditions which produced violence have been and continue to be nourished by the white South Africans, who "react with horror at the outcome of their lust for white domination...but they will do nothing to remove the root cause."[10]

Another reason cited for the riots was the fear that many white South Africans have of sharing power with blacks, whom they regard as "barbaric and hostile." Luthuli perceived the response of many whites to riots by blacks as the making of "stronger chains." While applauding some of the actions of the white police in containing situations of violence, he also viewed it as continuing to prod the Africans, "demanding this, ordering that, and hurling abuse." He recalled the provocation which took place in East London where "police charged into a prayer meeting, charged again, and then began shooting. They continued to shoot from their vehicles as they drove about the location in large numbers."[11] In noting that the Defiance Campaign was too orderly for the Government to respond effectively, Luthuli observed that the

---

[8] Leo Kuper, *Passive Resistance in South Africa* (New Haven, CT: Yale University Press, 1957), 126-127.

[9] Kuper, 125.

[10] Luthuli, 126.

[11] Luthuli, 127.

white supremacists were faced with the prospect of making endless arrests. The strategy of the campaign organizers was to replenish the civil resisters who were jailed with new recruits, who then would seek to be arrested. By pursuing such a course in a nonviolent manner, the protesters robbed their opponents of the initiative in the struggle. Luthuli warned that to pursue the opposite strategy would be disastrous since "violence by Africans would restore this initiative to them," causing them "to bring out the guns and the other techniques of intimidation and present themselves as restorers of order."[12] The Government sought to show a linkage between the riots and the Defiance Campaign, so as to create a negative perception of blacks in the minds of the whites. In the meantime, the Government displayed its repressive attitude, by adopting the Criminal Law Amendment Act and the Public Safety Act, which imposed harsh penalties upon those participating in "any defiance of passive resistance."[13] Such action by the Government did much to weaken the Campaign.

When it appeared that Luthuli had become too active in the Defiance Campaign, he was summoned to the headquarters of the Native Affairs Department for a reprimand. Prior to beginning the discussion of the chief's protest activities, however, the secretary for Native Affairs, raised the question as to why the ANC opposed the government plan for land rehabilitation, maintaining that "any educated person should appreciate schemes to restore the land and prevent erosion." Luthuli, speaking for himself rather than the ANC, noted that while the proposed government solution might appear to be sound, in practice, "the overcrowding of African areas by man and beast is the direct result of the 1913 and 1936 Land Acts," which the Government had imposed. Luthuli considered the solution symbolic of the type of "oppressive and restrictive legislation" imposed upon the blacks.[14]

After the preliminary discussion, the secretary proceeded to inquire as to how Luthuli, as chief, could ask the people to break the law of the land. He was told that as an officer he was expected to keep the law, not encourage people to defy it. Luthuli did not deny having engaged in activities to achieve the aims of the ANC, but he insisted that the course which the organization had chosen to follow, was the only way to show opposition to laws which were without a moral basis. The Chief noted that the people had not been

[12] Luthuli.
[13] Luthuli, 128.
[14] Luthuli, 120-121.

asked to perform in a criminal manner; instead, they were being encouraged to take part in a campaign that would highlight the plight of the oppressed. The Defiance Campaign was designed to reflect the refusal of non-whites to consent to be governed by "criminal laws". Luthuli stated that he had experienced no conflict between his dual roles, noting that he had kept them separately. He insisted that not only had he refused to discuss matters of the ANC at the tribal council, but also he had resisted efforts of others to do so. The Chief was advised that he had not been summoned to be told to resign his membership in the ANC, instead, to be warned that he could not be both "Jeckyl and Hyde." Luthuli was given two weeks in which to make a decision as to his future.[15]

The Chief resented the implication that one had to have a split personality in order to "object to the immoral laws, whose main purpose is to uphold white supremacy"--a repugnant creed. Luthuli insisted that he was not in the ANC in spite of being a chief; instead, because of the extent to which his eyes had been opened as a result of his chieftainship. In his reply to the Native Affairs Department, Luthuli stated that he had no intention of resigning from either of his positions, since he did not perceive a contradiction between being a chief and holding a leadership position in the ANC. Shortly thereafter, the Government removed him from his post as chief of the Umvoti Mission Reserve.[16]

In his prepared statement concerning his removal, Luthuli noted that for more than thirty years, both as a school teacher and chief, he had sought to promote the progress and welfare of his people and the achievement of a multiracial society in South Africa. He regarded his course of moderation as a failure since the Government had responded by adopting more repressive legislation. Luthuli defended his joining the ANC, perceiving membership in the organization as a legitimate nonviolent means of expression. While not challenging his dismissal, he did suggest that the Government should "define more precisely and make more widely known the status, functions and privileges of chiefs. "According to Luthuli, a chief "is the voice of his people in local affairs...part and parcel of the tribe," and not a local agent of the government." In the pursuit of tribal interest, he may use all legitimate modern techniques, even if the demands are considered "unpalatable to the

[15] Luthuli.

[16] Luthuli, 123.

Government of the day." Luthuli contended that chiefs could not serve their tribes effectively "without cooperating with other leaders of the people, both the natural leaders (chiefs) and leaders elected democratically by the people themselves.[17]

Luthuli insisted that in a country like South Africa where the laws and conditions tend to debase human personality, a chief who is worthy of the name must fight fearlessly against these evils. If as a result the Government finds it necessary to remove such chiefs, then it will put itself in the predicament of having to remove many chiefs or cause the people to "dismiss from their hearts chiefs who are indifferent to the needs of the people through fear of dismissal by the Government." Luthuli did not feel that the Government should place chiefs in such dilemma.[18]

In spite of his removal from the post of chief, Luthuli vowed to continue his struggle for justice through nonviolent passive resistance techniques. As a Christian, he sought the aid of God in this task, for he anticipated an uncertain fate—"ridicule, imprisonment, concentration camps, flogging, banishment and even death." While he exhibited no fear for his own safety and life, he was concerned for the welfare of his family. He placed the matter in God's hand, noting that "it is inevitable that in working for freedom some individuals and some families must take the lead and suffer: The Road to Freedom is via the Cross."[19]

President-General of the ANC

Shortly after Luthuli was deposed as chief, he was elected president-general of the ANC. His election was made possible as a result of the loss of credibility of Dr. James Moroka, the incumbent, following his decision to dissociate himself from his fellow-accused by having his lawyer defend him, separately. According to Luthuli, by taking such action, Moroka "appeared unready to go the whole way in defiance;" instead, was asking whites "to shield him from the consequences of white laws, and from the consequences of his own stand."[20]

[17] Luthuli, 237.
[18] Luthuli, 238.
[19] Luthuli.
[20] Luthuli, 129.

Once Luthuli assumed the office of president-general, he terminated the Campaign of Defiance, contending that it had served its purpose. He praised it as an outstanding accomplishment, which will occupy a prominent position in the political history of South Africa. According to Luthuli, the campaign had a profound effect, both upon the enemies of apartheid, and those who sought to preserve the status quo. It also was credited with further internationalizing the issue of racial discrimination, making it difficult for the Government to deceive the world by insisting that the issue was a domestic one. In assessing its impact on non-whites, as a whole, Luthuli concluded that "it accelerated greatly the political consciousness of the people, giving them a new awareness of the potency of united and cooperative action among all oppressed people irrespective of colour or class."[21]

In the wake of the Defiance Campaign, the Nationalist Party, under the leadership of Daniel Malan, "steam rolled" through the Parliament the Criminal Law Amendment Act, which was justified on grounds that there was a need for means to deal with "mass disobedience." According to the law, any person, who was accused of engaging in protestor any campaign against any law, could be subject to whipping, a fine, or a three year jail sentence, or a combination of any two. The law also provided more extensive penalties for "persons whose words or actions were calculated to cause another person to commit an offense as a means of protest."[22]

Also enacted was the Public Safety Act, which gave the Government the power to declare a state of emergency, if it was believed that a serious threat to public order existed. Once such an emergency was declared, the Government could arrest and detain persons, arbitrarily, provided that it submitted the names of persons to the Parliament after thirty days. Under the declaration of emergency, which could be of one year duration, parliamentary and judicial functions could be suspended. Also the state of emergency could be renewed, if deemed necessary. As was expected, Luthuli and other ANC leaders protested the adoption of the two bills, but to no avail.[23]

During the 1954 campaign, the ANC waged a major battle against the removal of thousands of Africans from the Western Areas of Johannesburg. Because of the national importance of the issue, it became the essential feature

---

[21] Luthuli, "Presidential Address at ANC Annual Conference of December 18-20, 1953 in Karris and Carter, III, 121.

[22] Karis and Carter, 6.

[23] Karis and Carter.

of the "Resist Apartheid Campaign." Being aware of Chief Luthuli's intention of addressing a Sophiatown rally on July 11, the police issued to him his second banning order upon his arrival at the Johannesburg airport. Because of the ban, he was unable to address the rally, nevertheless, he issued a statement, which pledged support of the ANC to those who were about to be uprooted from their "sacred shrines and castles," which had been "acquired through hard-earned savings." Referring to the act as "legalized robbery," Luthuli warned that "the Western Areas Removal Plan of the Government represents their major implementation of their *apartheid* policy and, no doubt, is a forerunner to what will be done in other centres; and so our Resist *Apartheid* Campaign in connection with this scheme must be firm and decisive."[24] Because the fate of Africans in other cities in South Africa was perceived as being determined by the stand taken at Johannesburg, he pledged that the leaders of the ANC would do everything possible "to consolidate the country to oppose the carrying out of this outrageous tyrannical scheme." Luthuli expressed appreciation to the other human rights organizations which had pledged their support to the Resist Apartheid Campaign. He reminded his followers that although they were voteless they were not necessarily voiceless. They were urged to help mobilize others in the fight against the racist conditions of South Africa.[25]

In spite of Luthuli's determination to prevent the removal of Africans from the Western Area, his banning restricted his effectiveness in opposing the change. Other factors which contributed to the failure of the campaign were inadequate communication, internal friction, and conflicting interest. In the end, thousands of Africans either were forced to move from the area or did so willingly. In their assessment, Karis and Carter concluded that the strength of the protest was undermined by tenants who appeared to be happy to move from "the squalor of a congested and expensive slum to less crowded and cleaner housing at modest rents, although with increased transportation costs." The South African Government was perceived as building better houses in the new area than at first intended, in order to bribe a larger number of Africans to relocate, willingly.[26]

Another major struggle waged by the ANC in 1954 was the campaign against the Bantu Education Act. Hendrik F. Verwoerd, Minister of Native

[24] Luthuli, "Message to Resist Apartheid," July 11, 1954, in Karis and Carter, 132.
[25] Karis and Carter.
[26] Karis and Carter, 25-26.

Affairs, contended that "education must train and teach people in accordance to the sphere in which they live." Consistent with this belief, the Government introduced a system of education where each child was to be taught in his mother's tongue. Perceiving no place for the Bantu in the European community, Verwoerd insisted that he be trained to serve his own community. The system had the effect of isolating the African by denying him educational contact with Europeans and members of other tribal groups.[27] In his assessment of the impact of the "limited education" upon Africans, Melville Harcourt observed that:

> by a stroke of the pen Africans were permanently barred from entry into the larger world of Western life and culture, because without education--the one passport to independence in any technocrat society--the African was ill-suited to perform the skills of modern industry and totally unfitted for the liberal professions.[28]

Luthuli deplored the passing of the outrageous act, noting that it foretold "the end of all true education for Africans." He envisioned three alternatives which were available to Africans--accept the change without protest, conduct a temporary boycott, or withdraw their children from the schools, permanently. He rejected the first, observing that "... we could not simply sit by and listen to some Cabinet Minister telling us that since no protest had been made, the whites could be assured that we are delighted with Bantu Education." Likewise, Luthuli was aware that many parents, even though they opposed the new system, preferred to have their children receive some education, rather than roam the streets. Although limited in terms of his leadership, by the ban which had been imposed upon him, he did confer with some of the delegates who later attended the National Conference of the ANC which convened in Durham. The advice given by Luthuli was that some action should be taken, but the type should be determined by the readiness of the people. The Conference adopted a resolution which called for a "permanent and total boycott of all education" until the Bantu Education system was abandoned. In terms of implementation, the ANC found itself in a dilemma. Luthuli observed that the leadership could not afford to move slower than the general members, but on the other hand, if it decided to boycott, many areas

[27] Karis and Carter, 29.
[28] Melville Harcourt, *Portraits of Destiny* (New York: Sheed and Ward, 1966), 155-156.

would not be ready. The National Executive Committee decided that certain areas could proceed with boycotts with its permission.[29]

As efforts were being made for a boycott of schools in April 1953, Verwoerd attempted to frustrate those plans by issuing an ultimatum that proclaimed that children who were absent from school on April 25, 1955, would not be readmitted; and that schools or classes which were empty that day would lose teaching posts and the money allocated for those schools would be transferred elsewhere.[30] As a result of the boycott, approximately 7,000 students were dismissed from school, and 116 teachers were fired because they were no longer needed. In 1956, however, the minister agreed to readmit the students, provided that no other trouble occurred. According to Carter, the Government made "the future education of these children dependent on the acceptance of the Act both by their communities and by the African National Congress."[31]

As was the case with the campaign against the Western Areas Removal Plan, the ANCs efforts suffered several weaknesses, including the ineffectiveness of the leadership of Luthuli due to his illness, and the restrictions imposed upon him because of the ban. Another weakness was the division within the African community concerning the proper response to the imposing of the new educational system upon them. The determination of the Government to inflict heavy penalties upon those engaged in passive resistance activities, also, tended to be a restraining force. While the protest of Africans did not prevent the Government from "turning back the hands of time," it did signify to the rest of the world that apartheid would never be willingly accepted by them.

A third undertaking of the ANC during 1954 was the preparation for the Congress of the People, an idea introduced by Professor Z. K. Matthews. In order to accommodate Luthuli, whose movements were restricted because of the ban, the joint meeting of the executive committee of the ANC and other participating Congresses met at an Indian school in the Lower Tugela to make plans for the Kliptown Rally of June 25-26, 1955. The other sponsoring organizations were the South African Indian Congress (SAIC), South African Coloured People's Organization (SACPO), and the Congress of Democrats (COD) which was composed mostly of sympathetic whites. Also attending the

---

[29] Luthuli, *Let My People Go*, 147-148.
[30] Gwendolen M. Carter, *Politics of Inequality* (New York: Praeger, 1958), 109
[31] Carter.

meeting were observers from the Liberal Party, who later withdrew from the planning committee after complaining that they were not invited to participate until the foundation had been laid. The sponsors rejected the criticism, maintaining that the Liberal Party did not respond to the initial invitation.[32]

Representatives of the various congresses established a committee to solicit advice for provisions to be included in the Freedom Charter. According to Luthuli, a major weakness of the charter-drafting process was the inability to organize properly the material which had been submitted by the various sources, due to the lateness of its arrival. He admitted that, as drafted, the Charter contained unnecessary details in some sections, while in others, it was too vague, but he considered the document to be a true expression of "the hopes and aspirations of the people who desire South Africa to be one homeland for all its inhabitants."[33]

On January 25 - 26, 1955, delegates of every South African race met at Kliptown, near Johannesburg, to hear the reading of the Freedom Charter, and to adopt it. Its preamble, perhaps, best summarized its purposes:

> We the people of South Africa, declare for all our country and the world to know:
>
> - that South Africa belongs to all who live in it, black and white, and that no government can justly claim authority unless it is based on the will of all the people;
> - that our people have been robbed of their birthright to land, liberty and peace by a form of government founded on injustice and inequality;
> - that our country will never be prosperous or free until all our people live in brotherhood, enjoying equal rights and opportunities;
> - that only a democratic state, based on the will of all the people can secure to all their birthright without distinction of colour, race, sex or belief;
> - and therefore we, the People of South Africa, black and white together--equals, countrymen and brothers--adopt this Freedom Charter. And we pledge ourselves to strive together sparing neither strength nor courage, until the democratic changes here set out have been won.[34]

---

[32] Luthuli, 156.
[33] Luthuli, 158.
[34] Luthuli, 239.

The Charter speaks of the right of all people to participate in the government, enjoy equal human rights, share in the country's wealth, work, own homes, receive an education, and be guaranteed equality before the law. The Charter anticipated a South Africa where all could live in peace and friendship. Luthuli praised the Charter as both practical and relevant, and giving "a flesh and blood meaning *in the South African setting,* to such words as *democracy, freedom, liberty.*" Luthuli concluded that the Congress of the People was an awakening force for the Government of South Africa, warning the oppressor of the seriousness in which the Africans regarded the struggle.[35]

Inasmuch as the Congress of the People was an ad hoc assembly, the participating organizations were called upon to ratify the Freedom Charter. Although it was anticipated that the ratification by the ANC would take place, immediately, such was not the case. As a prelude to consideration by the annual conference in December 1955, discussion of the document took place at the branch level. The Natal Provincial Conference, in which Luthuli played an active role, adopted resolutions which congratulated the four organizations which sponsored the Congress of the People Rally, and expressed general agreement with the principles of the Charter. The conference, however, observed, that there was an overemphasis of racial distinctiveness, and recommended that greater stress be placed upon the building of a united South Africa.[36] Later in the year, Luthuli's special presidential message was read to the 1955 annual conference. He deplored the ideological feud which had erupted within the ranks of the ANC over the "ownership of South Africa," viewing the struggle as dissipating energy which otherwise could be better used in the fight against apartheid. He envisioned an "all inclusive African Nationalism" designed to assure freedom for all who reside in South Africa, without regard to racial or geographical origin, as long as they "paid their undivided loyalty and allegiance" to the country.[37]

Luthuli's views, however, were not shared by all members of the ANC. A faction of the organization, which called itself the Africanists, deplored what they perceived to be the dominant role played by non-Africans in the drafting of the Freedom Charter. They viewed the struggle for liberation of South

[35] Luthuli, 159.
[36] Karis and Carter, 65-66.
[37] Luthuli, "Special Presidential Message," Annual Conference of Dec. 17-18, 1955, in Karis and Carter, 213-214.

Africa as one that should be waged, primarily by Africans.[38] Another issue that caused division within the ranks of the ANC was that of Communist influence. Critics questioned whether Luthuli had allowed himself to become a tool of Communists.[39] The Chief minimized the role of the Communist in the movement, maintaining that the major concern of the ANC is liberation, and that it would not be "sidetracked by ideological clashes and witch hunts."[40]

As it had done on previous occasions, the Government reacted to the Congress of the People Rally, and the adoption of the Freedom Charter in a very repressive manner. The police raided the homes and offices of leading members of the various organizations, seizing documents, and arresting 156 persons on the charge of high treason. Included among those arrested and detained were many of the leaders of the Congresses which had participated in the drafting of the Freedom Charter.

In spite of the repressive actions by the Government of South Africa, the ANC continued to mobilize opposition to racism. According to Luthuli, the organization had created a "climate of resistance" which encouraged the launching of one of the most successful campaigns against injustice by people at the grass root level. As a response to the increasing of fares by the subsidized bus company (PUTCO), Africans in the Alexandra Township, near Johannesburg, began to walk rather than use the bus. The apparent success of the boycott led the press to charge that many of those participating in the protest were responding to intimidation--a charge which Luthuli denied. In the meantime, the Government sought to break the boycott by utilizing "systematic police persecution on the route between Alexandra and the heart of Johannesburg." The undue harshness of the police caused many whites to become sympathetic, and in some cases, use their cars to assist boycotters. Luthuli applauded the courage and endurance of those who met the challenge, especially the infirmed--many of whom began their walks before sunrise and returned home very exhausted long after darkness had fallen.[41]

Efforts to arrive at an honorable settlement of the boycott were facilitated by the "good office" of the Bishop of Johannesburg, and the willingness of the

---

[38] Karis and Carter, 65.

[39] Richard Gibson, *African Liberation Movements* (New York: Oxford University Press, 1972), 53.

[40] Karis and Carter, 64.

[41] Luthuli, *Let My People Go*, 174-176.

Chamber of Commerce to subsidize the company indirectly. According to Luthuli, the Chamber, apparently recognized that tired workers did not aid the cause of production. Because the boycott was considered to have been a success, some expressed the desire to continue it, even though the original demands had been met. The ANC objected to this approach, fearing that differences of opinion in regard to it might cause a lack of enthusiasm for the strike; therefore, making it possible for the Government to triumph in the end.[42]

By 1957, Luthuli's leadership of the ANC had become seriously affected by his illness, the restrictions imposed upon him by the ban, and the time that was being consumed in preparation of his appearance at the treason trial. In spite of the limitation placed upon his ability to protest against unfair governmental actions, he was determined not to remain silent. In May 1957, Luthuli wrote a letter to Prime Minister Strijdom, complaining about the current treatment of Africans, and suggested ways in which the grievances could be redressed. He decried "the denial to the African people of the democratic channels of expression and participation in the government of the country." The restrictions were perceived as causing much of the stresses and strains which Africans undergo. Luthuli advised the Prime Minister that African people viewed the oppressive laws as "weapons of attack on their very existence as a people." Three types of laws were cited as illustrations: the Land Laws, Pass Laws, and Master and Servant Acts. Luthuli attributed the extremely congested conditions to the Land Laws, which had allocated only 13% of the land of South Africa to the Africans. These laws denied them the right to own land in both rural and urban areas. Also coming under attack were the Pass Laws, which were regarded not only as denying Africans their freedom of movement, but generally, were enforced in a manner so as to create "unnecessary suffering and humiliation." The third group of laws criticized, were the Master and Servant Acts, which limited African participation in industry and commerce to unskilled categories. Luthuli also expressed opposition to oppressive legislation, which was pending before the Parliament, including a bill that would extend apartheid to university education, a bill designed to increase indirect taxation on the already poor African people, and a bill that would prevent the operation of alternative bus services in situations where the boycott weapon had been used effectively "to

[42] Luthuli, 177-178.

redress economic injustice." In order to relieve racial tensions, Luthuli suggested the calling of a multi-racial convention to resolve critical national problems. He indicated, however, that if the Government did not find his proposals acceptable, the ANC would continue to wage its struggle for racial justice.[43]

As the 1958 general elections approached, consideration was given to ways in which Africans, who were voteless, could make their voices heard in matters which concerned them. A decision was made by the ANC leaders to conduct a "stay at home" campaign, which would coincide with the elections of April 16. One of the slogans selected for use in the campaign was "Away with the Nationalist." Even though the slogan was designed as an expression of disapproval of the ruling Nationalist Party, it was not intended to imply support for the United Party, its opposition. The ANC, in a message directed to white voters, suggested that any one interested in a South Africa that would embrace all races and colors could never support either parties contesting the elections. Recalling the train of abuses which had been visited upon Africans during the ten year rule of the Nationalist Party, Luthuli warned that its "policy of blatant oppression and racialism" had created "a legacy of bitterness and hatred," which, if allowed to continue, would almost certainly have a devastating effect upon the country. In his appeal to white voters, once again, he sought to clarify the goals of the ANC, pointing out that it did not support "white supremacy nor black supremacy, but a common South African multi-racial society, based upon friendship, equality of rights and mutual respect."[44]

Because a major concern of Africans in 1958 was that of economics, the organizers of the "stay at home" campaign sought to capitalize on this dissatisfaction by using the slogan, "A Pound a Day." This slogan was perceived as having the dual effect of mobilizing Africans for the campaign, while simultaneously, dramatizing for the white voters the plight of the blacks.[45]

As preparations were being made for the campaign, the Government was making plans to cripple it. Bans were issued by various ministers against the meeting of large crowds. As in other cases, the repressive actions of the

---

[43] Luthuli, "Letter to Prime Minister Strijdom," May 28, 1957, in Karis and Carter, 396-403.
[44] Luthuli, "A Message to Every Voter from the African National Congress," Flyer signed by Luthuli, and issued before the general elections of April 16, 1958, Karis and Carter, 426-427.
[45] Luthuli, *Let My People Go*, 182.

Government contributed, heavily, to the failure of the campaign. According to Luthuli, another factor was the inability of the leaders of the campaign to command effectively. He observed that because the effort was undertaken by local groups which subscribed to the general policies of the ANC, "the call was made with too many voices, and the great mass of the people, too often misled by dubious statements publicised in the white press, were in doubt about whence the call came."[46] Luthuli also regretted the negative impact, which the ideological split within the ANC had upon the campaign, accusing the Africanists of attacking the policy of the organization, not from within, but in the public forum. When this fact was publicized by the white press, it confused many of the would-be supporters. Luthuli regarded the stay-at-home campaign as having at least one redeeming feature, however, the creation within the electorate of an awareness of the demands of the Africans.[47]

Another issue that was of major interest to Luthuli was the proposed creation of Bantustans, which he perceived as seeking "to wipe Africans off the South African political map." His concern was that the world might be confused as to the true meaning of this action, inasmuch as the South African Government was conducting a propaganda blitz to sell the idea that Bantustans were designed to provide self-government for the Africans based upon their traditional values. Luthuli rejected this contention, maintaining that the proposed resettlement plan was only a "march back to tribalism," with tribal chiefs serving as "minor puppets and agents of the Big Dictator"--the South African Government. He did not envision this scheme of "territorial segregation" as providing any new formulas of fairness in regard to the division of the land, since Africans, who composed 70% of the population still would be relegated to 13% of the land. Luthuli also questioned whether the placing of factories "on the edges of the destitute Reserves" was designed to enhance the economic prosperity of the Bantustans, or to capitalize on the available cheap labor. He described the Bantustan as "the home of disease and miserable poverty, the place where we shall be swept into heaps in order to rot, the dumping ground of 'undesirable elements,' delinquents, criminals created especially in towns and cities by the system." Luthuli viewed it as the dumping ground for the old and sick from the cities, who had given up their "strength, youth and labour" for the system. The home for Africans in South Africa was perceived as being in the "white man's garbage can." Luthuli

[46] Luthuli, 183-184.

concluded that the Bantustan Act was "the white man's solution, at ruthless cost to the African, of the white man's problem."[48]

In 1959, the ANC achieved success in a potato boycott, which it undertook in reaction to an arrangement between jailers and white farmers, whereby more than a half million pass offenders per year were released from jail into the safe-keeping of farmers. On these farms, they dug potatoes and were treated, virtually, as slaves. To dramatize the issue, the ANC called for a boycott of all potatoes for a month, but because of the enthusiastic support of the protest it continued for more than three months. When Luthuli, with the backing of the ANC Executive Committee, terminated the demonstration, many criticisms were raised by those who wanted it to continue. He justified his action on the basis of the hardship it was inflicting upon Africans, who depended upon the potatoes as essential parts of their daily diets, and because the goal they had sought had been achieved.[49]

In order to emphasize his opposition to the despised pass system, Luthuli, in March 1960, defied the Government by burning his pass. This act of defiance was the climax of protest against Pass Laws, which had been taking place for years. In 1956, opposition escalated when the Government enacted new laws which required women to carry passes. The strategy was to issue passes, first of all, to the women of the farms and country, and after having accomplished this goal, to begin the process in the towns, where opposition was greater. The rural women, however, were not cooperative. According to Luthuli, the unyielding courage of the women prevented the authorities from issuing the passes, except by "guile or brute force, and at the cost of lives." A delegation of Zulu women, including Mrs. Luthuli, took their grievances to the Zulu paramount, whose wife had already accepted a pass. While he agreed to relay their opposition to the proper authority, he did not seem enthused. No positive result was achieved at the meeting.[50]

In October 1959, protesting women held a mass demonstration in Johannesburg, in which more than 2,000 were arrested and detained. Aware of the growing opposition, the annual conference of the ANC, which was held in December, approved a resolution which called for the intensification of the campaign against passes. As leaders of the organization, Luthuli always had

[47] Luthuli, 183-184.
[48] Luthuli, 203.
[49] Luthuli, 218-219.
[50] Luthuli, 193-194.

insisted upon the proper preparation of the people before launching protest activities, but because of the hostile action by the rival Pan-African Conference concerning the pass system, he was "forced" to act before he considered the time appropriate. Robert Sobukwe, the leader of the Pan-African Congress called upon all Africans to follow him and leave their passes at home, and to make this clear to the police. The initial response of the police to this strategy was, for the most part, to arrest a handful of the leaders and to ignore the followers. According to Luthuli, "the followers were thus placed in a position where they were still in possession of their passes, and their protest against them was being overlooked." Luthuli had anticipated "an orderly, carefully mounted campaign with a deliberately-timed climax,"[51] but events were moving in the opposite direction, especially in Sharpeville, where 69 Africans lost their lives and 180 were wounded while demonstrating, peacefully, against the pass system.

As a response to the tragedy of Sharpeville, Luthuli, who at that time was in Pretoria because of the treason trial, called for a national day of mourning to be observed March 28, 1960. The response was commendable, with many churches opened for prayer. According to the ANC leadership, passive mourning and active prayer "no longer seemed adequate to deal with a system which was causing deaths, and sending large numbers of people to jail." A call was made by the ANC for the burning of passes, and as leader, Luthuli insisted upon leading the way. The Government reacted by arresting him, and declaring both the ANC and the Pan-African Congress unlawful organizations. Luthuli was sentenced to six months, without the option of a fine, but it was suspended for three years because of his ill health.[52]

Luthuli prepared a statement, which he intended to read at the time of his sentence, but because of the advice of his lawyer, and due to ill health, he did not present it. In the undelivered statement, he pleaded legally not guilty, insisting that the action was taken because he and most of the African people considered the pass system to be "the cause of much evil and suffering." He referred to it as "nothing less than an instrument of studied degradation and humiliation" of the African people, and "a badge of slavery, a weapon used by the authorities to keep us in a position of inferiority." Luthuli used the occasion to express appreciation to the "growing number of fellow-white South Africans" who displayed concern over the plight of their black brothers.

---

[51] Luthuli, 220.

He questioned, however, whether anyone, other than victims, comprehended what it was like to undergo a pass raid, which usually was characterized by "the fear of a loud, rude bang on the door in the middle of the night, the bitter humiliation of an undignified search, the shame of husband and wife being huddled out of bed in front of their children by the police and taken off to the police cell". He also questioned whether there was any country in the world in which it was "a criminal offense for husband and wife to live together," or which "separates eighteen-year-olds from their parents."[53]

Turning to the tragedy of Sharpeville, Luthuli considered it a shocking and horrified experience for all decent South Africans, and an outrage to humanity. Noting the large number of people who had lost their lives and had been wounded, he advised that "if ever the cup of bitterness against the Pass Laws ran over, it was then". The result was the responding of Africans to the call of the ANC to observe a day of mourning and to burn their passes--"the symbol of bondage". Considering the occasion as one in which he had to take a stand, Luthuli burned his pass. He viewed it as an appropriate demonstration of his conviction and willingness to live up to the demands of the cause. He maintained that he could not have done less since he had to live with his conscience. Luthuli observed, "I would rightly lose the confidence of my people, and earn the disrespect of right-thinking people in my country and in the world, and the disdain of posterity."[54]

---

[52] Luthuli, 222-226.
[53] Luthuli, 244.
[54] Luthuli, 245-247.VI The Archbishop and His Crusade for Justice.

Chapter 6

The Archbishop and His Crusade for Justice

> There is no peace in Southern Africa. There is no peace because there is no justice. There can be no real peace and security until there be first justice enjoyed by all the inhabitants of that beautiful land.[1]
> Desmond Tutu

Archbishop Desmond Tutu's religious commitment propelled him into the struggle for a just society. Perceiving Christianity as more than attending church on Sundays, he sought to exemplify it in every aspect of life. His efforts were not limited to personal and direct methods of eliminating evils, but also to influencing others to take active roles in the South African liberation struggle, especially the Church and the broader international community. In pursuit of his goal, he placed heavy emphasis upon the use of the appeal to the conscience.

Seeking Meaningful Dialogue with the Government

Essential to any solution to the South African problem is meaningful dialogue, yet governmental leaders too often have refused offers, considering it below their dignity to confer with the Africans. In spite of the Government's intransigence, Desmond Tutu was persistent in his effort to accomplish

---

[1] Desmond Tutu, *The Rainbow People of God: The Making of a Peaceful Revolution*, (New York: Doubleday, 1994), 92.

meaningful dialogue. Shortly after his elevation to the post of Anglican Dean of Johannesburg, he wrote an open letter to Prime Minister John Vorster warning that unless the Government became more sensitive to the conditions of the Africans, bloodshed and violence would become the inevitable results. He reminded the Prime Minister that "a people made desperate by despair, injustice and oppression will use desperate means" to achieve liberation. Tutu expressed fear that the time was rapidly approaching "when events will generate a momentum of their own, when nothing will stop their reaching a bloody denouncement which is too ghastly to contemplate."[2]

In his letter, the Bishop advised the Prime Minister that Africans are "exceedingly patient and peace-loving." Recognizing the reality of politics, Tutu suggested that since the Government could not be expected to alienate its political supporters, it might make some genuine concessions that would indicate that the Government and the whites, generally, mean business when they proclaim their interest in peaceful change. He called upon the Government to:

1. Accept the urban Black as a permanent inhabitant of what is wrongly called White South Africa.
2. Repeal the pass laws which demonstrate to Blacks more clearly than anything that they are third-rate citizens in their beloved country.
3. Call a National Convention made up of the genuine leaders (i.e. leaders recognized as such by their sections of the community), to try to work out an orderly evolution of South Africa into a non-racial open and just society.[3]

In conclusion, Bishop Tutu advised Vorster that although his new position as Bishop of Lesotho would require him to reside outside his beloved country, he intended to retain his South African citizenship. In his usual manner, Tutu sought the blessings of God for the Prime Minister and his Government, and appealed to God to inspire him to "hear the cry of the Africans before it was too late." He concluded by expressing his willingness to meet with Vorster to discuss the critical issues raised in the letter.[4]

---

[2] Tutu, *Hope and Suffering* (Grand Rapids, MI: William B. Eerdmans Publishing Co., 1983), 32-33.

[3] Tutu, 34.

[4] Tutu, 35.

According to Tutu, Vorster dismissed the letter as "a propaganda ploy somehow engineered by the Progressive Federal Party." The Prime Minister's reaction was interpreted as questioning whether a black person had the intelligence to articulate the grievances of black people.[5] Tutu's warning was prophetic, with hundreds of Africans being killed in the Sharpeville tragedy which occurred slightly more than a month after the release of the letter.

The "deaf ear" approach of Vorster, however, was not followed by his successor, P. W. Botha, who in 1980 conferred with Bishop Tutu and several other religious leaders. The Prime Minister was warned that unless the root cause of oppression was removed, the Government could expect further unrest in the country. Bishop Tutu and others in the delegation suggested that the Government could take meaningful steps toward power-sharing by abolishing the despised pass law system; discontinuing its practices of detention without trial, and arbitrary banning; and establishing a uniform system of education. The religious leaders also urged the immediate ending of forced population removal, and called upon the Government to declare a commitment to "a common citizenship for all South Africans in an undivided South Africa."[6] Bishop Tutu expressed dissatisfaction with the outcome of the conference with the Prime Minister, noting that while the religious leaders were discussing in good faith, the Government was using the Christian League as a front organization to "subvert, malign and discredit" the South African Council of Churches. In the meantime, the Conference was criticized by militant Africans, who saw nothing to be gained by courting the favor of the white racist government.[7]

In spite of the Government's failure to consider seriously the recommendations of Tutu and the other members of the clergy, he continued to exert an effort to redress the grievances of fellow-Africans. He served in many delegations, which conferred with various governmental officials, especially in matters relating to forced population removal and education. These issues, along with those concerning the pass system, detention, banning, and the lack of political participation, received the constant attention of the Bishop. However, because governmental officials were not always willing to grant him an audience, often he had to "talk over their heads"--via the press and public addresses.

---

[5] "Tutu, Desmond [Mpilo]," *Current Biography Yearbook*, 1985, 419.
[6] Tutu, "Full Text of Press Statement," April 2, 1986.
[7] Tutu.

In his argument against forced population removal, Tutu gave a historic account of how the whites from Europe had deprived Africans of their land. As a result of legislative action, Africans, who constituted 80% of the population were confined to 13% of the land. According to the Bishop, in the attempt to make its racist and immoral policies less odious, and in an effort to "salve the conscience" of countries which also were participating in the exploitation of Africans, the South African Government introduced its plan for the creation of Bantustans. In the development of this plan, Africans, the major victims of this so-called program of separate development, had no meaningful involvement. According to the South African Government, its intention was that eventually these proposed homelands would become "autonomous sovereign nations." Tutu rejected this concept, maintaining that if the black community consisted of numerous nations, so did the white, which was composed of English, Afrikaners, and others. He also questioned the existence of "sovereign states," which except for the Transkei, had "no territorial integrity, or any hope of economic viability." Tutu perceived the so-called separate development scheme as implying the existence of a white South Africa, with borders determined by whites, and with territory including the "most prosperous and most developed" parts of the country. In pursuing its goals, the whites were viewed as seeking to co-opt the Indians and Coloured. According to Tutu, the strategy of the Government was to permit "some very specially blessed Blacks" to receive such benefits as relatively good education for their children and high salaries in order to assure their support of the status quo. He observed that "they will be co-opted into the system as a Black middle class to be a buffer between the *have*-Whites and *have not*-Blacks."[8]

In a physical sense, the only way to arrive at an all white South Africa, would be to relocate millions of Africans. According to Tutu, often they have been moved from places where they have had reasonably adequate housing and work and have been forced into "inhospitable areas," with inadequate accommodations. He contended that at times when black labor was needed even well-to-do farmers were forced to work for wages, in order to pay taxes which were imposed upon them, but when that labor was no longer needed, they were forced out of the urban areas. In rejecting the "separate development scheme," Tutu maintained that "the cost in terms of human suffering is incalculable," noting the serious impact which undernourishment,

[8] Tutu, *Hope and Suffering*, 92-96.

starvation, and malnutrition had upon growing children. He also was concerned about the "legacy of bitterness, anger, frustration and hatred," which were being passed on to the next generation. Tutu considered it a miracle, that given the oppression, deprivation, and exploitation of the Africans, they continue to seek a non-racial state, and to work for the achievement of justice and reconciliation in a manner so as to avoid a blood path. Tutu warned, however, "Blacks are going to find it difficult to forget what Whites have done and are doing to us in the matter of population removals."[9] For Tutu, the forced population removal scheme had a special meaning. Even though he was not forced to move into a Bantustan, like other Africans, he was stripped of his national citizenship. The Bishop noted that he did not have a South African passport, in the real sense; instead, he had a travel document which described his nationality as "undetermined at present."[10]

Among the other evils in which Bishop Tutu focused his human rights campaign, was that of opposition to the despised pass system, which Luthuli earlier had referred to as "a badge of slavery." From the outset, Africans found the system repugnant; thus, they frequently demonstrated against its use. In 1979, when Tutu took his publicized stand against the pass system, he was aware of statistics, which had revealed that during the previous year, there had been an increased use of pass raids. He perceived these frequent raids as means employed by the authorities to intimidate unemployed Africans, and thereby accomplish their removal from urban areas into the Bantustan. According to Tutu, arrests also were made of Africans who were employed, and those who were students--many of whom were not given adequate time to produce documents. The Bishop made futile appeals to the authorities to discontinue the nuisances and humiliation of Africans. In warning that the pass raids are highly provocative in an already tense situation, Tutu challenged white South Africans to break their silence and demonstrate their opposition to a situation which could have calamitous consequences.[11] The Bishop did not carry a pass; instead, he used for identification a driver's license, or his travel document, when it was not in the possession of state officials.

---

[9] Tutu, 96-99.

[10] Tutu, "The Nobel Laureate and His Message," *New Direction*, (Howard University, Jan. 1985), 27-28.

[11] Tutu, *Crying in the Wilderness* (Grand Rapids, MI: William B. Eerdmans Publishing Co., 1982), 72-73.

Bishop Tutu, also, has maintained a steadfast opposition to banning and arbitrary detention. As was seen in the case of Luthuli, banning was a device that was frequently used to lessen the effectiveness of a leader. In order to point out the inhumaneness of the banning process, Tutu recalled two visits he made to the home of Winnie Mandela, who was not permitted to leave her home because of a ban imposed upon her by the Government. On the first occasion, in which he went to celebrate the Holy Communion, the ritual had to be performed in his car since he was not permitted to enter her home. On the second occasion, she could not leave her yard; thus, the Bishop conducted the ritual from the street, while Mrs. Mandela stood in her yard.[12] Under a typical ban the victim was prohibited from communicating with any other person. Tutu also called upon the Government to refrain from lengthy periods of detention without trial, and to release Nelson Mandela and other political prisoners. Since he regarded Mandela as the most likely first prime minister of a liberated South Africa, he could see no advantage which the Government could gain by continuing to hold him in detention.[13]

The sharing of political power was also one of the demands made by Bishop Tutu. Africans were legally prevented from participating in the political process. He complained that even though he was 53 years of age and a bishop in the Church, he was not permitted to vote, but a white boy who was only 18 could enjoy such a privilege. Tutu regarded the 1983 Constitution as an unacceptable document, since it was, in essence, "an instrument of the politics of exclusion." He contended that although Africans composed 73% of the population of the country, they played no part in the political process. The Bishop did not consider the new Constitution to be "remotely democratic," even though it did include provisions for Colored and Indians to participate in the Government for the first time. He suggested that because the document provided for three legislative chambers that were racially defined, "racism and ethnicity were entrenched and hallowed in the Constitution." In order to express their opposition to the document, Africans demonstrated peaceably, but according to Tutu, the South African Government responded with violence.[14]

Consistent with his long-time opposition to the state-designed Bantu Education System, Bishop Tutu called frequently for a uniform system of

[12] Tutu, 68-69.

[13] Tutu, 96.

[14] Tutu "Dismantling Apartheid, *Social Education*, Sept. 1985, 454-455.

education. Indeed, it was because of the introduction of this segregated form of education that he gave up teaching, and carved out a career in the ministry. According to the Bishop, the Bantu Act "took the education of black children out of the hands of the Church and placed it into the hands of a neglected civil authority."[15] The Soweto riots of June 16, 1976 were a response to the further tampering with the education of Africans by a governmental decree that required all courses to be in Afrikaner. Tutu insisted that the Government provide education for Africans that is equal to that of any other resident of South Africa.

Because Tutu failed to achieve the desired reforms through other means, during the summer of 1985 he sought, once again, to confer with President Botha. According to the Bishop, he wanted to talk as "one grandfather to another, as one Christian to another." The State President's response was that he was too busy to see him privately, but would see him as part of a group of other church leaders in a meeting on August 19. The Botha Government was reported as viewing Tutu as an enemy who did not deserve "any special recognition as the leading emissary of the black community." The Bishop rejected the invitation to be a part of the delegation, suggesting that his effort to confer with the State President had begun to jeopardize his credibility among the blacks of South Africa.[16] His refusal to attend the conference led to indirect criticisms by the Reagan Administration. The Bishop, however, justified his not attending the meeting since he perceived it as not having been in the best interest of black Africans.[17]

In June 1986, however, the violence which swept the country during the week prior to the tenth anniversary of the Soweto uprising set the stage for a meeting between Botha and Tutu. During the 90 minute conference, the Bishop warned the President that the emergency decree which had been declared was not likely to restore law and order, due to the failure to deal with the underlying causes of the riots.[18] On July 21, 1986, slightly more than a month later, the two met again in a two hour conference, but like the first meeting, it appeared to be unproductive. The Bishop urged the President to lift the state of emergency and legalize the outlawed African political

[15] Tutu, *Crying in the Wilderness*, 17.

[16] *Time*, Sept. 2, 1985.

[17] "Pretoria Lifts Ban on Winnie Mandela: Tutu Calls for Sanctions," *Washington Post*, April 3, 1986.

[18] Michael Sherrill, "The Boot Comes Down," *Time*, June 23, 1986, 42.

organizations. Botha defended the state of emergency, noting that because of the breakdown of law and order following the lifting of the previous one, it was necessary to reimpose it. According to the President, "since its reimposition, a greater sense of safety had returned to the Black townships and economic faith in the country was recovering." In the meantime, the Bishop was told that as a South African he was expected "to oppose foreign intervention in the country's affairs.[19]

At the urging of Tutu, President Botha agreed to ask members of the cabinet to investigate specific cases which had been raised concerning political detainees, and the harassment of the clergy. The major reason given by the Bishop for holding the conference with the President was because of the Church Council's request that he intercede in behalf of bishops and priests who were being held in jail. The meeting of Bishop Tutu and President Botha, at a time when the latter was using extremely repressive measures against Africans, was perceived as damaging the image of the Bishop among young African militants. According to Zwelakhe Sisulu, the meeting was viewed as giving "a false impression that the government is prepared to talk to the real leaders of the black community." In the meantime, Botha, who had failed to see the Bishop for six years, appeared to have used the two recent conferences to rebuild the image of the country abroad.[20]

In spite of critics who warned that talks with Botha were futile, Tutu, who by this time had become archbishop, continued to seek dialogue. He held a meeting with the South African President in March 1988 to appeal for leniency for the "Sharpeville Six," who had been sentenced to death for violation of state of emergency decrees. According to Tutu, "after an amicable discussion of the issue at hand," Botha began to bluster and scold, to which he responded, "one thing you've got to know is that I'm not a small boy. You're not going to talk to me like that. You are not my headmaster." The Archbishop admitted to a reporter that they both behaved like little children, with each accusing and counter-accusing and "finger-wagging." At the end of the meeting, Botha handed Tutu a note which demanded to know whether he was "acting on behalf of the Kingdom of God or the Kingdom promised by the ANC," and the South African Communist Party.[21]

---

[19] Allister Sparks, "Botha, Tutu Meeting Results in No Progress," *Washington Post*, July 22, 1986, A14.

[20] *Washington Post*.

[21] Tutu, *The Rainbow People of God*, 145 - 146.

In a letter of April 8, 1988, the Archbishop cited scripture to justify the concern of the Church in obtaining justice. He described the racial policies of South Africa as not only "unjust and oppressive;" but also "positively unbiblical, unChristian, immoral, and evil". He proceeded to advise Botha that too much time had been lost trying to "beautify apartheid through cosmetic improvement while the pillars of a vicious system remain firmly in place." Acknowledging that he was a Christian religious leader, the Archbishop maintained that he was "committed to the work for a nonracial, just and democratic South Africa," and that he rejects atheistic Marxism" the same as he rejects "apartheid, which he considered "equally abhorrent and evil."[22]

In defending the activities of the Church, Tutu informed Botha that "the aim of the church is to bring about social justice" and that "if the present system does not serve this purpose, the public conscience must be roused to demand another." According to the Archbishop: "If the church does not exert itself for justice in society, and together with the help she can offer also be prepared to serve as champion for the cause of the poor, others will do it."[23] He warned that the followers of Jesus are mandated to be concerned with the "least of these."

In August 1989, Frederick W, de Klerk assumed the presidency of South Africa and about two months later, October 11, he and his Constitutional Development Minister Gerrit Viljoen conferred with Archbishop Tutu; Rev. Allan A. Boesak, president of the World Alliance Reformed Churches; and Rev. Frank Chikane, general secretary of the South African Council of Churches. During the conference, the Church leaders reemphasized the need for adopting six major steps immediately: the rescinding of the 40-month old emergency decree, the lifting of restrictions on political activity, the releasing of detainees who were being held without trial, the legalizing of political organizations, the releasing of political prisoners and clemency for those on Death Row. The same demands had been made earlier by the outlawed ANC. The Church leaders also called upon the South African Government to repeal the various apartheid laws, allow exiles to return home and begin negotiation for a new South Africa. They insisted that both the African National Congress and the Pan Africanist Congress be involved in the process. De Klerk informed the delegation that his government was giving a high priority to the

[22] Tutu, 153.
[23] Tutu, 151.

lifting of the emergency decree. He also advised them that his government was involved in a "step by step process of change in which one step had to be completed before another could be taken." The President expressed the hope that the conference be viewed as a step ahead.[24]

After reflecting on the conference, Archbishop Tutu suggested that de Klerk be judged by his actions and not by his words. According to Tutu, the President will need time for the planning and implementing of his program. He suggested that Africans observe the first 100 days to see what has been accomplished, then evaluate carefully the President's message to the opening session of Parliament next year and afterward "give him, say three months after that to make the necessary changes."[25]

The apparent cordial relationship which existed between Tutu and de Klerk was in stark contrast to the association which the Archbishop had with John Vorster and P. W. Botha, the former leaders of South Africa. Perhaps, perceiving the potential influence of the church leaders, de Klerk sought to involve them in discussions relative to the achievement of a multiracial state. Tutu declined the invitation, however, insisting that his role was largely one of a facilitator and not that of a mediator. Instead, he advised the Government to utilize leaders of banned organizations in the process. Shortly thereafter, the South African Government legalized the African National Congress and released Nelson Mandela from prison, whom de Klerk began to consult with concerning the future of the country. With the return of Mandela to the political scene, Tutu was contented to move from the center of the spotlight, satisfied that he had paved the way for meaningful dialogue on the future of South Africa.

Leading, Consoling and Inspiring the Oppressed

In the struggle to achieve racial justice, not only did Archbishop Tutu petition the Government for redress of grievances, but he also participated in demonstrations to appeal to the consciences of both South Africa and the international community. John Webster perceived him as an important component of the African community, since "he gives hope to people and

[24] John D. Battersby, " Tutu and deKlerk 'Talk About Talks'" *New York Times*, Oct. 12, 1989, I, 3:1.

[25] Desmond Tutu, "Judge Mr. deKlerk By His Action," *New York Times*, Oct. 20, 1989.

communicates the feelings of the oppressed to those in power."[26] Typical of Tutu's involvement was his participation in a protest demonstration against the arrest of the Reverend John Thorne, the former General Secretary of the South African Council of Churches. On May 26, 1980, the Bishop and more than fifty other church leaders marched toward John Vorster Square in Johannesburg, singing "Onward Christian Soldiers." The protesters were greeted by South African officials who arrested them for marching without a permit.[27] Five years later, Tutu led a similar demonstration of South African religious leaders in a protest against the six month detention which had been given to an African priest. On this occasion, however, the Johannnesburg police did not arrest them, but merely took their names and photographed them.[28]

In later years when the South African Government banned public demonstrations, the Archbishop reacted by using his pulpit as an alternative. In March 1988, Tutu addressed a congregation at St. George's Anglican Cathedral following the Government's cancellation of a scheduled protest rally by the newly organized Committee for the Defense of Democracy. In his message, he deplored the totalitarian practices of the South African Government.[29] Several months later, the Archbishop further angered the Government by calling for a boycott of segregated nationwide elections which had been scheduled for October 26, 1988. Although his action was in defiance of the state of emergency decrees, he was not arrested. For violating the decrees, he could have been imprisoned for upward to ten years and given an $8,000 fine. The Archbishop insisted that he was not defying the Government, but was obeying God. When he repeated his protest call almost a week later, the police broke into the church and began filming his sermon, but took no additional action.[30] In spite of police threats, Tutu continued his opposition to the segregated elections.

Funerals and memorial services also have been used to rally support for the liberation cause. Father Buti Thlagale noted that:

---

[26] Tutu, *Crying in the Wilderness*, 22-23.
[27] John F. Burns, " South Africa Arrests Two Anglican Bishops at Protest," *New York Times*, May 27, 1980, A3.
[28] Pico Iyer, "Rising Defiance," *Time*, April 15, 1985, 78.
[29] *New York Times*, Sept. 5, 1988.
[30] *New York Times*, Sept. 10, 1988.

> in calling for and participating in commemorative services or personally attending funerals of the victims of apartheid, the Bishop has persistently sought to uphold the Black People's right to be heard. These public gatherings, always under close observation by the security police, are an expression of solidarity amongst the oppressed.[31]

At the memorial services for Steve Biko in August 1977, Bishop Tutu praised the founder of the Black Consciousness Movement as an "instrument of God's peace" and "a man of real reconciliation" who was "unshakeable in his commitment to the liberation of all South Africans, black and white striving for a more just and more open South Africa." The Bishop also used the occasion to inspire his followers to continue the struggle, challenging them to dedicate themselves anew to the liberation struggle. He maintained that many of the supporters of the racist regime know in their hearts that "they are upholding a system that is evil and unjust and oppressive, and which is utterly abhorrent and displeasing to God."[32] The Biko incident represented one of the worst features of South African life--brutality in its prisons. The African activist died mysteriously in prison on September 12, 1977 after having been beaten.

Similarly, Bishop Tutu paid tribute to Robert Sobukwe in memorial services on March 6, 1978. The deceased, who had been instrumental in the founding of the Pan Africanist Congress, was arrested several times and was required to serve sentences on Robben Island. The Bishop reminded the mourners that some of the better Africans had been sacrificed for the "struggle of justice and the ending of oppression and exploitation." He assured them that freedom will eventually come to South Africa since God was a God of liberation.[33]

Because of the nationalist fervor generated at funerals, the Government tried frequently to curtail large commemorative services. In February 1981, Bishop Tutu angered the Government when he arranged memorial services for members of the outlawed ANC, who had been killed by the South African army in a raid in Mozambique. Tutu defied the governmental ban and

---

[31] Tutu, *Hope and Suffering*, 20.

[32] Tutu, *Crying in the Wilderness*, 64.

[33] Tutu, 67.

performed the services, insisting that those who were killed had friends and relatives in South Africa.[34]

In August 1985, the township of Daveyton encountered difficulty as it prepared for the funeral services of two girls who had been killed in a demonstration. In anticipation of the services being "politicized," the Government had on duty a massive military/police presence. *Time* offered this description of the tension which existed: "Stones were picked up, but none were thrown. Army weapons were held at the ready but no shots were fired. Police dogs appeared atop armored cars, but none were unleashed. Police whips were brandished, but none were used."[35] At the funeral of one of the victims, increased tension developed as the mourners insisted on marching the short distance from the funeral scene to the burial ground in defiance of the state of emergency decree, which forbade marches in funeral processions. During the services, Bishop Tutu informed the mourners that he had asked that the dead be allowed to be buried in dignity. In his appeal to the Government, he urged that salt not be rubbed into the wounds of the mourners, suggesting that they already had been hurt too much. He advised the Government that as humans, when confronted by death, we too cry and feel despair. After the funeral, the police commander warned the crowd that they were violating the law and would have to disperse. When told that the convoy to the cemetery could only be by vehicles, the Bishop responded by requesting the commander to provide busses since the people did not have vehicles, and in the absence of such transportation an ugly scene might erupt. After about an hour, with the police providing the necessary busses the funeral procession began. Tutu thanked the colonel and told him that "in trying to maintain unreasonable laws," he had behaved in a reasonable manner.[36]

Africans, who were determined to bury their dead in dignity, were confronted by a government that was equally determined to restrict their funeral rituals. In early September 1985 when thousands gathered to honor 24 Sowetans, who had been killed by police gunfire, they were denied entrance to the stadium, and were forced to disband by the unleashing of canisters of tear gas. Earlier, the Government had announced restrictions designed to prevent mass funerals. According to *Time* more than 8,000 blacks gathered at the

---

[34] Percy Qoboza, "South Africa: Rights Leader to Visit US This Month," *Washington Star*, March 3, 1981.

[35] William Stewart, "A Burial with Dignity," *Time*, Aug. 19, 1985, 25.

[36] *Time*.

cemetery to bury the slain. They sang "forbidden songs of freedom and chanted banned slogans." The security forces reacted by spraying gas causing the crowd to disperse, leaving some of the dead half buried.[37]

Prior to the funerals, the Government imposed restrictions on political gatherings, and sent the police from house to house in Soweto to inform the people that there could be "no mass funerals, no outdoor ceremonies, no flags, no slogans, no gatherings of more than 200 mourners." Families of the deceased were asked to sign papers agreeing to observe the above rules, and funeral home directors were warned "not to release any bodies for burial without official permission."[38] Fearing the violence which might result if funeral services were held at St. Paul's Church, Tutu, who by this time had become Archbishop of Cape Town, advised church officials "to call off the planned funerals and have everyone return home peacefully." There were dual reactions to the suggestion--some of the mourners went home as requested, while others joined the thousands who had already gathered at the Jabavu Stadium.[39]

In April 1991, on the eve of the liberation of South Africa, one of the strongest foes of apartheid was assassinated--Chris Hani, the General Secretary of the South African Communist Party. In reaction to his death, more than 2,500,000 persons were believed to have taken part in eighty-five events during a national day of mourning on April 14. At some of these sites violence took place with seventeen persons killed. Once again, Tutu emerged as a peace maker. At the same time, he demonstrated courage in honoring one who was a Communist in a country which proclaimed itself as a bulwark against Communism. In addressing the crowd of more than 100,000 who attended Hani's funeral, the Archbishop noted that they had gathered to "bury a great son of the soil," one who "was dedicated to peace, to reconciliation, to negotiation."[40]

Tutu also used the occasion to demand democracy and freedom. In these words he consoled the people:

> My friends, we are marching to victory. We are marching to victory of freedom over the oppression of apartheid. We are marching to victory, the victory of justice over the injustice of apartheid. We are marching to victory,

---

[37] Jill Smolawe, "Battle at the Burial Grounds," *Time*, Sept. 15, 1986, 39.
[38] *Time*, 40.
[39] *Time*.
[40] Tutu, *The Rainbow People of God*, 253.

the victory of light over the darkness of apartheid. We are marching to victory, the victory of life over the death of apartheid.[41]

SEEKING PEACE WITHIN

As an instrument of peace, Tutu also sought to eliminate "Black on Black" violence. When an angry mob attempted to kill a man who was accused of being a police informer, the Archbishop interrupted the religious services, and "waded into the crowd and flung himself across the victim's body." After having restored the peace, he continued the services. Tutu also expressed dismay over the beating and burning of a woman who had been accused of complicity with the police. He warned the audience that such violence must cease, and if it continued, he would be inclined to leave his homeland, and take up residence, elsewhere. Such violence, he insisted, made it difficult for him to speak for the cause of liberation. He challenged the crowd of 30,000 that in seeking to obtain liberation not to stoop to the methods used by their enemies. Being aware of the importance of international opinion to his cause, Tutu expressed fear that the picture of the burning woman would have a negative impact on the campaign for social justice. He observed that "when they saw that woman burning on television, they must have said that maybe we are not ready for freedom." Tutu urged his followers not to destroy the good will they had obtained by using methods of violence.[42]

In spite of Tutu's warning, "Black on Black" violence continued. He was especially sadden when, on what appeared to be the eve of the ending of the struggle against apartheid, very serious internal fighting erupted among the Africans. In an effort to end this senseless killing, the Archbishop attempted to bring rival African leaders together to seek means of ending the violence. Such a conference was convened in his official residence on November 29, 1990, but it did not achieve the desired results due to the absence of Chief Buthelezi, head of the Inkatha Freedom Party. Among those present were Nelson Mandela, deputy president of the African National Congress, and representatives of the Anzanian People's Organization, Pan-Africanist Congress, and nominally self governing ethnic homelands. In order to defend his absence, Buthelezi issued a letter complaining that the ANC was not

[41] Tutu, 254.

[42] William E. Smith, "Black Rage, White Fist," *Time*, Aug. 5, 1985, 26.

interested in working for reconciliation. He proposed a personal meeting with Mandela to resolve the problems.[43] To the dismay of Tutu, Africans continued to kill other Africans as they advanced toward a new South Africa.

CHRISTIANIZING THE CHURCH

Since an effective nonviolent campaign is dependent upon the success of its appeal to the conscience of humankind, the Church is perceived as having a major role to play. In South Africa, its role became even more important after the banning of all major nationalist organizations. The South African Council of Churches (SACC), an ecumenical organization, composed of most of the churches in the country tended to fill a major void by facilitating communication among Christians of different races. According to Majorie Hope and James Young, the organization constitutes one of the few places in which Whites could "become familiar with Black opinion and experiences," and "for Blacks it is almost the only forum where they can air their aspirations and frustrations."[44]

Prior to his elevation in 1978 to the top leadership post of the SACC, Tutu had worked hard for the cause of racial justice, but after he assumed his new post, his involvement escalated greatly. As the first African general secretary of the Organization, he became the spokesperson for approximately thirteen million Christians in South Africa, of whom more than 80% were Africans. Tutu was determined to make the Church a greater instrument of social justice and peace.

Before Tutu's selection to the highest post in the SACC, the ecumenical organization had incurred the wrath of the South African Government. During the early 1970s, it was called upon to react to activities of the Programme to Combat Racism (PCR) of the World Council of Churches (WCC). Many South African churches, apparently, were caught off guard when the PCR announced in 1970 the funding of special grants to "oppressed racial groups and organizations supporting the victims of racial justice." Leaders of the SACC reacted by expressing support for other projects of the PCR, while

[43] Christopher S. Wren, "South African Blacks Meet to End Strife", *New York Times*, Nov. 30, 1960, A3.

[44] Majorie Hope and James Young, *The South African Churches in a Revolutionary Situation* (Maryknoll, NY: Orbis Books, 1981), 86.

objecting to the funds granted to liberation movements which used violence. Vorster was not satisfied with their mere objection, insisting that churches withdraw from the WCC because of its anti-South African and revolutionary stance. Hope and Young credited the opposition of Africans to the withdrawal as the major reason why some of the churches refused to take such action. For Africans, "the real issue was not membership in the world body, but rather, how real was the commitment by their churches to the struggle against racism."[45]

The Prime Minister reacted bitterly to the refusal of the churches to withdraw from the WCC, which was accused of "introducing innocent South Africans to all manner of evil ideas and expectations." He threatened reprisals against churches which did not break ties. In the end, Vorster could only count on the support of the Dutch Reformed Church(DRC), in which most of the Afrikaners belonged. Like the Government, the DRC had a major obsession with the WCC, one which Ernie Regehr concluded had resulted from its perception of a betrayal by Western Christians. He noted that:

> "as bulwarks of reformed Christianity, committed foes of atheistic communism and agents of western civilization on a continent seeking models of development, Afrikaners sincerely believe they should receive the thanks, rather than the wrath, of Western Christians."[46]

As additional grants were made in later years, the controversy intensified. In an interview on South African television on November 26, 1978, Bishop Tutu was challenged on how as a man interested in "methods of peace," he could support grants from the WCC to the Rhodesian Patriotic Front, which had murdered missionaries and civilians, had shot down civilian aircraft, and had massacred survivors. In referring to a statement attributed to the Bishop, the television commentator observed that while Tutu was not "personally a violent man," he supported violence against governments. The Bishop denied having supported the grant in question, noting that he, alone with the SACC, had opposed grants to both the Patriotic Front and the South West African People's Organization. He called attention, however, to a statement which had been issued by the Lambeth Conference of Anglican Bishops, which convened in England in 1978, that read: "in many parts of the world there are those

[45] Hope and Young, 91.

[46] Ernie Regehr, *Perception of Apartheid* (Scottdale, PA: Herald Press, 1979), 206-207.

involved in the struggle for human rights at great cost to themselves, and often the struggle may become violent...we must not abandon them even when the struggle becomes violent."[47] While acknowledging his condemnation of actions of violence by terrorists within the country, at the same time, he deplored the violence being perpetrated against neighboring states by the South African armed forces.[48]

During Bishop Tutu's first year as general secretary of the SACC, the annual conference adopted resolutions and pronouncements on principles, which it perceived as necessary to guide the behavior of investors in South Africa. Its action was justified on the basis of the need of the Church to exert its influence on all aspect of life. The SACC envisioned this as being necessary since investors do not usually "regard themselves as being bound by Christian moral principles or by the interests of the majority of local people." A second reason for focusing upon investments and loans was because they are usually made "within the context of a political and economic order that is considered by the church to be fundamentally unjust." The Conference called upon foreign countries and organizations, in the name of justice, "to revise radically their investment policies and employment practices in regard to South Africa, in such a way as to benefit the total population of South Africa." Although the Conference did not demand withdrawal of investments or a moratorium, it did establish minimum acceptable conditions for investments--to secure better living conditions for African workers, who were viewed as foreigners in their homeland. According to the SACC, better conditions could be obtained by businesses negotiating with African trade unions, rather than recruiting migratory workers.[49]

A year earlier, the 1977 SACC conference adopted a more comprehensive list of conditions which were to be met as a prerequisite to the granting of loans to South Africa. Some of the demands were:

- Non-segregation of the races in all eating, comfort and work facilities.
- Equal pay and fair employment practices for all employees.
- Initiation and development of training programs that will prepare in substantial numbers, Blacks for supervisory, administrative, clerical and technical jobs.

---

47 Regehr, 276.
48 Regehr.
49 Regehr, 245-246.

- An increase in the number of Blacks in management and supervisory positions.
- Improvement in the quality of employees' lives outside the work environment.
- Immediate recognition of trade unions as a basis for future management of labour negotiations.
- Introduction of voluntary 2% self-tax on gross profit for contribution to education for Blacks.
- The locating of Black-initiated and controlled projects for support and encouragement.
- Refusal to continue to use migrant labour unless married accommodation is provided.
- Investment of a certain proportion of any investment portfolio in banking institutions which will utilise funds sorely for the benefits of Blacks.
- Active reduction of the number of foreign skilled workers and replacement of them with adequately trained Blacks.
- Refusal to invest in or assist projects which have to do with the manufacture of arms.[50]

Under the leadership of Bishop Tutu, the SACC, in its search for a just society, assumed many responsibilities. One of the most controversial of these was that of caring for the needs of political prisoners, detainees, and banned persons.[51] Recalling that Jesus said, "When I was in prison you visited me," the Bishop viewed this as giving the SACC a mandate to act in a similar manner. Through its Dependent Conference, it sought to facilitate the readjustment of released political prisoners to normal life by aiding them in acquiring proper means of self support. Also it has provided legal defense for those accused of political crimes. Providing for their defense was not perceived as necessarily condoning their alleged crimes, but rather assisting in the "proper administration of justice." According to Tutu, an acquittal rate of between 70 and 75% was achieved in cases where legal assistance was provided, in contrast with a conviction rate of approximately 80% in cases where the accused were not defended. The Bishop observed that in a normal

---

50 Regehr, 246-247.

51 Tutu, *Hope and Suffering*, 179.

country, he would have won the praise of the Government for his assistance in the administration of justice. Perceiving it to be the right of each person to receive the best defense possible, Tutu pledged to continue his effort. He insisted that in spite of government intimidation, he would continue, since it was his duty to obey God rather than man.[52]

In order to weaken the influence of the SACC, the South African Government bombarded the country with propaganda. The former, through its Division of Justice and Reconciliation, sought to respond by keeping the churches and the general public informed on such vital issues as nationalism, population removal, Bantustan policies and foreign investments. Although reconciliation was a major goal, the SACC realized that it could not become a reality until justice was obtained; thus, Tutu considered his most important battle to be that of dismantling apartheid, which he proposed to do by peaceful means.[53]

Noting that the SACC tried to use negotiation, discussion, and dialogue in the achievement of its goals, Tutu suggested that the Government use similar approaches. Consistent with this philosophy, he called upon the Government to convene a national convention in which the "authentic leaders of all sections of the South African society would be represented." On several occasions, the Archbishop made it clear that he regarded the imprisoned Nelson Mandela as a credible voice of Africans, who should be heard on issues relative to national policies. Tutu's campaign of negotiation, discussion and dialogue caused him support in the African community, where some viewed him as being too willing to compromise. He defended his action on Biblical grounds, noting that "Moses went to Pharaoh several times even when he knew that it was futile."[54]

Although the Archbishop angered the Government, it was not able to silence him due to the respect which he held as a religious leader. Nevertheless, it attempted to place obstacles in his way. Tutu rejected restrictions imposed upon him, contending that where man's law is in conflict with that of God, he will obey the latter.[55]

---

[52] Tutu, *Crying in the Wilderness*, 47.
[53] Tutu, *Hope and Suffering*, 180-181.
[54] Tutu, 181.
[55] Tutu, 187.

BUILDING A COALITION AGAINST INJUSTICE

In order to achieve justice in South Africa, Archbishop Tutu endeavored to take his message beyond the confines of the African community. He spoke on various university campuses and to predominantly white groups, generally. In an address at the University of Witwatersrand, Tutu described the plight of Africans and discussed their non-violent efforts to obtain justice. In denouncing the evils of apartheid, he informed the students that not only are the choices of the Africans limited by their evil system, but that of whites, as well. The Archbishop challenged the students to join the oppressed in their struggle for liberation by discarding "lethargy, and the apathy of affluence," and by working for a "better South Africa." He appealed to the students to "uproot all evil and oppression and injustice of which blacks are victims and you whites are beneficiaries, so that you won't reap the whirlwind."[56]

To the white community, Tutu offered a hand of reconciliation, appealing to it to assist in bringing about a more equitable sharing of the resources of South Africa. They could do this, he suggested, by voluntarily agreeing to lower their "high standard of living," in order to avoid a situation of bloodshed and chaos which could result in their losing everything. The Archbishop advised his audience that the blacks seek nothing more or less than the whites seek—"a stable family life where husband lives with wife and children, adequate housing, and proper free and compulsory education for our children."[57]

The Archbishop contended that white businesses could do more to aid the cause of the oppressed. He criticized the former for making their profits in black communities, while behaving as if they were doing them a favor. Tutu noted, in particular, the refusal of building societies and banks to make loans to blacks, while using their money to enable whites to secure housing. Advising blacks that these institutions could do more to agitate for racial justice, he suggested that "many building societies and banks would feel a cool draught if we withdrew our savings." The Archbishop also was very critical of white newspapers, which he accused of reporting the news as if blacks did not constitute "an important part of their readership." He challenged blacks to exert their influence as consumers and "let white South

---

[56] Tutu, *Crying in the Wilderness*, 43-44.
[57] Tutu, 44-45.

Africa know about it, so that they negotiate with us [blacks]as those who have that power."[58]

As were the cases of King in the United States and Luthuli in South Africa, Tutu realized that liberation could become a reality only by joint efforts of a coalition against racial oppression. Experiences obtained during his tenure as general secretary of the SACC aided him in building effective coalitions in later years. Prior to its banning, the Archbishop coordinated his activities with the United Democratic Front--an umbrella group for anti-apartheid groups. In February 1988 when it was banned, Tutu joined with Rev. Allan Boesak and others in organizing the Committee for the Defense of Democracy. Before the new organization could launch its first campaign, it too was banned. With these efforts aborted, Tutu began to use the Church more in order to fill the vacuum.

Tutu did not restrict his coalition efforts to South Africa; instead he toured numerous countries seeking support for his cause. The Archbishop sought friends in the United States both in and out of Government. Not only did he seek to influence the Reagan Administration and Congress, but state and local officials as well. In addition, he campaigned for support in the religious, academic and business communities. In general, he appealed to the rank and file to aid him in his struggle against racial injustice. During his tours of Western nations, the Soviet Union and China, Tutu sought support for his cause. His international campaign, however, is discussed more fully in the next chapter.

RECONCILING THE NATION

As the struggle against apartheid neared its end, Archbishop Tutu perceived all South Africans as being "wounded and traumatized" by the evil of apartheid and in need of healing. Perceiving the church as the agent to facilitate national reconciliation, he called upon the church which had been divided between supporters and opponents of apartheid to first reconcile itself. A step was taken in that direction in November 1990 when a conference of church leaders was held to discuss issues of confession, forgiveness and national restitution for the wrongs committed under apartheid. In order to achieve reconciliation, according to Tutu, "the victims of injustice and

[58] Tutu, 97-98.

oppression must be ever ready to forgive." This he said is a "gospel imperative." Equally important, the archbishop insisted that those who have committed wrongs must be willing to say:

> We have hurt you by this injustice, by uprooting you from your homes, by dumping you in poverty-stricken homeland resettlement camps. By giving your children inferior education. By denying you humanity and trampling down on your human dignity and denying you fundamental rights. We are sorry, forgive us.[59]

Once this is done, he insisted, they must be willing to pay restitution and reparation.

Having led the church in efforts of reconciliation in the religious community, the Archbishop in 1995 had the opportunity to play a major role in achieving national reconciliation. Following the passage of the *Promotion of National Unity and Reconciling Act*, President Mandela selected the Archbishop to head the seventeen member Truth and Reconciliation Commission (TRC). The Commission was composed of three committees--Human Rights Violation (also headed by Tutu), Reparation and Rehabilitation and Amnesty. The members represented a cross section of the South African people in regard to race, religion, political views, and geography.

In order to fulfill its mandate, Tutu considered it necessary to give a limited meaning to "gross violation of human rights" since in effect, every black person because of apartheid could be considered a victim of such crime. For the TRC, the term was used only in reference to victims of killing, abduction, torture and severe ill treatment.[60]

When Tutu opened thc first meeting of his committee, he prayed and then made this statement:

> We are charged to unearth the truth about our dark past; to lay the ghosts of that past so that they will not return to haunt us and that all will thereby contribute to the healing of a traumatized and wounded people--for all of us in South Africa are wounded people-- and in this manner to promote national unity and reconciliation.[61]

---

[59] Tutu, *The Rainbow People of God*, 222.
[60] Tutu, *No Future Without Forgiveness*, 105.
[61] Tutu, 114.

Among the critics of the final report of the TRC was the ANC, which accused the Commission of having "grossly misdirected itself in its findings on the African National Congress, through the pursuit of objectives which are contrary to the spirit and the intention of the act under which it was established." It appealed to the high court to prevent the issuing of the report until it had an opportunity to respond to the pending charges, but the court refused to issue an injunction.[62]

The dismay of the ANC was perceived as being based on the perception that the TRC was judging both the freedom fighters and apartheid advocates on the same standards. Recalling that the Commission was criticized for what was called "criminalizing the liberation struggle and insulting those who engaged in it by placing them on the same level as the upholders of apartheid," Tutu insisted that the TRC obeyed the provisions of the act, noting that "a gross violation is a gross violation whoever commits it and for whatever motive."[63] His statement read:

> We stated categorically that apartheid was a crime against humanity. Equally vehemently we asserted that the liberation movements were conducting a just war because they had a just cause. But the Geneva Convention and the principles of the just war are quite clear that justice of war requires justice in war. A just cause must be fought by just means; otherwise it may be badly vitiated.[64]

Tutu noted that the ANC, itself, had made inquiries relative to abuses in its camps outside of South Africa and made apologies for these excesses.

Speaking out against Inequality Abroad

As was the case with Martin Luther King, Jr., Archbishop Tutu considered it to be his duty to condemn injustices regardless of where it existed. Addressing a crowd of approximately 15,000 in Kinshasa, Zaire in February 1989, he decried the suffering which Africans were experiencing as a result of wars. He mentioned in particular the ones in Angola, Mozambique, Ethiopia,

---

[62] "ANC Statement on the Final Report of the TRC," issued by the Department of Information and Publicity of the African National Congress, 30 Oct. 1998.[On-line] http://www.anc.org.za/ancdocs/misc/trcreply.html

[63] Tutu, 106.

[64] Tutu, 107.

Eritrea, Uganda and Sudan. Noting that Africa was producing more than its share of refugees--most of whom were "refugees from injustice and oppression in their motherland." Tutu also expressed dismay over Africa's record of human rights violations, which, for the most part, resulted from the many military dictators. In criticizing them, he observed:

> In many places, all that has changed for the people who suffer is the complexion of the oppressor. In colonial times the oppressor was of a different complexion. Sadly, today the complexion of the oppressor is the same as the complexion of the oppressed.[65]

Similarly, Tutu delivered a powerful anti-tyranny messages when he preached in Panama City on March 20, 1989. Earlier he had met with the de facto head of government, General Manuel Noriega and raised questions relative to "allowing independent observers at the elections and freedom of the press." During his sermon, he made clear that his remarks on tyranny referred to South Africa, nevertheless, they could have easily applied to the Panamanian dictator.[66] Typical of the warning, Tutu gave were these:

> The good ruler will redeem the lives of the needy from exploitation and outrage because their lives are precious in his sight. If you are a ruler and you are not this kind of ruler, you are in trouble. You are in real trouble. We try to tell oppressors everywhere. You are not God! You are just an ordinary human being....[67]

In December 1989, the Archbishop had the opportunity to express his opinion concerning the crisis in the Middle East. During a Christian pilgrimage to the Holy Land, he expressed hope that his presence there, would "give hope and encouragement to the victims of oppression." Tutu advised the Palestinians of his support for "their struggle for justice, peace, statehood and independence." Simultaneously, he affirmed "the right of Israel to its independence and territorial integrity." He found it impossible, however, to "pretend that there is no violence in the country." The Archbishop also perceived a parallel between "the ways the Governments of Israel and South Africa react to unrest." He suggested that if he were "to change the names, a

---

[65] Tutu, *The Rainbow People of God*, 158.
[66] Tutu.161.
[67] Tutu, 105.

description of what is happening in the Gaza Strip and West Bank could describe events in South Africa."[68] The controversial visit by the Archbishop was criticized by the Israelis and Jews throughout the world. He responded to the criticisms by defending his comparison, suggesting that he was compelled to tell the truth and "to speak up for justice everywhere whether in South Africa, the rest of Africa, the Middle East, Eastern Europe or China." He advised his critics that "denouncing injustice is for us a religious duty and not a political act." Criticisms of Tutu were not limited to the Jewish community, but extended to Palestinians as well. In response to a question from a Palestinian reporter, he observed that it was not his place to determine or suggest that the PLO serve as the legitimate representative of the Palestinian people.[69] Being a man of peace often requires one to make enemies on both sides. Because the Archbishop is aware of this, he was not disturbed by his critics.

Concluding His Mission

After having played a crucial role in the nonviolent campaign for the liberation of South Africa and having devoted a major effort to achieve reconciliation, Tutu decided that it was time to step down from his more publicized role as a national leader. This was made possible by the return of Nelson Mandela from prison and the unbanning of political groups. In a change of roles he came to the United States where he served as a visiting professor at Emory University, and while here received treatment for prostate cancer. Tutu returned home in August 2000 determined to live a more relaxed life. Although South Africa has not rid itself of all of its racial problems, the despised system of apartheid has been dismantled; therefore, with this accomplished, Archbishop Tutu was willing to leave the challenge to others.

---

[68] Alan Cowell, "Tutu, Visiting Jerusalem, Backs Palestine Statehood," *New York Times*, Dec. 24, 1989, A3.

[69] Alan Cowell, "Tutu Cool to Pretoria Offer to Join Talk," *New York Times*, Dec. 26, 1989, A3.VII Internationalization of the Cause.

Chapter 7

INTERNATIONALIZATION OF THE CAUSE

> Apartheid is a threat to word peace. We owe it to future generations to end it. Let us be part of the exhilarating enterprise of liberating South Africa for all its people, black and white together. And we shall remember who helped us to be free. [1]
>
> Desmond Tutu

Throughout history, the international community has been concerned about events which have taken place within the borders of a member state; therefore, it has sought to influence the outcome. During the human rights campaigns of Gandhi, King, Luthuli and Tutu foreign nations displayed vested interest in the internal struggles of their respective nations. Being aware of the international concern, each of the leaders attempted to appeal to the consciences of nations, and international organizations in order to enhance the causes for which they campaigned.

MOVEMENT FOR A FREE INDIA

The status of Mohandas Gandhi assured the early internationalization of the Indian struggle for independence, with his words and actions being reported throughout the world. During the decade of the forties, the Second World War further internationalized the struggle for India's independence.

---

[1] Desmond Tutu, *The Rainbow People of God: The Making of a Peaceful Revolution*, (New York: NY: 1994), 103.

Realizing the importance of India to the cause of the Allies, Gandhi used the occasion to appeal to the conscience of the world. It was not his intention to bring about the defeat of the British, nevertheless, he insisted that India could play a meaningful role in the Second World War, only if it was a free nation.

During the First World War, Gandhi had contended that inasmuch as he had accepted the benefits and protection of the British Empire, he had an interest in not seeing it destroyed. Likewise, he made valuable contributions to the British cause during the Boers War of 1899-1902, and the Zulu Uprising of 1906. As a result of his loyalty and that of his fellow-Indians, Gandhi hoped that the British would respond by granting independence to his country, but such was not the case. As a result of this betrayal, he became less enthused over India's involvement in the Second World War when Great Britain was threatened. Although critical of the aggressors in the war, Gandhi sought to exact from the British independence for India as a price for the participation of Indians in the war.

On the eve of the war, some of Gandhi's critics expressed fear that he might take advantage of the crisis to drive the British out of India with the aid of the Japanese. He replied by noting that in the effort to throw off its foreign yoke, India would not seek the aid of any nation. Gandhi contended that his country would not exchange the rule of the British for that of domination by another foreign power. He did not perceive the Axis powers (Germany, Italy, Japan and others) as coming to India as deliverers; instead, as "sharers in the spoil."[2] He insisted that it was better to be occupied by the enemy he knew than the one he did not know. Gandhi denied having pro-Japanese sentiments, advising his critics that if he discovered that he had made a miscalculation and had been aiding the cause of the Japanese, he would not hesitate to retrace his steps. He informed the world that Indians would lay down their lives to resist Japanese intrusion as much as they would resist the British.[3]

Having allayed, somewhat, the fears of the British and their allies concerning his alleged Axis sympathies, Gandhi appealed to the United States to use its influence in persuading the British to arrive at an honorable settlement with India. The United States was perceived as being in a position to exert a substantial impact because of its financial and military support of the British. The Mahatma contended that inasmuch as the United States was

---

[2] *Gandhji's Correspondence with the Government, 1942-44* (Ahmedabad: Navajivan Publishing House, 1957), 182.

[3] *Gandhji's Correspondence*, 185.

the "predominant partner in the Allies cause," it was a partner in "Britain's guilt."[4]

About two weeks later, Gandhi wrote to President Roosevelt, informing him that in spite of his hatred of British rule, he had nothing but good wishes for the United States. The Mahatma maintained that the Indians' demand for immediate withdrawal of the British from the country was motivated by friendly intentions. He advised the President that he was seeking to convert ill will toward Great Britain to good will; thus, making it possible for millions of Indians to participate in the war. Gandhi insisted that under foreign rule, however, the Indians had no contribution to make to the war efforts of the British. As he had done on previous occasions, he challenged the assumption that the Allies were fighting "to make the world safe for the freedom of the individual and for democracy," noting the British continued exploitation of Indians and Africans and the United States' policy of racial discrimination. Gandhi informed President Roosevelt that the Allies need not have fear concerning India's freedom, inasmuch as they would be permitted to keep troops in the country in order to prevent aggression by Japan and to defend China. He maintained, however, that such troops could be stationed there only by a treaty with Free India. In support of his proposal for independence, he solicited the aid of the President.[5]

Similarly, Gandhi sought the aid of China, an ally of Great Britain, in his struggle to gain the freedom of India. In August 1942, he wrote a letter to Generalissimo Chiang Kai Shek, expressing India's sympathy with the plight of China, and advising him that the appeal which had been made for the withdrawal of British troops from India was not intended to weaken the Indian defenses against the Japanese or embarrass the Chinese. In emphasizing that he would not "be guilty of purchasing the freedom of India at the cost of China," Gandhi pledged the support of his fellow-countrymen in preventing Japanese occupation of either country. but warned, once again, that India could play a role only if free. He expressed dismay over the British response to the Indian overture of cooperation. Gandhi perceived the "failure of the Cripps mission" as leaving deep wounds in his country, observing that "out of

---

[4] *Gandhji's Correspondence*, 177.

[5] M. K. Gandhi, "Letter to Franklin D. Roosevelt," in Homer A Jacks, ed., *The Gandhi Reader* (Bloomington, Indiana: University Press, 1956), 357-358.

that anguish has come the cry for immediate withdrawal of British power so that India can look after herself and help China to the best of her ability."[6]

As the situation in Asia worsened, and the Chinese leader realized the sincerity of Gandhi's position, he sought the aid of the United States on behalf of India. He warned, in a letter to President Franklin Roosevelt, that "if India should start a movement against Britain or against the United Nations (the Allies) this will cause deterioration in the Indian situation from which the Axis power will surely reap benefits." Chaing advised the President that because the latter's view was generally acceptable to the British, and because the United States was "the leader of this war of right against might," he should use his influence to bring about a resolution of the Indian problem, The President reacted by sending Chaing's letter, which was marked "strictly confidential," to the British Prime Minister, with a personal message. Clement Atlee, who headed the British Government at that time, warned that his country would respond with stern measures if mass civil disobedience erupted in India. Following the arrest of Gandhi, Nehru, and other Indian leaders, Chaing, once again, appealed to Roosevelt to use his influence, but the latter replied that neither he nor Chaing had the moral right to force their feelings on either the British or the Congress Party.[7]

Gandhi perceived the success of his internationalization efforts as depending strongly upon the ability and willingness of President Roosevelt to use his influence on behalf of the Indian people. As events unfolded, however, they appeared to suggest that the President's ability was limited, and that, for the most part, he was not willing to exert his influence, if such an attempt was offensive to his British ally. James Burns, in his biography of Roosevelt, recalled that following the entry of the United States into the Second World War, the President suggested that Great Britain might use the American experiment with the Articles of Confederation as a model from which to organize a temporary government in India. Churchill quickly rejected the advice, considering the matter to be strictly internal. Later, in 1942, Roosevelt, again, appealed to the British Government, urging it to continue negotiations with India rather than recall the Cripps Mission, but the appeal fell on deaf ears.[8]

---

[6] Gandhi, "Letter to Chiang Kai-Shek," in Jack, 352-353.

[7] James M. Burns, *Roosevelt: The Soldier of Freedom* (New York: Harcourt, Brace, Javanovich, Inc., 1970), 240-241.

[8] Burns, 220-221.

In a sense, the issue could not be viewed strictly as a British internal matter since it was affecting the course of the war. At times, it appeared that the British were more concerned with holding on to its colonial possessions than defeating the Fascist powers. Typical of this attitude was Churchill's rejection of the Roosevelt interpretation of the application of the rights stated in the Atlantic Charter to all humanity. He insisted that he had not become "the King's first minister in order to preside over the liquidation of the British Empire."[9]

The United States' response to the Gandhian appeal, at best, could be viewed as sending mixed signals. Roosevelt, on two occasions, dispatched personal envoys to India, in spite of the fact that it was not an independent nation. Once, the representatives had reported their findings to the President, out of deference to the British, he ignored their reports.[10]

As the war neared its end, India was still under British domination, but an unrelenting Gandhi did not give up his struggle. On the eve of the opening of the San Francisco Conference, which drafted the Charter of the United Nations, he warned that peace would be possible only if there was a willingness "to hammer out a real peace based on the freedom and equality of all races and nations." Gandhi suggested that "Freedom of India will demonstrate to all the exploited races of the earth that their freedom is near and that in no case will they henceforth be exploited."[11] When the Charter was adopted, it reflected such Gandhian principles as "self-determination of peoples," "respect for human rights," and the "use of peaceful means to redress grievances." Shortly after the organizing of the United Nations, India received its independence, and became a model for other dominated countries as they marched to nationhood.

As Gandhi had envisioned, once India achieved its independence, it utilized the United Nations as a means by which to internationalize issues of colonialism and racism. As a result, when Luthuli, King, and Tutu waged their later campaigns for racial justice, they were doing so before a global audience.

---

[9] Burns, 379.

[10] Burns, 220-221.

[11] Louis Fischer, *The Life of Mahatma Gandhi* (New York: Harper and Row Publishers, 1950), 409.

THE CIVIL RIGHTS STRUGGLE IN THE UNITED STATES

At the close of the Second World War, racial discrimination in the United States constituted a serious barrier to a successful foreign policy; thus, it was assumed that in order to achieve desired "cold war" objectives, it would be necessary for Americans to adjust their racial attitudes and practices. It was the belief of policy-makers that it would be easier to point out defects of the Communist system if domestic race discrimination was eliminated. Therefore, the seriousness of the ideological struggle between the Soviet Union and the United States combined with the appearance of numerous African states into the international arena, to provide an opportunity for linking the domestic civil rights campaign to the broader issue of international politics.

The importance of domestic race relations to the successful struggle against Communism was recognized by President Harry S. Truman as early as 1946. In his search for a solution to the problem of racial discrimination, the President appointed a committee on civil rights. In its report, *To Secure These Rights*, 1947, the Committee perceived the United States' leadership in the international community as being compromised because of shortcomings in domestic race relations. As a follow-up to the Committee's report, President Truman recommended the adoption of several proposals designed to enhance the civil rights of African-Americans. In his message to Congress, February 2, 1948, the President noted, "If we wish to inspire the peoples of the world whose freedom is in jeopardy, if we wish to restore hope to those who have already lost their civil liberties, if we wish to fulfill the promise that is ours, we must correct the remaining imperfections in our practice of democracy."[12]

In later years, the advice of President Truman was repeated many times by other governmental officials. In 1961, a Senate Study Mission on Africa reported that "racial discrimination in the United States was the most important of all the national barriers to a better understanding between Africa and this country."[13] A similar opinion was expressed by Secretary of State Dean Rusk, who considered problems of discrimination in the United States to be "the largest single burden we bear in the conduct of our foreign relations."

---

[12] President Harry S Truman, "Civil Rights Message," 80th Cong., 2nd. sess., House Document 516, Feb. 2, 1948.

[13] US Congress, Senate *Study Mission to Africa*, 87th Cong., 1st. sess.1961, 3.

He called upon the United States to move promptly "to establish the fact that American citizens are American citizens in every sense of the word."[14]

Simultaneously, Africa was expressing opinions concerning American race relations. Shortly after the arrival of Ghana on the international scene in 1957, its representative to the United Nations General Assembly noted its special responsibility and obligations to "all African peoples and to peoples of African descent throughout the world."[15] A similar interest in American race relations was expressed by Jaja Wachuku, the Nigerian Foreign Minister in 1961, when he combined his assessment with a warning. While complimenting the United States for its attempt to build "a truly multi-racial society based upon justice and equality," he warned that the treatment of blacks in the United States as second and third-class citizens had to be quickly eradicated in order for it to win the full support of Africa.[16]

The 1963 summit of African leaders, which convened in Addis Ababa, Ethiopia, also expressed concern over the treatment of African-Americans. It noted, however, that the National Government of the United States was taking steps to end racial abuses, which appeared to threaten the harmonious relationship of African countries and the U.S.[17] A year later, when the Heads of States and Governments of the Organization of African Unity met in Cairo, they indicated their pleasure over the recently enacted Civil Rights Act, but also expressed concern over the continuing manifestation of racial bigotry and oppression in the United States.[18]

Because the American Government appeared to have been aware of the need to improve race relations, civil rights leaders envisioned an advantage of increasing the internationalization of the struggle. King's efforts in this regard were made easy due to the emergence of television as a major form of international communication. People in areas, once considered remote, were able to follow the civil rights campaign--witnessing the bombing of churches, and the attacking of children by police dogs. Likewise, what King said or did was heard by a global audience; therefore, his strategy, in part, was designed with that thought in mind.

---

[14] Transcript of a television interview of "CBS Reports: An Hour with the Secretary of State," Department of State Document 700, Nov. 28, 1962, 8.

[15] Ako, Adjei, Address to the United Nations General Assembly, Sept. 19, 1957.

[16] Eighth National Conference of the US National Commission for UNESCO, *Africa and the United States*, Boston, 1961, 6.

[17] Conference of Independent African States, *Resolutions*, May 25, 1963.

[18] Organization of African Unity, *Resolutions* July 1964.

For King, there was a clear linkage between the problems of African-Americans and events around the world. To him, the American Civil Rights Movement was simultaneously, "a special American phenomenon" and "a significant part of a world development." He applauded the fact that the cry of freedom by liberation movements was spreading throughout the world like a fever, and that "the great masses of people are determined to end the exploitation of their races and lands."[19] Because the people of Ghana represented such a force, King derived a great pleasure in being one of those who received a special invitation to observe the birth of that nation in 1957. It was in recognition of his outstanding achievements in civil rights endeavors that he earned the respect of Prime Minister Nkrumah; thus, the invitation. As suggested, even without discussing the civil rights issues, they were further internationalized by his mere presence in Ghana. King used the occasion, however, to point out the resemblance of colonialism in Africa and Asia to racial discrimination in the United States. Being disturbed over the conditions he observed in Nigeria, he suggested that it was a blessing that the sun no longer rises and sets on the British Empire.[20]

Two years later, King responded to an invitation of the Gandhi Peace Foundation and made a pilgrimage to India. While there, he paid homage to the great nonviolent leader, and consulted with high officials of the Indian Government. As in the case of Ghana, it was because of his accomplishments in the civil rights struggle that he earned the admiration of the Indian people. In the discussion with Prime Minister Nehru, King compared the American civil rights campaign with the Indian struggle for independence, King was impressed with how the Government of India was atoning for the centuries of injustices which had been inflicted upon the untouchable. He credited the leaders of India with throwing their moral and legal support behind the laws against discrimination, in contrast to the lack of leadership here in the United States. During his stay in India, King visited many parts of the country, informing his audiences of the struggle which he was conducting in the United States.[21]

By 1964, King had become a permanent feature of the televised evening news in many foreign countries. The viewers saw him as he fought the battle against segregation in Birmingham, and heard him as he delivered his "I Have

[19] King, *Where Do We Go From Here,* 169.
[20] Oates, 117.
[21] David Lewis, *King: A Biography*, 199-205.

a Dream" address during the March on Washington. Some foreigners joined in his effort to achieve that dream by contributing financially to the cause. King's international prestige enabled him to receive many invitations from abroad. He visited both East and West Germany, delivering sermons in each of the countries. The civil rights leader also preached at St. Paul's Cathedral in London, and held a private audience with the Pope.[22]

The greatest international recognition of King's civil rights struggle came during the fall of 1964 when he was designated the recipient of the Nobel Peace Prize. In bestowing the honor upon him, Gunnar Jahn recalled the segregated society in which King had lived and the suffering he had encountered in his effort to bring about a just society.[23] King used the august occasion to speak to the world concerning the issue of racial injustice, which he perceived as a global problem. He applauded the "magnificent drama of independence" which was unfolding in Asia and Africa, as well as "the gradual demise of the system of racial segregation in the United States." Both the Supreme Court's decision of 1954, which ended the doctrine of "separate but equal," and the passage of the Civil Rights Act of 1964, which provided for equal accommodations, were cited as progressive steps. He reminded his audience that much remains to be done, however. In pledging to continue the struggle for racial justice, King insisted that the Civil Rights Movement will not "seek to liberate Negroes at the expense of the humiliation and enslavement of whites. It seeks no victory over anyone. It seeks to liberate American society and to share in the self-liberation of all the people."[24]

During the spring of 1966, Martin Luther King, Jr. and Harry Belafonte undertook a tour of European cities, in which they were well received. In Sweden, the visit was sponsored by the Martin Luther King Fund of Sweden, with Professor Gunnar Myrdal as honorary chairman. An account was established at the Bank of Sweden in order to enable Swedes to make contributions to aid the efforts of the American Civil Rights Movement. In Paris, the sponsoring committee was composed of Americans in France, and French Protestants.[25]

---

[22] Lewis, 254.

[23] Gunnar Jahn, Speech delivered on the occasion of the awarding of the Nobel Peace Prize for 1964, in Frederick W. Haberman, ed., *Nobel Lectures, Peace, 1951-1970* (New York: Elsevier Publishing Co., 1979), 326-332.

[24] King, "The Quest for Peace and Justice," in Haberman, 337.

[25] "King and Belafonte Tour of the European Cities," *SCLC Newsletter*, III, Mar-Apr. 1966, 6.

To his European audience, King portrayed the United States as "the world in miniature" with African-Americans representing "the key to understanding the process of building one nation of many backgrounds." Considering racial discrimination, political domination, and economic exploitation as major evils which the Civil Rights Movement was seeking to eliminate, King noted the progress which had been made in regard to the first two, while the third remained a major problem. Economic exploitation in the United States was not envisioned as only an American problem, but a global one, as well. Vowing to continue the struggle, King suggested that the "grand experiment" being conducted in this country could be of tremendous relevance to other countries as they seek to obtain social justice.[26]

King's internationalization of the civil rights struggle also extended to Canada, our neighbor of the North. In 1967, he taped a series of addresses for the Canadian Broadcasting Corporation, one of which recalled the relationship that has existed between Canadians and African-Americans since the time of slavery. For his audience, King explained his nonviolent campaign, the resistance which it encountered, the outbreak of violence, and the white backlash which followed.[27] Through the years of struggle, the Civil Rights Movement had counted among its supporters, Canadians, who joined in demonstrations, held sympathetic rallies, and contributed financially to the campaign for social justice.

While King was not able to visit all of the countries in which he had supporters, he was able to convey his message to them through articles in popular magazines, interviews with foreign reporters, and three books, which depicted the civil rights struggle: *Stride Toward Freedom, Why We Can't Wait* and *Where Do We Go From Here.*

As indicated earlier, King did not wage his campaign for social justice only to enhance the status of African-Americans, but for deprived peoples throughout the world, as well. He warned that, "however deeply American Negroes are caught in the struggle to be at last at home in our homeland of the United States, we cannot ignore the larger world house in which we are also dwellers. Equality with whites will not solve the problems of either whites or

[26] "Speech by Dr. Martin Luther King, Jr. during European Tour," Mar. 1996, King's Papers, MLK/CNSC.

[27] King, *Trumpet of Conscience*, 3-17.

Negroes if it means equality in a world society stricken by poverty and in a universe doomed to extinction by war."[28]

King's international efforts could be viewed from two perspectives: enlightening the world of the struggle for racial justice in the United States, and convincing the American Government to assume the leadership in the campaign to achieve human rights for people throughout the world.

The Struggle for Liberation in South Africa: Luthuli

Race relations in South Africa was considered at the first session of the United Nations General Assembly when it convened in 1946. The newly created organization was requested to consider the issue of discrimination against people of Indian descent in South Africa. Six years later, the United Nations confronted the racist system in a more general sense by creating a three member commission to study the racial situation in the Union of South Africa. Since that time, annual consideration has been given to the threat to world peace caused by the system of apartheid, which has been characterized by the United Nations as an "offense against humanity." Thus, at the time Luthuli began his campaign against apartheid, the issue already had become internationalized.

Writing in *Let My People Go*, a book which was banned in South Africa, but sold in other parts of the world, Luthuli observed that even though his country had tried to live in isolation, "it finds itself on a rapidly awakening continent and in a world which watches it closely." He noted that because "the indignation of other countries can have a practical bearing on the course events follow in South Africa... Africans have watched the growth of this indignation with rising hope." According to Luthuli, the blacks of the country were not anti-South Africa, but they were "anti-white-supremacist." Although he did not encourage other countries to engage in war against the whites of South Africa, he conceded that "the disapproval and ostracism of other countries will have the affect, if properly directed, or shortening the day of bloodshed and bondage."[29]

---

[28] King, *Where Do We Go From Here*, 167.
[29] Luthuli, *Let My People Go*, 207.

In the struggle to influence world opinion in regard to racism, Luthuli applauded the role of India in exposing the evils of apartheid through the channels of the United Nations. Ghana's African leadership also was regarded as having made a valuable contribution to liberation efforts in South Africa. Luthuli praised the Accra Conference which convened in December 1958, as "the fulfillment of a long-cherished hope," for the Africans. He perceived the All African People's Convention as providing direction for the oppressed people, who had not yet realized the independence of their nations.[30]

In 1961 when Dag Hammorskjold, the Secretary-General of the United Nations, visited the country, the Government made it impossible for Luthuli to meet with him. After the visit, the latter complained that Hammorskjold had conferred only with government-appointed chiefs and others who were not representatives of the African people. He suggested that if the Secretary-General had not found it possible to meet elected leaders, "it might have been better for United Nations prestige if he had met no non-white groups." Hammarskjold was advised by some of the Africans who conferred with him that "the chiefs in the Bantu areas were no longer recognized by the people." Instead, "men like ex-chief Luthuli and some others who had been suppressed were regarded as the real leadership."[31]

On the eve of the Commonwealth Prime Ministers' meeting in London in 1961, a major attempt was made to awaken the conscience of the world against apartheid. In an appeal in the *Times* of London, Luthuli sought to persuade member nations to deny continued membership in that organization to South Africa. His action was provoked by a letter to the *Times* from the Anglican Archbishop Joost de Blank, who had suggested that "if South Africa is expelled the non-whites will feel more than ever deserted and hopeless." He implied that on many occasions, he had talked with representatives of non-whites of South Africa, and was convinced that the majority of them wanted the country to remain in the Commonwealth. The efforts of the Archbishop, however, proved to be futile, since the Prime Minister, perceiving the outcome, announced that South Africa would not seek to retain its membership.[32] Luthuli rejoiced over the decision.

---

[30] Luthuli, 210-211.

[31] Edward Callan, *Albert John Luthuli and the South African Race Conflict*, Revised edition (Kalamazoo, MI: Western Michigan University Press), 1965, 28.

[32] Callan, 28-29.

The winning of the Nobel Peace Prize afforded Luthuli a rare opportunity to take his campaign for racial justice abroad. Although under banishment, the South African Government reluctantly permitted him to travel to Oslo, Norway to accept the award. In presenting the prize to him, Gunnar Jahn, chairman of the Nobel Selection Committee, describing the racial conditions which existed in South Africa, and the efforts which Luthuli was making to improve the plight of the oppressed of his country. The struggle for racial justice in South Africa was perceived by the Committee as demonstrating to other nations that human rights campaigns can be waged without violence.[33]

Using the Norwegian podium as a means from which to address the world, Luthuli called attention to the historic wrongs which had been perpetrated to redress those evils. He expressed thanks to those who had given support to the fighters for South African freedom, including the people and government of Norway--the host for the Nobel presentation.[34] Likewise, he acknowledged the role played by his fellow Africans, the World Council of Churches, the United Nations and other sympathetic international organizations. In recognition of the support of the international community, Luthuli observed that alone the blacks of South Africa would have been weak, but with the aid of friends from abroad, the obstacles have been less difficult. While recognizing that South Africans had benefited from the support of the international community, he insisted that the freedom of Africans cannot come as a "gift from abroad." Luthuli maintained that it must be won by the Africans themselves.[35]

In his attempt to gain foreign support, Luthuli was aware of the argument that a South African government dominated by Africans would be hostile to the interest of foreign business enterprises; therefore, he sought to allay the fears of interested parties. In an article, published in *Ebony* entitled "What I Would Do If I Were Prime Minister," Luthuli made clear that foreign investments would be welcomed, but they would be governed by the interest of South Africa.[36]

Utilizing channels of the Anti-Apartheid Movement, Luthuli was able to reach out to the rest of the world from his remote South African village to

---

[33] Gunnar Jahn, "Speech delivered on the occasion of the awarding of the Nobel Peace Prize in 1960," in Haberman, 216.

[34] Albert Luthuli, "Africa and Freedom," *Vital Speeches*, XXVIII, Feb. 15, 1962, 271.

[35] Luthuli.

[36] Luthuli, "What I Would Do If I Were Prime Minister?" *Ebony*, Feb. 1962, 29.

which he had been banned. In May 1963, he appealed to the international community to implement the resolution on sanction, which had been approved earlier by the United Nations. The resolution called upon nations:

> To break off diplomatic relations, or refrain from establishing them; close their ports to all vessels flying the South African flag and enact legislation prohibiting their ships from entering South African ports; boycott all South African goods; refrain from exporting goods, including arms and ammunitions to South Africa, and refuse landing facilities to South African aircraft.[37]

While applauding the actions of the United Nations, Luthuli noted that the resolution also expressed regrets over the fact that some Member States, by their actions, were encouraging the perpetuation of segregation in South Africa. In order to secure compliance with the resolution by those states, he appealed to "those who are still free to speak and act" to demonstrate their abhorrence of such violations. Specifically, Luthuli called for united efforts against the shipment of arms to South Africa. He directed appeals to both individuals and their governments. To the workers of the world, whom he regarded as sharing with South Africans a "common suffering and hardship," Luthuli appealed "to make their voices heard and to show their unity with us not only in words but in actions."[38] He was dismayed that some of the governments which were providing "terrifying weapons of destruction" to South Africa had a proud record of defending human liberties. Great Britain was cited as being foremost among such countries. Luthuli challenged the nations and governments to:

> cast aside your hypocrisy and deceit; declare yourself on the side of oppression if that is your secret design. Do not think we will be deceived by your pious protestations as long as you are prepared to condone, assist and actively support the tyranny in our land.[39]

He strongly urged that no arms be supplied to South Africa.

On June 12, 1964, following the sentencing of Nelson Mandela and other anti-apartheid leaders to life imprisonment, Albert Luthuli issued a statement,

---

[37] Luthuli, "No Arms for South Africa," in Solidarity Committee of the German Democratic Republic, *Luthuli Speaks*, 1982, 87.

[38] Luthuli, 89.

[39] Luthuli, 90.

which was read to the United Nations Security Council by the representative from Morocco. The statement noted the futile efforts of the ANC to redress the evils of the racist system by non-violent means. According to Luthuli, those sentenced represented "the highest in morality and ethics in the South African political struggle," and their policies were "in accordance with the deepest international principles of brotherhood and humanity." His statement was an appeal "to save these men, not merely as individuals, but for what they stand for." Luthuli issued a special appeal to Great Britain and the United States, South Africa's two strongest allies, "to take decisive action for full scale action for sanctions that would precipitate the end of the hateful system of *apartheid*.[40] The appeal also was directed to peoples, governments, organizations, and institutions throughout the world. In his call for the imposing of sanctions against South Africa, he warned that such action was necessary in order to "bring about the vital necessary change and avert what can become the greatest African tragedy of our times."[41]

As Luthuli waged his campaign for sanctions against South Africa, he was confronted with the constant argument that the ones who would be hardest hit by the proposed restrictions would be the Africans. In response, he acknowledged that Africans would be called upon to suffer as a result of sanctions, but he insisted that since suffering has been a regular part of their lives, additional suffering would not affect them seriously. According to Luthuli, Africans are willing to undergo the temporary hardships, if such suffering brings about the end of apartheid.

Luthuli's death in 1967 did not bring an end to the internationalization efforts of leaders of the anti-apartheid movement. Through the channels of the United Nations and friendly countries, Africans continued their campaign for racial justice. Among those who assumed a leadership role was Desmond Tutu, whose efforts focused heavily upon the internationalization of the struggle.

---

[40] Luthuli, "Statement Following the Rivonia Verdict," in Karis and Carter, 799.
[41] Luthuli.

CAMPAIGN FOR A NEW SOUTH AFRICA: TUTU

Although he conceded that the struggle for racial justice had to be fought mainly in South Africa, Bishop Tutu envisioned the international community as playing a vital role.

In his campaign, he attempted to convince governments, businesses and peoples of foreign countries that the African cause was a just one. As he spoke out against the evils of the South African system and the need for the outside world to join in the struggle to reform it, he placed himself in constant danger of punishment. His first encounter with the Government occurred in 1979 during a visit to Denmark where he called for "increased censure of South Africa by the international community." The Bishop urged Denmark to refuse further purchase of coal from his home country until it made meaningful changes in its racial practices. The Government of South Africa responded by lifting the Bishop's passport.[42]

Following the return of the passport early in 1981, Bishop Tutu traveled to Europe and the United States, where he, once again, criticized the policies of the South African Government. Speaking before a conference sponsored by the National Council of Churches (USA), he called for the applying of political, diplomatic, and economic pressures on South Africa to bring about the end of apartheid.[43] Likewise, in an article written for the African-American Institute, the Bishop suggested that the international community could play a vital role in the peaceful resolution of the South African crisis by applying pressure on its government to force it to negotiate with the authentic leaders of the various sectors of the population.[44]

When questioned concerning the argument that the United States can achieve more through quiet diplomacy than through public condemnation of apartheid and economic sanction, Tutu observed that during the more than twenty years since the tragedy at Sharpeville, the United States has been talking to the Government of South Africa, and yet there has been no meaningful change in the behavior of the latter. Bishop Tutu's remarks angered the South African Government, but it refused to arrest him, possibly,

---

[42] Desmond Tutu, *Crying in the Wilderness*, 18.
[43] Tutu, 19.
[44] Tutu, *Hope and Suffering*, 129.

fearing the anticipated outcry which would have followed. Nevertheless, it did withdraw his passport for a second time.[45]

Of all the countries interacting with South Africa, Tutu considered the U. S. as being in a better position to persuade the racist government to initiate meaningful reforms. While he expressed pleasure with the efforts made by President Carter, he found President Reagan's "constructive engagement" policies to be disappointing. In contrasting the policies, the Bishop noted that under the former, the morale of the Africans was encouraged by the "rhetoric of disapproval" by the United States. Referring to the Carter Administration, he observed that "they seemed to care about our plight. They did not talk about the overriding strategic importance of South Africa with her wealth in key strategic resources as being more important than human freedom."[46] According to the Bishop, because of the attitude of the Carter Administration, Africans in South Africa held the United States in high esteem, but because of the Reagan policy of "constructive engagement," they felt a sense of despair. Tutu suggested that as a result of the general belief that if a war should occur in South Africa, Africans would not be able to count on the West for assistance, opponents of apartheid are being driven into the arms of the Soviets by the very country concerned about Soviet expansionism. The Bishop warned that once South Africa is free, the country will continue to be of strategic importance and Africans will remember those who aided them in their struggle. Given its present policy, he did not think that the Reagan Administration would be on the favorable list.[47]

As was the case with Luthuli, the receiving of the Nobel Peace Prize did much to enhance the international status of Bishop Tutu. The prize was presented to him as a "renewed recognition of the courage and patience shown by black South Africans for their use of peaceful means to oppose the apartheid system." It was the opinion of the Norwegian Selection Committee that the campaign in South Africa had "wide-ranging consequences for the whole of the African Continent and therefore also for the cause of peace in the world."[48] In his Nobel lecture, Tutu informed the world of the evils perpetrated on Africans by the system of apartheid, and invited the

---

[45] *TransAfrica News Report*, Spring 1981.
[46] Tutu, 116.
[47] Tutu, 116-117.
[48] Egil Aarvik, "Speech delivered on the occasion of the awarding of the Nobel Peace Prize for 1984," Oslo, Norway, Dec. 10, 1981, Norwegian Information Center.

participation of the international community in the effort to establish a just society in South Africa.

After having been proclaimed the Nobel Peace Prize winner for 1984, Tutu appeared before the Subcommittee on African Affairs of the United States House of Representatives and continued his assault upon the constructive engagement policies of the Reagan Administration. He perceived the policy as giving South Africa additional reasons for delaying its exit from Namibia, since it linked independence of that country with the withdrawal of Cuban troops from the sovereign nation of Angola. Considering apartheid to be evil, immoral an unChristian since it supported and collaborated with the South African Government. Tutu appealed to the United States to act consistently with its "great tradition of freedom and equality," and take a clear and unequivocal stand against injustices perpetrated against South Africans. Contending that decisions by the United States have a great impact on events in other countries, he suggested that many Africans will become adherents of democracy "if the United States is true to her real self." The Bishop urged this nation, which he considered as having "an extraordinary capacity sometimes for backing the wrong horse," to break with that tradition, and for a change, cast its lot with the victims of oppression.[49]

In his efforts to persuade the Reagan Administration to change its policies toward South Africa, Tutu met several times with Assistant Secretary of State Chester Crocker, but he failed to achieve his goal. On December 7, 1985, the Bishop conferred with President Reagan, but neither appeared to change the views of the other.[50] Later when he visited the United States to accept the Martin Luther King, Jr. Award, Bishop Tutu contrasted the Reagan Administration's support for anti-government rebel movements in Nicaragua and Angola with its failure to back South African rebels in their fight against their racist government.[51]

Frustrated over the entrenched position which the South African Government was taking, Bishop Tutu agreed with the efforts of the ANC to achieve a nonracial and democratic society, but he rejected violence as a method of obtaining that goal. Citing the Nazi example, the Bishop suggested

---

[49] U. S. Congress, House of Representatives, Committee on Foreign Affairs, Subcommittee on Africa, *The Current Crisis in South Africa*, 98th Cong., 2nd sess., Dec. 4, 1984, 8-9.

[50] Gerald M. Boyd, "Reagan Rejects Tutu's Plan for Tough Policy on Pretoria." *New York Times*, Dec, 8, 1984, A16.

[51] Alan Cowell, "Bishop Tutu Returns Home to Criticism," *New York Times*, Jan. 28, 1986, A4

that "there can come a time when it is justifiable to overthrow a government by violence. Otherwise, there would have been no justification for fighting Hitler and Nazism."[52] Tutu emphasized that if there were not meaningful changes in South Africa, he would call for punitive economic sanctions.

On April 3, 1986, Bishop Tutu followed through with his threat by calling upon the international community to impose punitive sanctions against South Africa in order to aid in bringing about a "new South Africa, non-racial democratic, participatory and just."[53]

By making a direct call for sanctions, the Bishop ran the risk of being arrested for treason. In suggesting sanctions, Tutu encountered critics who argued that such a tactic would destroy the economy of the country; therefore, worsening the plight of the Africans. To this he responded with a warning that unless the Government changed it intransigent attitude that with or without sanctions "the economy will be destroyed in the wake of violence, bloodshed and chaos that will ensue if a full-scale civil war breaks out." A second criticism raised was that foreign corporations were playing a useful role in South Africa, inasmuch as they had introduced reforms in the economy. While admitting that progress had been made in such areas as salaries and promotion of employees, Tutu contended that these gains have been made largely as a result of pressures applied by the disinvestment campaign. According to the Bishop, blacks did not want to ameliorate or improve apartheid, but to dismantle it. He warned the international community that there was no room for neutrality, noting that when one professes to be neutral in a conflict regarding injustice and oppression, that party has "decided to support the unjust status quo." Tutu raised these questions: "Are you on the side of injustice? Are you on the side of oppression or liberation? Are you on the side of death or of life? Are you on the side of goodness or of evil?"[54]

In order for sanctions to be effective, Tutu considered the support of the United States, Great Britain and other Western powers essential, but unfortunately these countries were not leading the way. The Bishop was especially dismayed over the failure of the Thatcher Government of Great Britain and the Reagan Administration to take stronger action against the racist government of South Africa. He applauded the action of the U.S.

[52] *New York Times.*
[53] Tutu, "Full Text of Press Statement," April 2, 1986.
[54] Tutu, "Sanctions v. Apartheid," *New York Times*, June 16, 1986.

Congress, however, in overriding the veto of the President in regard to economic sanctions.

In his efforts to destroy the racist system of South Africa, Archbishop Tutu placed heavy emphasis upon changing the attitudes of Western nations since he considered their investments and other forms of aid essential to the survival of the white minority government, however, he did not limit his campaign to those nations. The Archbishop later visited both China and the Soviet Union where he emphasized the need for the international isolation of South Africa. In 1988, Tutu angered his government when he visited the Soviet Union and praised it for its moral and humanitarian support. The pro government press criticized the Archbishop for praising a country which it perceived as guilty of church persecution and denial of religious freedom. Tutu replied by asking the question, "if Communists give you water, are you supposed to be so ungracious and ill bred as to take the water and refuse to say thank you to your helper." The Archbishop was in the Soviet Union for the observance of the 1,000 anniversary of the Russian Orthodox Church. During his five day stay there he conferred with the Soviet Deputy Foreign Minister, who assured him that the Russians were committed to a "non-violent solution to the problem of injustice in South Africa."[55]

Almost from its inception, the United Nations provided a forum for the foes of apartheid, and Archbishop Tutu has utilized this forum, when possible, in his struggle to build a better South Africa. In addition to conferring with the Secretary-General, he has appealed to various bodies of the United Nations for support. In 1984, he addressed the Security Council, deploring all forms of violence--" the violence of an oppressive and unjust society and the violence of those seeking to overthrow that society." The Archbishop appealed to the Council to "urge South African authorities to go to the conference table with the authentic representatives of all sections of the community."[56]

Again, in October 1985, in his address to the UN Special Political Committee, Tutu called attention to the nonviolent campaign being waged by Africans in South Africa. He reminded Western nations that they had obtained their independence by violent struggles. The Archbishop challenged the international community to match its words with action in aiding South Africans obtain their liberation.[57] In his address, he noted that Western nations

---

[55] *New York Times*, June 19, 1988.
[56] Tutu, "I Appeal to This Body to Act...," *UN Chronicle*, XXI, 9, 1984, 66.
[57] "You Don't Reform a Frankenstein...," *UN Chronicle*, XXII, 10/11, 1985, 17.

had declined to take a stand against apartheid because of South Africa's strong stance against communism. Tutu warned that "injustice and oppression are surely the best breeding grounds for Communism." He insisted that the behavior of the West "is giving free enterprise and capitalism very bad names" when it ally itself with the "vicious system of apartheid." Tutu reminded the West that many Africans consider capitalism and free enterprise to be exploitative. He did, however, acknowledge the support given by the Scandinavian countries, France and Canada in the fight for liberation in South Africa.[58]

In March 1988, Tutu appealed to the international community to use its influence to persuade President Botha to commute the sentences of a group referred to as the "Sharpeville Six". Among the leaders contacted by the Archbishop were US Secretary of State George Shulz, West Germany Chancellor Helmut Kohl and British Prime Minister Margaret Thatcher.[59] Again in 1989, when the nation was characterized by widescale demonstrations and police brutality, Tutu and Alan Boesak consulted with diplomats from twelve countries including ambassadors of Britain, the US, France, Federal Republic of Germany, Australia and Canada. They appealed to them to "condemn police excesses and to monitor the march.[60]

The constant appealing of Tutu and others yielded sufficient international support, which when combined with the systematic protest in South Africa forced the apartheid government to retreat from its position and agree to meaningful negotiations. By March 6, 1990, because sufficient progress had been made, a service of Thanksgiving was held in observance of the changes which had occurred in South Africa. On that occasion the Archbishop offered a prayer which, in part, thanked God for the international support, which they had received. He also used the occasion to solicit continued foreign assistance.[61]

---

[58] Tutu, *The Rainbow People of God*, 100.
[59] Tutu, 149.
[60] Tutu, 186
[61] Tutu, 197 VIII Enduring the Suffering

In today's world it is virtually impossible to isolate domestic events from international affairs. Because of their awareness of this, the prophets of social justice utilized the international arena as the best forum from which to conduct their struggles for a just society.

Chapter 8

ENDURING THE SUFFERING

> The way of nonviolence means a willingness to suffer and sacrifice. It may mean going to jail. If such is the case the resister must be willing to fill the jail houses of the South. It may even mean physical death. But if physical death is the price that a man must pay to free his children and his white brethren from a permanent death of the spirit, then nothing could be more redemptive. [1]
>
> Martin Luther King, Jr.

In order to be an effective participant in a civil disobedience campaign, one must be willing to undergo suffering. Those who participate, especially those who lead, must be aware that their opponents, when enraged, will inflict all manner of punishment upon them. Jesus, in his "Sermon on the Mount," attempted to prepare the righteous for such abuse, advising them that "whosoever shall smite thee on thy right cheek, turn to him the other also."

So impressed was Gandhi with those words of Jesus, that he constantly referred to them during his various nonviolent campaigns. He advised would-be followers that they should take pledges of nonviolence only after they give the matter serious consideration. Gandhi was aware of the many ordeals in which one who opposes the system would have to encounter; therefore, he attempted to prepare his followers by advising them that such campaigns might necessitate going to jail, being forced to perform hard labor, suffering from starvation, being flogged and mistreated, being fined heavily, under-

[1] Martin Luther King, Jr. *Stride Toward Freedom*, 216.

going illness, and even in some cases dying.[2] Such abuse can only be borne by the strong; thus, many who begin the struggle fall by the wayside, when the battle gets rough. Gandhi, King, Luthuli, and Tutu realized the danger which awaited them, therefore, they made proper preparation, and when the time arose, they performed their tasks in a fearless manner. In order to aid others in improving their conditions, they were willing to give up the "good life" as interpreted by the larger society.

Personal Sacrifice

For effective participation in nonviolent campaigns, Gandhi suggested the observance of perfect chastity, the adoption of poverty, the following of the truth, and the cultivation of fearlessness. The first two were considered precious sacrifices by those who were accustomed to enjoying the pleasures of life. According to Gandhi, "a man who is unchaste loses stamina, becomes emasculated and cowardly."[3] Believing this, he took the *Brahmacharya* oath, pledging himself to a life of celibacy, which he considered as being essential for one "aspiring to serve humanity with his whole soul." He felt that he would be unequal to the task if he "engaged in the pleasures of family life and in the propagation and rearing of children."[4]

Simultaneously, Gandhi sought to live a more austere life; therefore, he renounced comforts, luxuries, and pleasures. By the time of his renunciation, he had established himself as a noted lawyer with a respectable income, and one who could have afforded a luxurious life, but he chose to forego these earthly pleasures, and reside with other civil-resisters in a "cooperative commonwealth." In later years, when Gandhi returned to India, he and his followers lived in *ashrams*--places of discipline and service. For the average person, celibacy and poverty represent hardships, but Gandhi was able to endure them since he felt that his cause was worthy of such sacrifices. Renunciation was seen by Fischer as having a major advantage for a leader since it caused his followers to trust him more. He perceived this as being

---

[2] Gandhi, "The Advent of Satyagraha," in Homer A. Jack, *The Gandhi Reader* (New York: Grove Press, 1956), 63.

[3] Gandhi, *Indian Home Rule* (Ahmedabad, India: Navajivan Publishing House)1962) 84.

[4] Gandhi, *An Autobiography* (Boston: Beacon Press, 1957), 316.

especially important in Indian culture where one is generally suspicious of one who is willing to give so much for so little personal return.[5]

Not only did Gandhi make extraordinary sacrifices, but his family, as well. His wife gave up jewelry and other luxuries of life, and likewise, his sons were denied the benefit of formal college training in order that they might live more austere lives. In a letter to his son, Manilal, which he wrote while in prison in 1909, Gandhi reminded him that their lot was poverty, and as a general rule, he should be guided by the philosophy of "it is more blessed to be poor than to be rich." He advised him that a life of poverty is far sweeter than one of riches.[6] Since Gandhi had two families, his personal family often was deprived of his attention, in order that he might better serve his larger family, which, in a sense, included all Indians.

Gandhi's life had a major impact upon King, who after a visit to India in 1959 became very sensitive of the need to identify closer with the causes of the poor. At onetime, he entertained the idea of taking a personal vow of poverty, but having a family to support was one factor which caused him not to pursue it, according to his wife. Even though he did not take such a vow, he refrained from owning property since he believed that it would separate him from the masses. King once boasted that "he could travel around the world without a suitcase, with one suit only and a change of underwear." His desire to "remain poor" was especially noteworthy since King's status both in the national and international arenas made it possible for him to secure employment which could have brought him great wealth.[7]

Once King said, "a man who dedicates himself to a cause doesn't need a family." According to Coretta, it did not mean that he did not love her and the children; instead, because so much of his life had to be given to the Movement, he felt that he could not perform justly as a husband and as a father. As a wife of a major civil rights leader who devoted his "all" to the cause, Coretta played the dual role of mother and father. Her parental role was especially unique, inasmuch as she had to protect her children from insults which were directed at them because they were the children of Martin Luther King, Jr. Coretta recalled the children being teased by others, some of whom referred to their father as a jail bird.[8] While King, no doubt, enjoyed having a

---

[5] Fischer, *Gandhi: His Life and Message for the World*, 34.
[6] Fischer, *The Life of Mahatma Gandhi*, 92.
[7] Coretta Scott King *My Life with Martin Luther King, Jr.*, 160-161.
[8] King, 179.

family, it caused him special concern since he was interested in protecting their safety, and insulating them from insults.

As in the cases of Gandhi and King, the educational training of Albert Luthuli prepared him for a higher paying job than that of a chief, but his commitment to service motivated him to forego prosperous living and to accept, instead, a more austere existence. The more he became involved in the struggle for racial justice, the greater was the sacrifice he and his family were required to make. As Luthuli devoted more time to fulfilling the duties related to the presidency of the ANC, the harder his wife was called upon to labor in order to maintain the home. Recalling that the family had very little earthly possessions, and how public affairs often took him away from home, Albert acknowledged that his wife, Nakukhanya, had been very patient with him during the many occasions in which his work prevented him from performing family duties. According to Albert, not once did she raise questions during their "darkest hours" as to what would happen to her or to the family. He was grateful for the role she played in making the home a place that was "stable and constant and inwardly secure."[9] Although Luthuli realized the suffering his family was undergoing, he considered this mild, compared to the obstacles he anticipated his children would face in the South Africa of the future, if the present generation of Africans was unsuccessful in the reforming of the country.

The society in which Bishop Tutu lived was not too different from that which Luthuli knew. Like the latter, the former could have opted for a better life; instead, his commitment to racial justice caused him to cast his lot with the oppressed. When he became bishop, he could have selected to live in a more exclusive community, as an "honorary white," but he preferred residing in the black township. According to Tutu, his residence there could not be guaranteed, even though he was a bishop and general secretary of the South African Council of Churches. He noted that at any time the township manager could have decided that his "continued presence in Soweto was detrimental to its good ordering and peace;" therefore, could have ordered his removal.[10]

As can be seen, Gandhi, King, Luthuli, and Tutu--all made personal sacrifices in order to wage effective struggles against human injustices. Their families, as extensions of themselves, also were called upon to endure

[9] Luthuli, *Let My People Go*, 45.
[10] Tutu, *Hope and Suffering*, 99-100.

hardships. They lived under the constant threat of being harmed or even killed. In addition to the personal discomforts of these warriors of justice, they also were, too often, victims of both insults and acts of violence.

PERSONAL ABUSE

One of the often quoted verses of the Bible reads: "Blessed are ye, when men shall revile you and persecute you..." This verse was very meaningful to leaders of nonviolent campaigns who often had to refer to it for inspiration when they were abused by those who did not understand or appreciate their missions.

Gandhi recalled being personally abused in Durban, South Africa in December 1896 when whites reacted with outrage to a pamphlet which he had written during his stay in India. In the publication, Gandhi criticized the abusive treatment which Indians had to endure in South Africa. Adding fuel to the fire was the suspicion by whites that he was responsible for bringing more illegal Indians into the country. Even though Gandhi was stoned, slapped, kicked, and beaten until he was unconscious, the nonviolent leader reacted in a forgiving manner, advising officials that he would not prosecute the guilty parties since he did not consider them to be at fault. He observed that the information which they possessed, had been acquired from their leaders, and if true, he could understand why they would be excited and would react with indignation. Recalling that "excited crowds always tried to deal out justice in that manner," Gandhi suggested that if guilt was to be assigned, it should be attributed to the Government of Natal.[11]

Attacks upon Gandhi were not only made by whites who held anti-Indian sentiments, but fellow-Indians, as well. In 1908, he was beaten by an Indian extremist, who was disturbed because of an agreement which Gandhi had made with the Government concerning the voluntary registration of Indians in South Africa. As Gandhi led other Indians to the registration office, he was attacked--being struck on the head, then kicked, and beaten after he had fallen. Because of his dedication to the principle of suffering for the good of the cause, once again, he refused to prosecute, maintaining that those who had

[11] Gandhi, "Mobbed at Durban," in Jack, 75.

committed the act were not aware of what they were doing, and apparently were under the impression that he was doing something wrong.[12]

Not only did Gandhi suffer personal abuse in South Africa, but in India, as well. When he went to Calcutta in 1947 to aid in quelling the riots between Hindus and Moslems the house in which he lived was attacked. Suddenly, he was faced with rioters who attempted to harm him. A brick was thrown at him, and likewise, a rioter sought to strike him. Unable to calm the infuriated mob, the Mahatma admitted that "to put in an appearance before a yelling crowd does not always work." In view of his failure, he undertook a fast to achieve by that approach what his words could not.[13]

In the wake of the partitioning of India, hostility erupted between the Hindus and Moslems. Although Gandhi sought to mediate the disputes, his efforts were not appreciated by all Indians. On January 20, 1948, Madan Lal, a refugee from the Punjab sought to assassinate him, but the effort was unsuccessful. When the young man was seized, Gandhi requested that he not be molested. Instead, he suggested that an effort be made to convert him to "right thinking and right doing." The Mahatma informed the misguided youth that "those who differ with him [the youth] are not necessarily evil." At the same time, Gandhi urged other young people with similar ideas to "desist from their activity and try his method of resolving conflict."[14]

For the followers of Gandhi, the worst tragedy was yet to come. On January 30, 1948, ten days after the attempt on his life by Madan Lal, a co-conspirator, Nathuram Godse, who also was incensed over what he perceived to be Gandhi's pro-Moslem bias, shot and fatally wounded the Mahatma as he was on his way to prayer services. As Gandhi fell, he could be heard murmuring, "Oh God!"

Like Gandhi, King was aware that he would be called upon to undergo suffering; therefore, when the occasions occurred, he was prepared to endure it in a forgiving manner. One of his earlier encounters took place on September 3, 1958, when he was choked and kicked as he was arrested in Montgomery, Alabama. King informed the judge that he did not hold animosity or bitterness against the abusers; instead, he had compassion for those whom he regarded as being "brothers and fellow-human beings made in the image of God." He did not consider them responsible for their acts,

[12] Gandhi, "First Attack on His Life," in Jack, 75.
[13] Fischer, *The Life of Mahatma Gandhi*, 477-478.
[14] Fischer, 503.

maintaining that "these men, like all too many of our white brothers, are the victims of their environment." An environment which he considered to have been "blighted with more than 300 years of man's inhumanity to man as expressed in slavery and segregation."[15]

On September 20, 1958, King, once again, found himself a victim of personal abuse, but this time by a mentally deranged woman, who stabbed him in the chest while he was autographing copies of his book in the Bloomstein Department Store in New York. King did not show any bitterness against his assailant, indicating that she was not responsible for the violent act. He suggested that "she was in need of help--in need of healing rather than prosecution."[16]

Another test of King's commitment to nonviolence occurred in Birmingham in 1962, when he was attacked by a two hundred pound youth. He did not press charges against the "self-styled Nazi," who later was subdued by the police and delegates to the Southern Christian Leadership Conference convention. Instead, he requested that the attacker be allowed to remain at the convention. King expressed an interest in changing the system which had produced people, who express their disagreement with others by acts of violence, rather than punishing the perpetrator.[17]

Again, on January 18, 1965 during the Selma Campaign, King was personally abused after having checked into the all-white Hotel Albert. When a member of the National States Rights Party struck him, King's replied by literally "turning the other cheek.[18]

While some of the violence perpetrated against King was designed to frighten him, there also were attempts to eliminate him, completely. As the nation's foremost champion of civil rights, Martin Luther King, Jr. lived in constant fear of being killed or injured. The FBI reported that it had logged at least 50 assassination threats against him by the time of his death in 1968.[19]

In the midst of one of his addresses during the Montgomery Bus Protest, King became preoccupied with the theme of death, noting that "if one day you find me sprawled and dead, I do not want you to retaliate with a single act of violence, I urge you to continue protesting with the same dignity and

---

[15] Coretta Scott King, 341.
[16] King, 168-170.
[17] Oates, 133.
[18] Oates, 335.
[19] Oates, 486.

discipline you have shown so far."[20] While King was sure of his commitment to the cause, he had initial reluctance about asking his family to make similar sacrifices; therefore, he became disturbed when he received a telephone message warning "...Nigger, we've taken all we want from you. Before next week you'll be sorry you ever came to Montgomery." Being concerned with the potential danger of his task, he conceded his inability to face it alone; thus, he prayed for strength and courage to provide the necessary leadership for the cause. Having done this, he felt that he could "stand up for the righteousness, stand for truth" since he realized that God would forever be at his side.[21] With this experience, King concluded that he could face any obstacle and he did. Shortly thereafter, on January 30, 1956, the worst came to pass when his home was bombed. Fortunately, no one was killed or harmed. More than ten years later, however, an assassin found his mark, as the bullet from his gun wounded, fatally, the drum major for justice on April 4, 1968.

Luthuli also was the victim of physical harm. He gave an account of having been kicked and beaten as he addressed a predominantly Afrikaner audience in Pretoria. Although he was well battered and his jaw painfully swollen, he decided to proceed with his presentation, once the police had restored order. Luthuli considered the meeting to have been a good and encouraging one, with many of those attending, expressing shame and concern over the attack.[22]

Based upon the various sources analyzed, there appeared to have been no publicized personal brutality directed against Archbishop Tutu. Like the others, however, he was affected by governmental action to silence him through arrest and other forms of harassment.

ARREST, IMPRISONMENT AND BANISHMENT

Gandhi and King were arrested and imprisoned many times during their campaigns for social justice. Luthuli also was imprisoned, but the device used against him mostly was that of banishment. Tutu was usually deprived of the use of his passport; therefore he was limited in his travel abroad.

[20] Martin Luther King, Jr., *Stride Toward Freedom* 133.
[21] Coretta Scott King, 124.
[22] Luthuli, 212.

Mohandas Gandhi

Civil disobedience involves breaking unjust laws, and suffering the consequences of such violations. Thus, one who is involved in the struggle to end the wrongs of society anticipates being arrested and imprisoned. In pursuing his nonviolent campaigns in South Africa and India, Gandhi spent 2,338 days in jail/prison,[23] and might have served even more time, except that on numerous occasions, the authority considered it counter-productive to arrest and imprison him.

As leader of the movement against segregation of Indians in South Africa, Gandhi considered it his duty to lead the way in civil disobedience; therefore, he courted arrest by refusing to register as required by the Asiatic Registration Act of July 31, 1907, and encouraged others to do likewise. As anticipated, he was arrested and sentenced to two months in prison, but prior to serving, he was permitted to address the court. Being aware that some of his compatriots had received sentences of three month imprisonment with hard labor, he appealed for similar treatment, insisting that "if the men had committed an offense," then he "had committed a greater offense." His request was rejected, and he was sentenced to do a two month simple imprisonment. As the doors closed on him for his first prison sentence, Gandhi had initial concern about his future, but as more *satyagrahi* prisoners were brought in, he began to feel more at ease. Prior to their arrest, they had agreed to abide by all jail regulations, as long as their self respect was not compromised. Normally, prisoners who were serving simple sentences could wear their own clothes, or if they chose not to, could wear the special jail clothing. The *satyagrahi* prisoners chose the latter, but because there were so many of them, some had to be issued the type of clothing usually assigned to hard labor prisoners.[24] Shortly after the sentencing, General Smuts had Gandhi escorted to his office, where the two reached an accord in regard to the Asiatic Registration Act.

In 1913, as a result of his efforts to accommodate Indians who had gone on strike at the Newcastle Coal Mines, Gandhi was arrested three times in four days. He had actively courted arrest by attempting to march the strikers across the provincial border. Because of his responsibilities for the more than 8,000 pilgrims, he posted bond and was released after the first two arrests, but when he was apprehended the third time, he was held and tried on the first offense

[23] Jack, Appendix xxxiv.
[24] M. K. Gandhi, "First Imprisonment," Jack, 67-68.

of inducing indentured laborers to leave the province of Natal. He was found guilty and sentenced to a nine month imprisonment with hard labor. Then, he was tried on the charges related to the second arrest, and was found guilty of "aiding and abetting prohibited persons to enter transvaal." In order for the state to win the second case, however, it was necessary to secure the cooperation of Gandhi in providing witnesses who gave evidence against him. As was the rule of that time, the court could not convict a person merely on the plea of guilty. On the second charge, Gandhi was sentenced to three months in prison. Reacting to pressure, the Government released him after a month of imprisonment and began to negotiate with him concerning the grievances. Their agreement formed the basis for the Indian Relief Act of July 1914.[25]

After Gandhi's arrival in India in 1915, the British Government also made futile efforts to contain his influence through arrest and detention. His first arrest occurred on March 10, 1922 on charges of sedition, based upon the publishing of three articles in *Young India*. Specifically, the charges were "bringing hatred or contempt or exciting or attempting to excite disaffection towards His Majesty Government..."[26] To the charges, he entered a plea of guilty. In announcing sentence, the judge noted Gandhi's immense popularity among millions of Indians; nevertheless, he proceeded to sentence him to six years in jail. After having undergone surgery for appendicitis, he was released unconditionally about four years prior to the end of the sentence.[27]

When Gandhi, illegally took salt from the sea on April 6, 1930, he was not arrested, but approximately a month later, he was apprehended as he slept. In the arresting party were several pistol-carrying officers and more than 30 armed Indian policemen. Calvin Kytle noted that rather than give Gandhi another platform from which to speak to the world, the British bypassed the customary route, and charged Gandhi under "an obscure hundred-year-old regulation" that allowed the state to detain him without trial.[28] During his more than eight months in jail, he was able to obtain needed rest. Because of the apparent interest in having Gandhi and other leaders of Congress attend

[25] Fischer, *The Life of Mahatma Gandhi*, 111-116.
[26] K.P.K., "The Great Trial," Jack, 197-207.
[27] K.P.K. Gandhi, 206-207.
[28] Calvin Kytle, *Gandhi, Solider of Nonviolence* (Washington, DC: Seven Locks Press, 1982), 145.

the round table conference in London, Lord Irwin ordered his release in January 1931.

On August 8, 1942, the Congress approved a "quit India resolution", which was to be implemented by a civil disobedience campaign at a later date. The Government reacted by declaring Congress an unlawful association, and ordering the arrest of its leaders, including Gandhi. Also apprehended was Kasturbai, his wife, who had announced that she would substitute for him at a meeting in Bombay. Shortly after he had been jailed, Gandhi wrote a letter to Sir Roger Lumley, the Governor of Bombay, "protesting his own transportation from the train by automobile while his comrades were required to travel by motor truck." The Mahatma also requested the right to correct some grossly inaccurate statements made by the Government, but he contended that he could not do so without information from the outside. Although officials refused his request for newspapers, they gave him permission to communicate with members of the *Ashram* about personal matters, but not organizational affairs. Gandhi rejected the privilege.[29]

During this stay in jail, Gandhi experienced several personal tragedies. Firstly, he was disturbed over the widespread violence which erupted in the wake of his arrest, and he was sadden even more that because of his imprisonment he was unable to bring it under control. Likewise he was distressed that after having spent most of his life in non-violent efforts, he would be accused by the Government of perpetrating it. Secondly, during his stay in jail, he lost both a trusted friend and his wife whose deaths sadden him very much. Thirdly, Gandhi, himself, suffered a severe illness which almost took his life. On May 6, his last prison stay came to an end when he was released unconditionally.

Gandhi's many days in jail were spent in a variety of ways--rest, meditation, conversing, writing, teaching, and fasting. As a prisoner he tried to set a good example of discipline for his co-prisoners. He suggested that civil resisters, when serving sentences, should be honest, cooperate with prison officials, refrain from asking special favors and privileges, and perform their assignments to the best of their abilities.[30]

---

[29] Fischer, 384-386.

[30] M. K. Gandhi, "A Model Prisoner," *Young India*, Dec. 29, 1921.

Martin Luther King, Jr.

Police harassment, arrest, and detention also were weapons used to deflate the civil rights movement in the United States, but to no avail. Consistent with his strategy of using unearned suffering to better appeal to the conscience of Americans, King courted arrest, frequently. At the same time, law-enforcing officers, perceiving arrest and detention as means of weakening the civil rights efforts, too often, made frivolous arrests. The first of such arrests of King occurred on January 26, 1956 when he was apprehended by police, who attempted to intimidate him; and thus, bring to an end the Montgomery Bus Protest. Following his pick-up of three passengers, King was stopped by policemen and questioned concerning the ownership of the car. Afterward, he was allowed to proceed, but was trailed by motorcycled policemen who later stopped him after he had let out the passengers. He was ordered out of the vehicle and placed under arrest for traveling thirty miles per hour in a twenty-five mile speed zone. This experience for King was a horrified one, since he was aware of what it meant for an African-American to be imprisoned in the southern part of the United States. He had read many accounts of mobs seizing those who had been arrested and lynching them. At one time, King thought that his worst fears were being confirmed, as the arresting officers appeared to be driving in an opposite direction from where he believed the jail to have been located. According to King, when at last he saw the words "Montgomery City Jail," he was very relieved, feeling that "going to jail at that moment seemed like going to some safe haven."[31] Once he was booked on the charges, King was released on a recognizance bond. Two days later, the police court found him guilty and fined him ten dollars.

Within a month the police apprehended King, once again. This time, he and others were arrested after having been indicted for leading the Montgomery Bus Protest. After his arrest, he was released on bond and was later convicted and fined five hundred dollars, but this was suspended pending appeal. Because his lawyers did not complete the process within the allotted time, however, King was required to pay the fine. In the meantime, an arrangement was made by which the charges against other leaders in the protest and a group of white segregationists were dropped.[32]

---

[31] King, *Stride Toward Freedom*, 128.
[32] Coretta Scott King, 162.

On September 3, 1958, King was arrested, once again, and charged with loitering at the courthouse in Montgomery. He was in the building to see his lawyer when he was ordered by the police to move-on. Apparently, King was not recognized at the time of the arrest, but once his identification was known the charges were changed to disobeying an officer, then he was released on his own recognizance. In a conversation following the incident, King advised his wife that he would no longer accept bail, insisting that if he commits "a crime in the name of civil rights," he will serve his time in jail, if arrested. He contended that as a leader he should set an example for those whom he urged to suffer for the cause of justice.[33]

The next day, King was found guilty and was required to pay a fine of ten dollars, or serve fourteen days in jail. Even though he preferred remaining in jail, he was released because an anonymous person paid his fine. Later, King learned that the police commissioner had done so in order to avoid the bad publicity which the city would have received as a result of detaining the civil rights leader. At his trial, King was given permission to read a prepared statement in which he proclaimed his innocence, noting that he was a victim of police brutality, which at that time, was characteristic of the South. Simultaneously he defended the reason for African-Americans opposing such degradation, maintaining that they "can no longer silently endure conditions of police brutality and mob violence...because we are commanded to resist evil by God that created us all." King advised the court, however, that in the effort to overcome these unfortunate conditions, African-Americans will resort only to Christian love and nonviolent behavior. He expressed the belief that thousands of whites of goodwill also condemned mob violence and the inhumane treatment of African-Americans.[34]

Martin Luther King's next encounter with the police was in Atlanta, Georgia on February 17, 1960 when he was arrested on an Alabama warrant issued following an indictment of a Montgomery County Grand Jury on two counts of perjury. He was released on a $2,000 bond, and later was acquitted by an all-white jury on the charges of perjury relative to his 1956 state income tax return. The charges relative to the 1958 returns were dropped.[35]

---

[33] Coretta Scott King, 163.
[34] Coretta Scott King, 342.
[35] Lerone Bennett, Jr., *What Manner of Man* (Chicago: Johnson Publishing Co., 1964), Appendix.

In May 1960, King was arrested in DeKalb County, Georgia, near Atlanta, on charges of driving without a valid Georgia driver's license, and was released on bond. The arrest occurred when the Kings were returning Lillian Smith, the eminent writer, to the Emory University Hospital. It was believed that the policeman stopped King because of the presence of the white woman in the car. When King was questioned, it was revealed that he had failed to acquire a Georgia driver's license upon his move to Atlanta; therefore, he was driving illegally. King was fined twenty-five dollars and given a suspended sentence, then released on probation.[36]

Approximately five months later, King found himself, again, imprisoned. On October 19, 1960, when students launched a sit-in at major stores in Atlanta, King joined them at the demonstration at Rich's Snack Bar. He was arrested for trespassing and required to post a $5,000 bond before being released. Consistent with his belief, he refused to post bond, promising, instead, to stay in jail as long as necessary. He insisted that "in order to serve as a redemptive agency for the nation, to arouse the conscience of the opponent, you go to jail and you stay."[37] According to King, you don't pay the fine or post bail. He contended that in breaking a law that was inconsistent with moral law, you should be willing to bear the consequences, which in this case meant serving time. During King's incarceration, he shared a cell with student demonstrators, who viewed the experience as a retreat, and considered sharing a cell with the noted civil rights leader an honor. Much of their time was spent discussing such subjects as segregation, Gandhi, Christianity, nonviolence, love, and the Montgomery Bus Protest. Several days later, Mayor Hartsfield negotiated an arrangement whereby King and the students were released in exchange for a promise to call a temporary halt to their protest while negotiations took place.[38]

Although the students were released, King was held at the request of officials of DeKalb County, because of a violation of his probation on the previous traffic charge. According to the official, King's probation "required that he stay out of trouble with the law for one year, and his arrest in Atlanta violated that probation." When tried on October 25, 1960, he was found guilty and sentenced to serve four months of hard labor in a public work camp. King's incarceration in DeKalb County was of great concern to Coretta since

[36] Oates, 163.
[37] Oates, 162.
[38] Oates, 162-163.

she considered that county a haven for the Klan. Her fears intensified when the civil rights leader was moved at midnight to the Redsville Penitentiary approximately 300 miles away. After being fitted for the traditional white and green prison uniform, he was placed in a cell which had been reserved for hardened criminals. On October 28, after a show of concern by President John Kennedy and his brother, Robert, who was the US attorney general, Judge Oscar Mitchell reversed his decision and allowed King to post bond, and obtain release. In the spring of 1961, the Georgia Court of Appeals remanded the traffic charge to DeKalb County Court, which fined him twenty-five dollars and gave him a suspended six month sentence on the original charges.[39]

Albany, Georgia was the next scene of incarceration. On December 16, 1961, King was arrested, along with other demonstrators for obstructing the sidewalk and for parading without a permit. Refusing to post bond, King surrendered to the authority, in anticipation of spending Christmas in jail. He considered such an act as being necessary to bring needed life to the Albany campaign. After having been misled that a truce had been achieved, King allowed his bail to be posted. On February 27, 1962, King and Abernathy were found guilty of the charges, and on July 10 were fined $178.00 each, or 45 days in jail. They opted for the latter, but before long they were released and forced to leave the jail after an unidentified African-American paid the fine. It was King's belief that city officials or the police chief had really been responsible for paying the fine. Other suggested that the fine was paid by a "coalition of white segregationists and conservatives" who had hoped to deny King the moral victory which he sought. King was arrested, once again, however, on July 27, 1962 for conducting a prayer vigil at City Hall and was jailed for "failure to obey police officers, obstructing sidewalks and disorderly conduct." He was convicted and placed on a sixty day probation.[40]

On Good Friday 1963, King, expressing an interest in "wanting to be a good servant of his Lord and Master," decided to face arrest; therefore, he joined other volunteers in a downtown protest march in Birmingham. As they proceeded down the forbidden street which led downtown, they were permitted to go for several blocks before being arrested by the orders of Bull Conner, the police commissioner. Once placed in jail, King and his co-worker,

---

[39] Oates, 163-165.
[40] Coretta Scott King, 193-194.

Rev. Ralph Abernathy, were isolated, being placed in solidarity confinement for the first time. During King's incarceration, he had time to concentrate on problems of the movement and his family. He was greatly concerned about the status of the movement, its financial position, and the morale of the black community. King also was very anxious to communicate with his wife, who had not accompany him to Birmingham because of the recent birth of their fourth child. Likewise, Coretta was very frustrated over her inability to communicate with him. She reacted by placing a call to the office of President Kennedy, whom she had conversed with earlier when her husband was imprisoned at Reidsville, Georgia. Attorney General Robert Kennedy, the President's brother, returned the call, and was informed of the situation in Birmingham. Later that day, the President called from Palm Beach to reassure Mrs. King that he would look into the matter. Shortly after the call, King was permitted to phone his wife. Apparently, the President's intervention changed matters, considerably. To King, the solitary confinement was quite a revealing experience. He expressed confidence that God's companionship does not stop at the door of a jail cell, and although hidden from the light at that time, he had faith that once again he would see it.[41] It was during this stay that King wrote his historic "Letter from Birmingham Jail," which was a response to public criticisms concerning his reasons for having come to Birmingham.[42]

Later, King sought to generate what he referred to as "creative tension" in St. Augustine, Florida by marching on the Monson Motor Lodge. As a result of the protest, King was arrested and arraigned before being transferred to Jacksonville and placed in the Duval County jail, which state officials considered as providing greater safety for him. On June 13, 1964, bond was posted and King flew northward to deliver a commencement address prior to returning to St. Augustine to continue his campaign.[43]

On February 1, 1965, after having advised his followers in Selma that they might be required to go to jail in order to achieve their rights, King led a demonstration, and as a consequence, was arrested for marching without a permit. During his stay in jail, he and Abernathy used the time for fasting, praying, singing, meditating and exercising. It was also a time for holding conferences with SCLC aides and lawyers. King continued to direct the Selma Movement from his cell, maintaining close contact with Rev. Andrew Young,

---

[41] Martin Luther King, Jr., *Why We Can't Wait*, 72-75.
[42] King, Ch. V.
[43] Oates, 298.

one of his chief lieutenants. He also used the occasion, which had gained national attention, to write an open letter, which was published in the *New York Times*. King noted that by "jailing hundreds of Negroes, the city of Selma, Alabama, has revealed the persisting ugliness of segregation to the nation and to the world." On Friday, February 5, after having been bailed out of jail, he announced that he would go to Washington to ask the President to sponsor a voting rights bill.[44]

During his campaign for civil rights, King was arrested fourteen times, but unlike Gandhi, he was never detained for a long period of time. James Hanigan, in his analysis, considered this an "ironic misfortune" since "the kind of movement he [King] was attempting to lead and the vision he was proposing required time for reflection, meditation and the purification and renewal of one's own emotions and energies." Hanigan perceived jail as providing a retreat for King from the many demands made upon him.[45]

Albert J. Luthuli

Banishment was an instrument used by the South African Government to limit the effectiveness of Chief Luthuli. After having been elected president-general of the ANC, he was required to increase his travel around the country. It was during such travel in 1953 that Luthuli began to experience the Government's long arm of repression. While visiting Ficksburg in the Orange Free State (OFS), he was requested by the local chapter of the ANC to postpone for a day his arrival in Bethlehem. When Luthuli attempted to spend the extra day in Ficksburg, he learned, for the first time, of a regulation which forbade the staying in any one place for more than 72 hours without official permission. At the expiration of the deadline, a policeman informed him that he was to see the location superintendent, who interrogated him prior to entering charges against him. Luthuli was told that he could wait there for his case to be heard, or he could "pay an Admission of Guilt" fee. Because of the effect such a delay would have had on his program, Luthuli selected to pay the fine. At first, the police wanted to deny him the opportunity of returning to the

[44] David Garrow, *Bearing the Cross* (New York: William Morrows and Co., 1986), 330-331.
[45] James P. Hanigan, *Martin Luther King, Jr. and the Foundation of Nonviolence* (Lanhan, MD: University Press of America), 278.

area to secure his luggage, but after second thought, the officer gave him permission to remain in the territory until midnight.[46]

Shortly after this incident, Luthuli was banned, for the first time, as a result of his alleged violation of the Riotous Assemblies and the Criminal Law Amendment Acts. As a result of the ban, he was forbidden to enter the larger centers of the Union. While the restrictions did not prevent Luthuli from carrying out his duties as president-general of the ANC, it did cause inconveniences. Because of the ban, meetings of the executive committee had to be held more often than otherwise would have been the case, and had to be held in smaller towns in order to accommodate Luthuli.[47]

An important restriction that was imposed upon Luthuli by the ban was his inability to attend public gatherings anywhere. Since there was uncertainty relative to the attendance at church, he was advised by the Department of Justice that while it did not think that the police would interfere with his religious activities, he should apply for permission. Luthuli refused to do so, insisting that he did not intend to seek permission to worship God with his fellow-Christians. He maintained that no man "has the right either to grant or to withhold this privilege."[48] Not only was Luthuli banned, but ANC leaders through-out the country were placed under similar restrictions--perhaps, in hope of crippling the program. These bans, however, did not dampen the enthusiasm of the ANC supporters.

During the winter of 1954, the first ban on Luthuli expired, but after a brief taste of freedom he, again, angered the Government by going to Uitenhage, near Port Elizabeth to address the Cape Provincial Annual Conference. The new confrontation was precipitated when Luthuli visited Johannesburg, which he had planned prior to his first ban. Upon his arrival there, he was presented two documents; one which prevented him from attending public meetings and the other which confined him to his home area in the Lower Tugela for two years. He was allowed seven days of freedom before being required to return home.[49]

One of the immediate consequences of the ban was Luthuli's inability to attend the meeting in Freedom Square, Sophiatown, which would have been his first mass meeting in Johannesburg since his election as president-general

[46] Luthuli, 143-144.
[47] Luthuli, 145.
[48] Luthuli, 145-146.
[49] Luthuli, 151.

of the ANC. During his ban, he was free to move around the district, and was permitted to see visitors and receive messengers. Luthuli's work as head of the organization, however, was somewhat hampered since he had to miss a number of executive committee meetings. In urgent situations, however, the meetings were held in the Lower Tugela to enable him to participate. Otherwise, the restrictions were so rigid that when Luthuli suffered a stroke early in 1955, he could not be taken to a hospital until his wife had secured permission for him to be moved.[50]

During the winter of 1956, the two year ban ended; thus, Luthuli was able to deliver the presidential address at the ANC annual convention. His theme was "the struggle must go on, bans or no bans." Shortly thereafter, on December 5, 1956, he was arrested on a charge of high treason. To Luthuli, the charge was unexpected, even though for several months, members of the ANC had been accused of engaging in "seditious and traitorous" activities. After having bidden farewell to his family, Luthuli was taken by police car to Durban, and later was flown to Transvaal in a military plane, where he and others were placed in the Johannesburg Fort. At the time of his apprehension, there was no way of knowing how extensive was the arrest, but once Luthuli had entered the cell, he met men from places throughout South Africa, representing different religions and nationalities. Because of racial discrimination, however, the Europeans were held in separate facilities.[51]

For Luthuli, this was a new experience, since for the first time he was being detained within the walls of a jail. In order to uphold the good name of the Congresses, Luthuli and other leaders emphasized the need for order and discipline while in jail. It was ironic that so many resistance leaders were being held in one place, a situation which provided them the opportunity to confer on matters of common concern. According to Luthuli, "what distance, other occupations, lack of funds, and police interference had made difficult," now had been made easier because of their imprisonment. Luthuli observed that "delegates from the remotest areas were never farther than one cell away." To break the monotony of dealing with resistance affairs, different activities were organized, including debates, indoor games, lectures, music and regular religious worship. Among those detained were two Anglican priests who were instrumental in enhancing the spiritual life of the jail.[52]

---

[50] Luthuli, 155-157.
[51] Luthuli, 163-165.
[52] Luthuli, 166.

Religious worship always was an important aspect of Luthuli's life; thus, he recalled, vividly, the very moving services conducted by Father Calata on their last Sunday in jail. According to Luthuli, the prisoners gathered in a great circle and sang freedom songs, after which he led them in a pledge of "solidarity in the cause of liberation." He described the affair as "a touching little impromptu ceremony about which were both formality and dedication." Luthuli noted that without a doubt, "we had not languished in gaol [jail], our morale was very high."[53]

As they were moved to the Drill Hall for the preparatory examination, the people of Johannesburg turned out in force. According to Luthuli, the prisoners could do little to acknowledge the presence of their supporters because of the way they were being transported. What stood out most in his mind was how the waiting crowd sang the African National Anthem, which he compared to an angelic choir "whose rendition was perfect in every respect."[54]

Shortly thereafter, Luthuli, once again, encountered high blood pressure, and was excused from the trial for a month. During his illness, he was permitted to reside at St. Benedict's House in Rosettenville--an arrangement which was made possible by the Bishop of Johannesburg. This brief interlude provided Luthuli "a time of real spiritual and physical refreshment." Later, the treason charges against Luthuli were dropped, but for more than four years the charges against others were continued.[55]

In 1959, in an attempt to better educate whites concerning the plight of blacks in South Africa, Luthuli addressed a number of predominantly white meetings. As a result of his various activities, on May 25, he was silenced again and confined for five years. Seven days of grace were given before the beginning of the ban. As Luthuli made his way back to Groutville, enthusiastic supporters along the way applauded his courageous efforts. Large crowds saw him off at Durban, and similar ones greeted him at Johannesburg. As he neared the latter, however, he was warned by governmental officials that this ban was unlike previous ones, inasmuch as even a meeting between the Chief and one other person would be interpreted as violating the ban. In the meantime, the Great Congress meeting, which had been scheduled for May 31, was prohibited. By taking advantage of a technicality, however, nationalists were able to hold an indoor meeting in Gandhi Hall. Although

---

[53] Luthuli, 167.
[54] Luthuli.
[55] Luthuli, 169.

Luthuli was prevented from attending, his address was read. Shortly thereafter he returned to Groutville as required by the ban.[56]

In the wake of the Sharpeville tragedy of 1960, the ANC showed its resentment for the Government's repressive policies by calling for the burning of passes. Luthuli led the way and suggested that others do likewise. The Government responded immediately by declaring unlawful the ANC and the Pan African Congress, and by proclaiming a state of emergency. During this period, approximately 20,000 South Africans of all colors were arrested, including Luthuli, who, once again, was aroused from his sleep and placed in detention.[57]

Once placed in jail, a major effort was made to prevent Luthuli from mixing with other prisoners. Because his illness kept him restricted to bed for most of the day, his life was largely one of solitude, but his cell was not necessarily a place of boredom. He perceived it as a place of sanctuary where he could engage in religious meditation--an act which often in the past he had neglected because of his public activities. Luthuli wrote, "Frail man that I am, I pray humbly that I never forget the opportunity God gave me to rededicate myself, to consider the problems of our resistance to bondage, and above all to be quiet in His presence." He viewed his whitewashed cell as his chapel, and place of retreat.[58]

In the meantime, Luthuli was being required to give evidence in the treason trial. Unfortunately, during this period, he suffered an acute recurrence of high blood pressure; therefore, he was permitted by the Court to appear at the discretion of his doctor. Luthuli expressed deep regrets for being responsible for the lengthening of the ordeal of those being detained. Initially, he was not able to see other detainees, but later, was permitted to socialize with fellow prisoners while on the exercise field. He took advantage of this as often as his health would allow. After five weeks, however, this privilege was taken away because he was accused of stirring up trouble among inmates. According to officials, the detainees had begun acting unruly after Luthuli had started visiting the exercise area.[59]

When Luthuli was brought before the court, he was charged with 104 counts, including the burning of his Reference Book, and the disobeying of a

[56] Luthuli, 179.
[57] Luthuli, 214-215.
[58] Luthuli, 223.
[59] Luthuli, 225.

law by way of protest. The remaining 102 counts were for inciting others to act in a similar manner. When the trial was held, he was found guilty on the first two counts and consequently was sentenced to six months for the burning of the pass, without option of a fine, however, it was suspended for three years because of ill health. On the second charge, he was sentenced to a year in jail, or a fine of 100 pounds. His Black Sash friends paid the fine, and later were reimbursed by the Defense and Aid Fund.[60]

With this behind him, Albert Luthuli returned home to continue serving the remainder of his five year ban. Even though the restrictions placed upon him and the ANC, with-in themselves were very rigid, the South African Government, in 1962, attempted to go even further to ensure his political impotence. Acting under the provisions of the Sabotage Act, the Government barred even past statements and utterances of Luthuli from publication in any newspaper or magazine. The Minister of Justice was empowered to forbid him to communicate with anyone, or to prevent him from receiving visitors.

A day prior to the ending of the third ban, a fourth one was imposed, which confined him for five years to his home and the immediate area. In addition to being forbidden to publish, broadcast, or reproduce any statement for public attention, he was now prohibited from attending church services.[61] According to the Minister of Justice, Luthuli was guilty of engaging in prohibited activities, espousing the "cause of Communism," and cooperating with Nelson Mandela and Walter Sisulu in acts of sabotage.[62]

While under ban, Luthuli died tragically in a train accident near his home in 1967. As a tribute to the fallen leader, Alan Paton noted: "They took away his chieftainship, but he never ceased to be the chief. They took away his temporal power, but he never ceased to have his spiritual power. They took away his freedom, but he never ceased to be free. He was indeed more free than those who had bound him."[63]

---

[60] Luthuli, 224-225.

[61] Luthuli, 226-227.

[62] Edward Callan, *Albert John Luthuli and the South African Race Conflict*, Revised Edition (Kalamazoo, MI: Western Michigan University, 1965), 64.

[63] *Time*, June 5, 1964, 30.

Desmond Tutu

As had been the case with Luthuli, the South African Government attempted to derail the human rights campaign of Desmond Tutu through such means as arrest. Perhaps, because of his international standing in the field of religion, he was never detained for a long period of time, however. On May 26, 1980, the Bishop was arrested for participation in a march in Johannesburg, without a permit. He and his wife were among the religious leaders, who protested the earlier arrest and detention of Reverend John Thorne, the former General Secretary of the South African Council of Churches. Tutu and others were held in jail overnight, after having been charged with violating provisions of the Riotous Assemblies Act.[64]

The South African Government envisioned Bishop Tutu as being able to do more harm to the nation in the international arena than in domestic affairs; therefore, it did not seek to ban him to a certain geographical area of the country, but it did attempt to curtail his travel abroad. The Bishop first incurred the wrath of the Government in 1979 after a television interview in Denmark, in which he called upon that country to cease its purchase of coal from South Africa. The Government, perceiving him as damaging the prestige of the country abroad, lifted his passport.[65]

In January 1981, the Bishop's passport was returned, but it was not in his possession very long. During his tour of Europe in the winter of that year, once again, his passport was placed in jeopardy when he urged the international community to use its influence in bringing about the end of the racist policies of the Government of South Africa. Prime Minister Botha, noting that "granting a passport is a favor and not the responsibility of the state," ordered the withdrawal of the Bishop's passport.[66] Religious and political leaders from around the world deplored the action of the South African Government.

After the return of his passport, the Bishop made frequent trips abroad, and on virtually all of them, criticized the South African racist system and sought the aid of the international community in ending it. In response to Tutu's actions, the Government warned him that he is "walking on thin ice."

---

[64] Alan Paton, "In Memoriam: Albert Luthuli" *Christianity and Crisis*, XXVII, 5, Sept. 18, 1967, 206-207.

[65] "South Africa Arrests 2 Anglican Bishops at Protest," *New York Times*, May 27, 1980.

[66] *Current Biography Yearbook*, 1985, 419.

but it has restrained itself in imposing penalties upon him--perhaps viewing any action against him as being counterproductive.

In Archbishop Tutu's quest for racial equality, he suffered humiliation, but not defeat. On February 29, 1988, he and twenty-four other South African church leaders were arrested in Cape Town as they protested the banning of seventeen anti-apartheid groups.[67] As the Archbishop pursued acts of defiance in regard to emergency decrees, South African officials displayed greater tolerance than with other activists. Tutu noticed this disparity and challenged the Government to charge him with treason as it had done with others who had committed similar or lesser offenses. Perhaps, fearing the international outcry, the South African Government refused to accommodate the Archbishop.

At the outset, the prophets of social justice realized that they would be called upon to suffer for the cause. Each of them responded to the challenge in a way that inspired their followers; therefore, adding strength to the causes for which they sacrificed.

[67] "South Africa Plans to Crack Down on Critical Churchman Visiting US" *Washington Star*, Mar. 28, 1981.

Chapter 9

ENCOUNTERING THE CRITICS

> I had preached to them about my dream...I had urged them to have faith in America and in white society...Their hopes had soared. They were now booing because they felt that we were unable to deliver on our promises.[1]
>
> King

Because nonviolent resistance represented a moderate position of reform, it generated critics both on the right and left. On the right were those who perceived nonviolent resistance as being too confrontational; therefore, creating enemies among would-be supporters and on the left were those who considered it as being too moderate in its approach, therefore, inadequate in coping with problems which had their roots deep in history. As an alternative the latter advocated a more militant stance, including the use of violence.

Because of divergent points of view as to how to achieve the desired goals, too often friction developed within the ranks of the oppressed. Nonviolent resistance leaders sought to cope with such opposition in a manner so as not to weaken, seriously, the campaigns against oppression. The movements also were criticized by co-religionists--a group they assumed would support the nonviolent struggle for equality. This chapter will analyze criticisms encountered by the nonviolent resistance leaders and their responses to them.

---

[1] King, *Where Do We Go From Here*, 45.

The Movement and its Allies

Criticisms of the nonviolent struggle tended to focus on both the composition of the movement and the strategies which it pursued. Who should or should not be participants in the campaign was a question faced more seriously by Martin Luther King, Jr. and Albert Luthuli, since their efforts were more highly organized. The former headed the Southern Christian Leadership Conference, but his campaign relied upon the support of a coalition of other civil rights-oriented organizations and sympathizers. Similarly, Luthuli, although heading the African National Congress, sought to coordinate his efforts with those of coalition partners.

Composition of the Movement

Critics challenged King's multi-racial approach, maintaining that the struggle to obtain social justice for African-Americans should be waged by them, and not with the assistance of whites who might seek to control the movement. Although the issue had been raised earlier, it was during the "James Meredith March" in Mississippi that the argument received its most extensive publicity. Stokely Carmichael, leader of SNCC and Floyd McKissick, head of CORE, sought to replace the "Freedom Now" slogan with that of "Black Power." They contended that African-Americans must use approaches similar to those employed by the Irish, Italians and Jews in obtaining power.

King challenged the assumption that the Irish, Italians, and Jews had obtained power as a result of separatism, contending that while ethnic unity was important, they also benefited by "joining in alliances with other groups such as political machines and trade unions."[2] King suggested that in order "to succeed in a pluralistic society," which too often is hostile, African Americans need to approach their struggle with organized strength. He insisted, however, "that strength will be effective only when it is consolidated through constructive alliances with the majority group."[3] As King recalled the history of the Civil Rights Movement, he noted that the black-white alliance had played a very constructive role. While he applauded the "initiative, courage

[2] King, 50.
[3] King, 50.

and imagination" of African-Americans in the confrontations at Selma and Birmingham, he observed that their organized strength alone "would have been insufficient to move Congress and the administration without the weight of the aroused conscience of White America." King warned that "ten percent of the population cannot by tensions alone induce 90 percent to change a way of life."[4]

King rejected the argument that whites, generally, could not be expected to have a genuine concern for the programs of African-Americans; therefore, alliances should not be formed with them in order to secure civil rights for the latter. Critics maintained that "the white man's interest in collaborative effort is to diminish Negro militancy and deflect it from constructive goals." King conceded that "there are white elements that cannot be trusted," and since "no militant movement can afford to relax its vigilance against half-hearted associates or conscious betrayers," African-Americans must consider each of its alliances on its merit. He did not feel, however, that "occasional betrayals" should justify the rejection of the principle of alliances between the two races.[5]

King did not view "Black Power," in itself, as being a guarantee against social injustice. He warned that African-American politicians "can be as opportunistic as their white counterparts if there is not an informed and determined constituency demanding social reform."[6] He made a similar response to the argument concerning the gaining of economic power through separatism." In rejecting this assumption, King suggested that although there is a continued need to emphasize the pooling of economic resources by African-Americans, and their withdrawal of their business from discriminating firms, we should not become blind to the fact that "the larger economic problems confronting the Negro community will only be solved by federal programs involving billions of dollars." He questioned whether the pooling of resources by African-Americans and the selective use of their buying power could "create the multiplicity of new jobs and provide the number of low-cost houses that will lift the Negro out of the economic depression caused by centuries of deprivation." King contended that since the entire American society had to be altered in order to bring about greater economic justice, the

[4] King, 51.
[5] King, 50-51.
[6] King, 49.

combined efforts of liberal-labor-civil rights forces will be necessary to exert the required pressure upon the Federal Government.[7]

King advised African-Americans that within the white majority, there exists "a substantial group who cherish democratic principles above privilege" and have shown a willingness to cooperate with blacks in their struggle for racial justice. He also pointed to a larger group of whites who share "common needs" with blacks; thus they would constitute a natural ally in the struggle to achieve social justice. Blacks were advised by King that the entry into alliances "is a mark of our growing strength, not of our weakness." He contended that "in entering an alliance the Negro is not relying on white leadership or ideology; he is taking his place as an equal partner in a common endeavor." According to King, the organized strength of Blacks and their "new independence" will enable them to enter into alliances whereby they would be in a position to utilize such ties for "constructive and multiplied gains."[8]

One of the civil rights events which received criticisms because of too much white influence was the March on Washington of 1963. While most African-Americans applauded this interracial effort, there were others who perceived a conspiracy by the white power structure to control the March. Among the latter, were Congressman Adam Clayton Powell, Jr., Malcolm X, Louis Lomax, Julian Lester, and Calvin Henton.[9]

David Lewis, in his biographic study of King, discounted the "conspiracy theory," suggesting that Stephen Currier, president of the Taconic Foundation, in accepting the co-chairmanship of the Council for United Civil Rights Leadership, did not seek to use his position "to direct the course of the civil rights groups into quiescent channels." The major purpose of the organization, he insisted, was to raise the necessary funds to underwrite the March on Washington. Lewis, also, placed no credence in the charge that the "black leaders of the March betrayed their followers by accepting the financial support and political endorsement of liberal Whites."[10]

Building successful coalitions requires compromising one's position. Even if the participants in the March had represented only the major civil rights organizations, the goals of each would have had to be modified,

---

[7] King, 49-50.
[8] King, 52.
[9] Lewis, *King: A Biography*, 216.
[10] Lewis, 220.

somewhat, in order to achieve the desired unity. Organizers of the March could have settled for an all-black march, with fewer participants, or they could have opted for a larger more dramatic one, which would have been interracial in content. They saw much to be gained by the latter; thus, they selected to use that approach. Once President Kennedy became convinced that the March would take place, he became concerned with its size and content, since he perceived an unsuccessful march as having not only a negative impact upon the pending civil rights bill, but also his entire legislative program. The Kennedy Administration, therefore, worked through such individuals as Walter Reuther of the United Auto Workers to increase the participation of whites.[11] The President also was concerned about the orderliness of the proposed march, therefore, he exerted his influence in persuading organizers to "forgo the idea of a demonstration on Capitol Hill, in favor of a march from the Washington Monument to the Lincoln Memorial." Likewise, pressure was applied by administration supporters to convince John Lewis to revise his prepared remarks before delivery.[12] Critics cited the above illustrations to support their argument that the Kennedy Administration coopted the March. The March on Washington represented a mechanism by which civil rights organizations could achieve their objectives, while simultaneously, posing serious political problems for the President. Because of their shared interest in a successful march, it was inevitable that the two would collaborate, and where necessary, compromise so as to enable each to benefit from the March.

In South Africa, Luthuli faced criticisms similar to those of King. Friction developed within the ranks of the ANC over the role in which whites should play in the anti-apartheid efforts. According to Luthuli, the policy of his organization was to favor the inclusion of all resisters to white supremacy in the movement, while the splinter group, the "Africanists," preferred to follow a more isolated approach of not coordinating their campaign with those of Indian, white and colored opponents of apartheid. The Africanists based their position on the 1949 Programme of Action which they contended had envisioned an "African-only" resistance. While Luthuli conceded that point, he maintained that the movement now had gone beyond the 1949 declaration, therefore, should not cling to an outmoded outlook. He viewed the beginning

[11] Arthur M. Schlessinger, *Robert Kennedy and His Time* (Boston: Houghton-Mifflin Co., 1970) 350-351.

[12] Schlessinger, 351.

of cooperation among the races as one of the "most hopeful advances" of recent years, since it symbolized the "beginning of a non-racial South Africa." Luthuli suggested that "a racially exclusive resistance is the wrong reply to a racially exclusive oppression." He suggested that as a strategy, "the drawing in of our horns and the concentration of our forces may have some advantages, but in the long run it will obstruct the way to a South Africa which embraces all her citizens."[13]

The gap between the Africanists and the more established members of the ANC widened in the years following the organizing of the Congress of the People--an alliance which included the ANC, Indian Congress, Coloured People's Congress, and the European Congress of Democrats. The Africanists viewed the alliance as a betrayal, and expressed fear of a white takeover of the leadership of the ANC. They pointed to the Freedom Charter's opening paragraph which read: "*We the people of South Africa, declare for all our country and the world to know:* that South Africa belongs to all who live in it, black and white, and that no government can justly claim authority unless it is based on the will of the people." [14] The Africanists claimed that through the above statement, the ANC had summarily forfeited the Africans' inalienable right to full 'ownership' of South Africa. They criticized the Charter as failing "to recognize that Africans were still 'slaves' in their own land." According to the Africanists, other groups "had a right to remain in South Africa only if they recognize their position as 'guests' of the African nation and accepted rule by an African majority."[15]

Richard Gibson viewed the breaking point in the ANC feud as coming after the futile 1958 "stay at home strike" which the ANC had opposed initially, but later went along with the European and Indian members of the Alliance. With the failure of the strike came a call for disciplinary action against the Africanists who had openly opposed it. In April 1959, when a purge was undertaken, the Africanists reacted by organizing themselves into the Pan Africanist Congress.[16] In anticipation of its forming, Robert M. Sobukwe wrote in the *Africanist* in January 1959 that "cooperation is possible only between equals," not "between oppressor and oppressed, dominating and

---

[13] Luthuli, *Let My People Go*, 185-186.

[14] Luthuli, 239.

[15] Karis and Carter, *From Protest to Challenge, III*, 65.

[16] Richard Gibson, *African Liberation Movements* (New York: Oxford University Press, 1972), 55.

dominated." Considering such relations as the above as being "collaboration, not cooperation," Sobukwe contended that Africans should not collaborate in their own oppression.[17] Later in his inaugural address, he described multiracialism as "a method of safeguarding white interests, employing as it does, proportional representation irrespective of population figures." He considered such a system as a "complete negation of democracy."[18]

In his special presidential message of December 17, 1955, Luthuli defended the approach of the ANC, praising it for mobilizing all the "progressive forces regardless of race or class, into a growing, formidable army which in due course will cleanse South Africa of all traces of domination, racialism and exploitation."[19] Three years later, in an address to a predominantly white audience, he paid tribute to the efforts of such groups as the Congress of Democrats, Liberal Party, Labour Party, the Black Sash and many church leaders. Luthuli tried to assure the audience that his concern was not from whence different groups had come. Instead, he insisted that "since we are all here, we must seek a way whereby we can realise democracy, so that we can live in peaceful harmony in this land of ours."[20]

Another critic of the ANC was Jordan Ngubane, an African journalist, who broke with Luthuli because of what the former perceived as Communist influence within the Movement. While Ngubane did not regard the Freedom Charter as a Communist document, he envisioned the Communists as having had a motive for supporting the "deliberate vague document," which would "accustom Africans to the idea of nationalization and to commit them to an all-inclusive organization that would be controlled by a small Communist core."[21]

When confronted with the issue of inclusion of whites in the movement, who were former members of the Communist Party, Luthuli called to the attention of the critics the story of the blind man who was healed by Jesus, and reminded them that those persons who came to their aid might have had ulterior motives, his concern was that "they came to assist me fight racial

[17] Robert M. Sobukwe, "Future of the Africanist Movement," *The Africanist*, Jan. 1959, in Karis and Carter, 506.
[18] Sobukwe, "Inaugural Convention of PAC," Apr. 4-6. 1955 in Karis and Carter, 516.
[19] Luthuli, "Special Presidential Message," Dec. 17, 1955, in Karis and Carter, 212.
[20] Luthuli, "Freedom is the Apex," 1958, in Karis and Carter, 458.
[21] Karis and Carter, 64.

oppression, and they have no trace of racialism or being patronizing, just no trace of it at all."[22]

Accusations of Communist infiltration within the ranks of the African Liberation Movement, as well as the American Civil Rights Movement, were made not only by critics from within, but from their respective governments, as well . This subject will be explored in the following chapter.

PROGRAM OF ACTION

Nonviolent resistant leaders did not consider their strategies flawless; thus, they anticipated criticisms. Some critics appeared to have had constructive intents--being concerned with the overall improvement of the efforts; while other seemed to have had destructive designs, hoping to delay or derail the campaigns. Although Luthuli and King were the main targets of criticisms concerning the composition of their movements, all four of the nonviolent resistance leaders were criticized because of their strategies.

In spite of the fact that Gandhi was almost universally admired in India, he had his share of critics, including Jawaharlal Nehru, a very close friend and follower who later became India's first prime minister. Although perceiving Gandhi as representing India "to an amazing degree," and expressing its very spirit, Nehru, on occasion, felt compelled to criticize him. He disagreed with him on such issues as the termination of the civil disobedience campaign following the eruption of violence in Chauri Chaura, and he questioned Gandhi's rejection of modernization as a means of achieving a new India.

While Nehru deplored the violence which had occurred in Chauri Chaura, and considered it to be uncharacteristic of the spirit of the Movement, nevertheless, he raised questions concerning the sudden suspension of the campaign as a result of the action of "a mob of excited peasants in an out-of-the-way place." He contended that if there was justification for ending the "national struggle for freedom" because of such an incident, then the Movement might as well be considered dead, since it was impossible to train all of the would-be demonstrators in the "theory and practice of non-violent action." Nehru was concerned that even if those in the Movement were properly trained, there would be a problem of "the numerous agents

[22] Mary Benson, *Chief Albert Luthuli of South Africa* (London: Oxford University Press, 1963), 31.

provocateurs, stool pigeons, and the like" who would creep into the Movement and precipitate violence.[23] He maintained that if Gandhi's interpretation was correct, the movement would be at the mercy of the opponents who would always be in a position of creating circumstances that could force the abandonment of the struggle. In later years, however, to the satisfaction of the National Congress, Gandhi suggested that isolated acts of violence need not lead to the movement abandoning its efforts. He concluded that "if the nonviolent method of struggle could not function because of such almost inevitable happenings, then it was obvious that it was not an ideal method for all occasions, and this he was not prepared to admit." For Gandhi, "the method, being the right method, should suit all circumstances and should be able to function, at any rate in a restricted way, even in a hostile atmosphere."[24]

In the end, Nehru agreed that Gandhi had acted properly in suspending the civil resistance, but he questioned the reason the Mahatma had given for doing so. The reasoning was perceived as an insult to the intelligence of members of Congress, who unlike the members of Gandhi's *ashram* had not "taken all kinds of pledges and accepted a certain regime." Nehru questioned why should members of Congress "be tossed hither and thither" for what he considered to be "metaphysical and mystical reasons."[25]

Another point of disagreement between Gandhi and Nehru developed over the former's rejection of modernization. Gandhi contended that India's salvation consisted in "unlearning what she has learned during the last fifty years." This would have meant deemphasizing such symbols of modernity as railways, telegraph, hospitals, lawyers, doctors, etc.. Gandhi advised the so-called upper classes "to learn consciously, religiously and deliberately the simple peasant life, knowing it to be a life giving true happiness."[26]

Nehru interpreted Gandhi as viewing progress and civilization, "not in terms of a search for a higher standard of living; instead, a deliberate and voluntary restriction of wants, which promotes real happiness and contentment, and increases the capacity for service." Nehru considered Gandhi's advice as being wrong, harmful, and impossible to achieve. Speaking as a person, rather than as a leader of Congress, he expressed a

---

[23] Jawaharlal Nehru, *Toward Freedom* (New York: John Day Co., 1942), 80.
[24] Nehru, 83.
[25] Nehru, 310-311.
[26] Nehru, 314.

dislike for the "praise of poverty and suffering." perceiving them as undesirables which should be eliminated.[27]

In his khadi program (the wearing of home spun), Gandhi envisioned the development of an Indian mentality that would result in economic freedom and equality for all in the country. Within India would be developed a sense of self reliance that would lead to a free nation that would not be dependent upon a foreign power for its survival. Through the khadi mentality, Gandhi perceived the "decentralization of the production and the distribution of the necessaries of life."[28]

According to Louis Fischer, Gandhi had taught that in order to help the underdog, "you must understand him, and to understand him you must at least sometimes work as he does." By emphasizing khadi, Gandhi sought "to bridge brain and brawn, to unite city and town, to link rich and poor."[29] Many of the intellectuals in Congress, however, were less than enthusiastic. When Gandhi withdrew from the Congress in 1934, he noted the major differences which had developed between him and many of the Congressmen. In noting the hypocrisy, he observed that "the khadi clause of the Congress constitution has been almost a dead letter from the beginning." Some of his critics attributed the hypocrisy to Gandhi, whom they felt should have realized that the resolution was passed, not because of a deep conviction; instead, because of their loyalty to him. In spite of the fact that the khadi clause was not being observed, Gandhi opposed its removal from the constitution, perceiving such action as meaning the removal of the living link between the Congress and the million whom it has from its inception sought to represent.[30]

Gandhi also felt compelled to respond to critics of his nonviolent approach. He expressed regrets that for a majority of the members of Congress, the Khadi program was merely a policy, while for him it was a "fundamental creed." Not wanting to blame his critics, Gandhi assumed responsibility for the unenthusiasm for his nonviolent approach, attributing it to his faulty presentation and faulty execution, those were the only reasons which he could give for the failure of congressmen to accept his view.[31]

---

[27] Nehru, 314.

[28] Gandhi, *Constructive Programe*, Reprint (Ahmedabad, India: Navajivan Publishing House, 1961), 12-16.

[29] Fischer, *The Life of Mahatma Gandhi*, 231.

[30] D. G. Tendulkar, *Mahatma* (New Delhi: Ministry of Information and Broadcasting, Government of India, 1951) III: 296.

[31] Tendulkar, III: 297.

Throughout the country there were those who rejected the Gandhian method, and chose, instead, the pursuit of violence. The Mahatma's response to these critics have been adequately discussed elsewhere in this study.

The high priority which Gandhi gave to the issue of untouchability also caused some of the staunch supporters of Indian independence to criticize him. Although others considered it to be a secondary issue, for the Mahatma, it was a deeply religious and moral commitment; thus, he felt obligated to take a strong stand against it. As suggested in an earlier chapter, he considered the problem of untouchability a major issue, which had to be resolved before there could be a true free India.

Gandhi's approach to the resolving of religious tension in India also was bitterly opposed by some of his fellow-Hindus, who regarded him as: leaning over backward to accommodate the Moslems. These critics were especially disturbed over his advice that they should welcome back the Moslems whom had fled, and to compensate them for property which they had lost.[32] In the breaking down of religious hatred, Gandhi challenged Hindus, who constituted the majority of the population, to take the lead. Speaking to about 500 members of a highly disciplined organization of young militant Hindus, Gandhi advised them that "if Pakistan was mistreating Hindus that was no justification for their mistreating Moslems."[33]

Gandhi also rejected criticisms of those who suggested that Hindus be advised to abandon areas under attack by Moslems, and move to more secure areas. His contention was that the exchanging of population would be conceding that India could not remain united. He perceived it as a denial of his belief that "an affinity exists or can easily be established between people who are different or think themselves different."[34]

In January 1948, Gandhi's approach to the Hindu-Moslem conflict led to an attempt on his life by a militant Hindu. The Mahatma expressed forgiveness, noting that the young man probably viewed him as an enemy to Hinduism. Less than a month later, another young Hindu critic demonstrated his dismay with Gandhi's position by assassinating him.[35]

As anticipated, King's strategies for achieving a just society did not receive the endorsement of all of its advocates. During his campaign in

[32] Fischer, 461.
[33] Fischer, 482.
[34] Fischer, 450-451.
[35] Fischer, 502-505.

Montgomery, he encountered skeptics on both sides--those who thought that his actions were too aggressive, and those who preferred a more radical approach. As he expanded his efforts, he was confronted by even more critics. Illustrative of this were the criticisms which surfaced following his organizing the SCLC. Supporters of the NAACP viewed the entry of a new civil rights organization in the field as the introduction of another element of disunity, which the movement did not need. Because the SCLC was church-based, and had clerical leadership, it was envisioned as being in a better position to obtain mass appeal; therefore, weakening the NAACP, especially in the South. In addition, the new organization was criticized for its adherence to the nonviolent direct action approach.

As King attempted to recruit African-Americans for his campaign, he found that his efforts were being impeded by a misunderstanding of his method, with some thinking that nonviolent direct action was intended to replace other approaches. The matter became more complicated and distorted by the two adversaries, with the defenders of the legal approach deploring direct action, and those who defended direct action condemning the legal method. To King, direct action was not a substitute for legal action; instead, a complement of it. He praised the NAACP for providing the legal support for persons arrested while actively opposing racial segregation. King viewed direct action as providing the test cases which enabled the courts to make important civil rights decisions.[36] Even though he preferred direct action, he advised African-Americans to support the NAACP, praising it for the historic role which it has played in the civil rights field.

Roy Wilkins, the executive secretary of the NAACP, also was conciliatory, noting that since there were many complex problems associated with the improvement of race relations, there was work for "many hands and hearts." He warned, however, that because of the strength of the opponent, any division among those fighting for civil rights would be disastrous to the overall cause.[37] Initially, Wilkins expressed concern over a statement attributed to King describing sit-ins as "a moving away from tactics which are suitable merely for gradual and long-term change." According to the NAACP leader, such remarks might easily be interpreted as a rebuke of his organization and its procedures. Wilkins advised King that the primary

---

[36] King, *Why We Can't Wait*, 33-34.

[37] Roy Wilkins, *Standing Fast* (New York: Viking Press, 1982), 269.

interest of the NAACP was the securing of first-class citizenship for black Americans as speedily as possible, and although it will use a variety of methods to achieve its goal, the Association believes that "citizenship had to be firmly secured in law." In spite of their differences, the two leaders maintained admiration for each other, and they sought to resolve later disagreements within the family.[38]

King's campaign for racial justice also encountered critics on the left. During the march through Mississippi in 1966, the Deacons for Defense argued that inasmuch as self defense was essential, nonviolence should not be considered a prerequisite for participation in the civil rights march. They were supported in this view by some of the activists of CORE and SNCC. King, however, opposed the idea, viewing it as impractical and disastrous to precipitate a "violent confrontation in Mississippi." He perceived the use of force as serving the cause of white segregationists and the government of Mississippi, which would welcome the violence as a pretext for killing scores of African-Americans. While King did not quarrel with the idea of blacks defending themselves as individuals, he did question the use of guns in an organized demonstration. He feared that "if they lowered the banner of nonviolence...Mississippi injustice would not be exposed and the moral issues would be obscured."[39]

When King launched his campaign in Birmingham in 1963, he found that many African-Americans were unenthused about his efforts. He and his followers were criticized and referred to as "outsiders" who had come to town to wage a civil rights campaign, but had refused to keep the local people informed. Although King could understand why the people of Birmingham would not want to become involved in something which they had no part in helping to organize, he defended the need for secrecy. He did not consider it wise to entangle the civil rights demonstrations in the current city election campaign.[40]

The cry of "outsider" was heard again in the Chicago campaign by such critics as Dr. Joseph H. Jackson, president of the National Baptist Association, and Ernest Rather, who headed the Committee of One Hundred. They attributed the civil disruptions in Chicago to the nonviolent techniques of King. They urged him to "return to the South, where there was a fertile terrain

---

[38] Wilkins, 269-70.
[39] King, *Where Do We Go From Here*, 27. King, *Where Do We Go From Here*, 27.
[40] King, *Why We Can't Wait,* 64-65.

of flagrant injustice for which his tactics were ideally suited."[41] Similarly, Rev. Henry Mitchell, serving as spokesperson for about a dozen ministers, and claiming to represent 50,000 African-Americans of Chicago, accused King of being an "outsider" whose marches had created hatred in the city. The ministers urged King to leave the city. A few weeks later, Rev. Carl Fuqua, the executive secretary of the Chicago branch of the NAACP, joined in the call. Because his organization embraced the largest number of members, its withdrawal from the Coordinating Council of Community Organizations (CCCO), constituted a major blow to efforts of Martin Luther King, Jr.[42]

Although King did not wage a major campaign in New York, he visited it at the request of Mayor Robert Wagner, in the wake of the riots of 1964. Among those who spoke out against his visit was Congressman Adam Clayton Powell, Jr., who protested that "no leader outside Harlem should come into the town and tell us what to do."[43] Even though King realized that his incursions into the North would cause many of his earlier supporters to desert the cause, he felt obligated to expand his campaign to oppose injustice, regardless of where it was found.

King also had to respond to the implied criticism of "Why Now." There were African-Americans who thought that the demonstrations in Birmingham were ill-timed; and would probably cause the election of a candidate least favorable to their cause. King suggested that they were "indulging in a false optimism about what would happen to Birmingham under the new government." He concluded that because of the unacceptable conditions which had existed in the city for years, many African-Americans were convinced that things would be better after Bull Connor had faded from the political scene.[44] Later, in his "Letter from Birmingham Jail," King provided a more extensive rationale for why the demonstrations could not be postponed.

As was true with King's campaign in the North, many of his former associates deserted him when he embraced the antiwar cause. Among those who disapproved of his position were Nobel Peace Laureate Ralph Bunche, Senator Edward Brooke, Columnist Carl Rowan, and leaders of the National Urban League and the NAACP. The latter approved a statement, which

---

[41] Lewis, 336-337.
[42] Lionel Lokos, *House Divided: The Life and Legacy of Martin Luther King* (New York: Arlington House, 1968), 273.
[43] Lewis, 245.
[44] King, 64.

regretted the merger of the anti-war effort and the civil rights campaign. The NAACP, in an attempt to dissociate itself with King's anti-war cause, emphasized that it was not "a peace organization nor a foreign policy association;" instead a civil rights organization, "committed to its primary goal of eliminating all forms of racial discrimination and achieving equal rights and equal opportunities for all Americans."[45]

While Senator Brooke did not question King's motives, he did express concern that he would take a position which was perceived as doing irreparable harm to the Civil Rights Movement. Carl Rowan also disapproved of King's position in regard to the war, noting that his outspoken criticisms made him "*personna non grata* to Lyndon Johnson," and was likely to cause the lost of friends in Congress. According to the columnist, King had created the impression that African-Americans were disloyal; thus, causing alienation from the civil rights campaign. Rowan perceived this tragic event as being of serious consequence to million of blacks who found themselves locked in poverty, and were depending upon the leadership of the President and Congress to provide the progress and laws that would open the doors to a better future. Rowan considered it "a tragic irony that there should be any doubt about the Negro's loyalty to his country--especially doubt created by Martin Luther King, who helped as much as any one man to make America truly the Negro's country too."[46]

How did King respond to the criticisms by those associated with the Movement? Certainly, not by retreating from his position. He reminded those critics who tried to convince him that he should not seek leadership roles both in the civil rights and peace movements that he had "worked too long and hard...against segregated public accommodations to end up segregating my moral concern."[47] He did not feel that his opposition to the war should be interpreted as meaning disloyalty to the country. Instead, he suggested that it was because of his love for America that he was speaking out against the war- - "not in anger but with anxiety and sorrow...and above all with a passionate desire to see our beloved country stand as the moral example of the world."[48]

---

[45] *The Crisis*, 74 (1967): 127.
[46] Carl Rowan, "Martin Luther King's Tragic Decision," *The Reader's Digest*, Sept. 1967, 42.
[47] King, *Trumpet of Conscience*, 24.
[48] King, "The Casualties of the War in Vietnam," an address delivered at the Nation Institute, Los Angeles, CA, Feb. 25, 1967.

As a postlude, millions of Americans, in later years, also regarded the war as a lost cause.

Luthuli also had his share of critics. As indicated earlier, a split developed within the ranks of the ANC in regard to the role played by non-blacks in the deciding of strategies for the anti-apartheid movement. Likewise, criticisms were expressed concerning the influence that was being exercised by the Communists. Since these subjects were discussed earlier in this chapter, our focus here will be on criticisms relative to more specific aspects of Luthuli's campaign. When to launch campaigns and when to end them were issues that generated many criticisms.

Shortly after Luthuli became active in the ANC, his approach was questioned, especially by those who preferred more militant action. Having recently assumed leadership of the Natal Branch of the organization, he appealed for more time before launching the Defiance Campaign. To his dismay, he was jeered and called a coward; nevertheless, he insisted that while there was a need for urgency, an ill-prepared campaign would be worse than none at all. Luthuli warned his followers that the Movement could not rely on sporadic demonstrations which often came at times "when patience has snapped for the moment" and violence erupted. He suggested the need of the people "to be briefed with clarity and care...and given the opportunity to signify their willingness and readiness to participate" before launching campaigns.[49]

By the time Luthuli had become president-general of the ANC, the Defiance Campaign had run its course; thus, he terminated it. This action provoked criticisms by those who preferred to see it continue. Luthuli dismissed such protest, maintaining that the Defiance Campaign was launched at the right time, and likewise, it was the proper time for ending it. While recognizing the accomplishments of the campaign, he noted that its back had been broken well before its formal ending.[50]

In later years, critics also raised their voices against what Mary Benson referred to as Luthuli's "serious act of misjudgment" in regard to the stay at home protest which he had called to coincide with the parliamentary elections of 1958. His decision was believed to have been influenced greatly by the Congress of Trade Union, an ally of the ANC. The protest, which ended in failure was bitterly criticized by the "Africanists" who openly and actively

[49] Luthuli, *Let My People Go*, 113.

opposed it. These ill-fated protest widened the gap between the rival factions of the ANC, and led to the eventual withdrawal of the Africanists from the organization.[51]

Like Luthuli, Tutu, as a moderate leader, encountered critics both on the right and the left. Typical of such opposition from the right were those who disagreed with his advocacy of economic sanctions against South Africa. These critics perceived a withdrawal of foreign business firms as creating a greater hardship for blacks than their white counterparts. Among those who opposed sanctions was Chief Gatsha Buthelezi, who is considered by many to be the spokesperson for the Zulu Tribe. On the other hand, there were those who viewed the situation in South Africa as being beyond compromise; thus, they considered Tutu's moderate stance as merely giving aid and comfort to the racist government of the country. These critics advocated a more militant approach.

The Religious Community

Among the most vocal critics of nonviolent resistance were religious leaders, whom King thought should have had a stronger commitment to the struggle for social justice. As an advocate of a socially relevant religion, he found himself at odds with many of the more traditional-oriented ministers. As noted earlier, one of his better known critics was Rev. Joseph Jackson, who at that time was the president of the National Baptist Convention, which consisted of approximately five million black members. The conservative leadership of this organization led to a revolt by some of the "younger more civil-minded and generally higher educated ministers," who formed the Progressive Baptist Alliance in1962. Jackson contended that it was the duty of the minister "to bring the good news of the Gospel to his flock, to save the members of his flock for Jesus, and to effect change by exemplary conduct."[52] Very early in life, King rejected this philosophy, concluding that "any religion which professes to be concerned about the souls of men and is not concerned about the social and economic conditions that scar the soul is a spiritually moribund religion only waiting for the day to be buried."[53]

---

[50] Luthuli, 130.
[51] Benson, 197-198.
[52] Lewis, 158.
[53] King, *Stride Toward Freedom*, 91.

The appeal to the conscience of white Americans was considered an essential part of the campaign for racial justice, and white ministers were perceived as having a major role to play in this effort. The convincing of these ministers proved to have been a formidable task since some of them actively opposed the nonviolent efforts. In a meeting held to resolve the Montgomery Bus Protest, the Reverend E. Stanley Frazier, a white minister, argued that "Blacks were wrong in boycotting the buses," and he deplored the leadership exercised by ministers of the Gospel in this illegal activity. He contended that "the job of the minister is to lead the souls of men to God, not to bring about confusion by getting tangled up in transitory social problems." Rev. Frazier urged African-American ministers to use their influence in ending the boycott and lead their people "to a glorious experience of the Christian faith." King retorted, that those in the Movement also knew Jesus and had an experience with Him. He could see no conflict between devotion to Jesus and the action pursued by the Montgomery Improvement Association, the organization that was spearheading the protest. King maintained that those who are truly dedicated to the religion of Jesus will involve themselves in efforts to end social evils. He recognized that in order to make the changes he envisioned, it would be necessary to go against the cherished traditions of the community, but he insisted that customs that are wrong must be changed. King regarded it as necessary to decide whether our allegiance will be given to "outmoded and unjust customs or to ethical demands of the universe." As Christians, he maintained, " we owe our ultimate allegiance to God and His will, rather than to man and his folkways."[54] King expressed admiration for the eloquence of Frazier, and questioned why the "children of darkness" are frequently more determined and zealous than the "children of light."

In later years, King felt compelled to respond to criticisms made by Christian ministers and Jewish rabbis. In his famous "Letter from Birmingham Jail," he defended his reason for bringing his campaign to that city, pointing out that injustice existed there, and like the prophets of the Old Testament, and Apostle Paul, he felt the need to carry the gospel of freedom beyond his own town. Rejecting the contention of his critics, King maintained that as president of the SCLC, he had organizational ties with the local chapter, and had come to the city in response to its invitation. In the historic letter, he criticized his fellow-clergymen for deploring the demonstrations, while at the same time

---

[54] King, 117.

showing little concern for the conditions that had made the demonstrations necessary. Although King expressed regrets for the need of the protest, he considered it more unfortunate that the white power structure of the city had left African-Americans no other alternative.

King also rejected the ministers' complaint that the direct action was untimely, contending that "freedom is never voluntarily given by the oppressor; it must be demanded by the oppressed." The civil rights leader noted that he had never engaged in a direct-action campaign that was "well-timed in the view of those who have not suffered unduly from the disease of segregation." According to King, African-Americans had waited for more than 340 years in order to achieve their constitutional and God-given rights.

The letter also was used to respond to the anxiety of the clergy concerning the willingness of African-Americans to break the law. King defined laws as both just and unjust, emphasizing that the former should be obeyed, and the latter disobeyed. He insisted that "one has not only a legal but a moral responsibility to disobey unjust laws."

King advised religious leaders that in the struggle for racial justice, the Church has fallen short in its commitment. While he commended Christian leaders who had taken an active role in the struggle, he noted that others were "more cautious than courageous and have remained silent behind the anesthetizing security of stained glass windows." In contrast with the early church, the contemporary church was described as "a weak, ineffectual voice with an uncertain sound," and too often acting as "an arch defender of the status quo." King perceived the power structure of the community as being "consoled by the Church's silent--and often even vocal--sanction of things as they are."[55]

While King had many critics within the religious community, there were far more who were willing to lend their aid to the civil rights cause. Their personal involvement in the campaign did much to facilitate the appeal to the conscience of the people, which was essential to the establishment of a just society.

During Luthuli's campaign for racial justice in South Africa, he also encountered opposition from his fellow-Christians. Illustrative of this was the very hostile position taken by the Afrikaner-dominated Dutch Reformed Church, which condemned such protest activities as the Defiance Campaign,

[55] King, *Why We Can't Wait*, Ch. 5.

and equated "obedience to the State with obedience to God." Given its traditional position in regard to race relations, it was not surprising that this church would take such a position. No other church, however, adopted such an unfriendly position even though some had ambivalent feelings concerning their support for the cause. Although the General Assembly of the Presbyterian Church expressed sympathy for the oppressed, and condemned the laws which provoked the demonstrations, simultaneously it "deeply regretted the Defiance Campaign." Likewise, the Methodist Church condemned the unfair laws, but expressed disapproval of the violent opposition to them. Its followers, however, were left with the freedom to oppose such laws by nonviolent means. In the meantime, while warning of the possible dangers which could result from the Defiance Campaign, the Anglican Archbishop considered it "a moral judgment upon the type of legislation being opposed, and upon the whites who had passed such laws." He advised Anglicans that according to traditional Christian teaching, there was no obligation Christians had to "obey unjust laws."[56]

When challenged to take a position in regard to the Defiance Campaign, the Christian Council, at first, sought to refer the matter to individual churches, since it perceived its major duty as being the coordinating of activities among the churches. As a member of the Council, Luthuli opposed the proposed actions, contending that the Council had an obligation to take a stand, inasmuch as "it was the duty of the Church as a whole, to give moral guidance at once while the issue was alive and while some Christians were in real confusion about the principles involved." Following the appeal of Luthuli and others, the Christian Council drafted a statement which called upon individual Christians "to bring their conscience to bear on the situation." They were advised that it was not unChristian to engage in a campaign against injustice, if such resistance was not inconsistent with the individual's conscience. Christians also were reminded that disobedience to man's laws could be justified only in "obedience to a higher law."[57]

Although Luthuli did not envision the Church as being the organizer of political movements, he did foresee a need for it to be involved with the improvement of conditions under which people live. He insisted that if it "stands on the outskirts, we cannot expect our religion to survive and be respected." Unfortunately, in a country which has placed so much emphasis

---

[56] Luthuli, 136-137.

upon its Christian foundation, too few people have been willing to interpret their Christian commitment to mean aiding the cause of the oppressed.

Years later, when Tutu conducted his campaign for social justice in South Africa, he also encountered critics from within the Church. As had been the case with King's ministry in the United States, there were those who insisted that the role of the Church should be limited to the "saving of souls." Critics insisted that the Church should not attempt to mix religion and politics, a contention which Bishop Tutu rejects. He maintained that the same type of furor was not raised when the white Dutch Reformed Church attempted to give Scriptural support to policies of the government on such matters as race relations. Tutu disagreed with those who argued that since God does not take sides, neither should the Church. He envisioned God as an intervener in cases of injustice and oppression and cited the exodus of the children of Israel from Egypt as an outstanding example.[58]

One of the major critics of Tutu was President P. W. Botha who on March 16, 1988, accused him of distorting the "true message of Christ" by involving the Church in the political struggle against apartheid. The South African President demanded to know whether Tutu was "acting on behalf of the Kingdom of God or the Kingdom promised by the ANC," which he perceived as seeking to establish an atheistic Marxist state. In reply, the Archbishop cited scripture to justify the concern of the Church in obtaining justice. He maintained that the racial policies of South Africa were not only "unjust and oppressive; but they are positively unbiblical, unChristian, immoral, and evil."[59]

Although the prophets of social justice desired a united front in regard to their struggles, they were realists; thus, they anticipated critics from within their movements. While they welcomed criticisms which were designed to improve their campaigns, they expressed dismay over the tactics of critics who sought to disrupt the movement.

---

[57] Luthuli, 137.

[58] Tutu, *Hope and Suffering*, 37-38.

[59] Tutu, *The Rainbow People of God*, 148X Efforts to Destroy.

Chapter 10

EFFORTS TO DESTROY

> It was soon clear that the Treason Trial had provided a new rallying point for the resistance. I must give credit where it is due. I doubt whether we could have devised so effective a method of ensuring cohesion in resistance and of enlarging its embrace, as did the Government when it set the Trial in motion.[1]
>
> Luthuli

The struggles of Gandhi, King, Luthuli, and Tutu were directed at the removal of social injustices and not necessarily the replacement of governments of the respective countries. Nevertheless, because in many ways, the governments were the major perpetrators of those injustices, they interpreted advocacy of social change as meaning agitation for their overthrow. Even when governmental leaders or agents realized that this was not true they continued to accuse nonviolent leaders of crimes of sedition, apparently in an effort to destroy them as effective leaders.

A CHARGE OF SEDITION

Perhaps, the most overt effort to discredit Gandhi was undertaken in the wake of the unsuccessful noncooperation campaign in Bardoli in 1922. At the insistence of the British Government, he was arrested on March 10, 1922 and was charged with sedition, based upon his publication of three articles in

---

[1] Luthuli, *Let My People Go*, 170.

Young India—"Tampering with Loyalty" (Sept. 19, 1921), "A Puzzle and Its Solution" (Dec. 15, 1921), and "Shaking the Manes" (Feb.23, 1922). Specifically, he was charged with "bringing or attempting to bring into hatred or contempt or attempting to excite disaffection towards His Majesty's Government, established by law in British India."[2]

In the article, "Tampering with Loyalty," Gandhi openly courted arrest and encouraged his followers to do likewise, by spreading "disaffection openly and systematically." He did not deny that sedition was the theme of Congress and that "every non-cooperator is pledged to preach disaffection towards the Government established by law." Gandhi conceded that although non-cooperation was a "religious and strictly moral movement," its aim was to "overthrow the Government."[3]

In the article entitled, "A Puzzle and Its Solution," Gandhi was more specific concerning the attitude of noncooperators toward the Government. He wrote, "We are challenging the might of this Government because we consider its activity to be wholly evil. We want to overthrow the Government. We want to compel its submission to the people's will. We desire to show that the Government exists to serve the people, not the people the Government."[4] According to Gandhi, the noncooperators were engaged in a war against the Government because of its breach of faith with Muslims in regard to the Khalifat issue, and because of the humiliation which had been inflicted upon the Indians in the Punjab.

The third article, "Shaking the Manes," was written as a response to the threatening words of the British Government that it would react to a disruption of governmental functions in India with all of its vigor and determination. Gandhi, insisting that India was prepared to cope with "all the hard fibre that can be transported across the seas," warned that it was not willing to settle for anything less than self-government and a full redress of the grievances involving the Khalifat and Punjab. He suggested that the British Government transform its empire into a "true commonwealth of free nations," with member nations accorded equal rights and the power to secede from the partnership. The failure to do so, according to Gandhi, would mean that all of the determination, the vigor and hard fibre of the British would have been

[2] K.P. K. Menon, "The Great Trial," in Homer Jack, *The Gandhi Reader*,(New York: Grove Press, 1956), 198.

[3] M. K. Gandhi, "Tampering with Loyalty," in Jack, 192.

[4] Gandhi, "A Puzzle and Its Solution," in Jack, 193.

exhausted in India in vain, since the effort would not have broken the spirit of the Indians.[5]

When Gandhi was summoned before the judge to respond to the charge of sedition, he entered a plea of guilty. In spite of this admission of guilt, the advocate-general insisted upon arguing the case. He sought to convince the court that not only did Gandhi use the three articles to spread disaffection openly, but earlier articles, as well. Considering the accusations of the advocate-general to be fair and accurate, Gandhi admitted that he had preached with a passion "disaffection towards the existing system of government," and he admitted that such preaching did not begin with his affiliation with *Young India*. He also agreed that he should be held responsible for the violence which had occurred at Bombay, Madras, and Chauri Chaura. In appealing for a rigid sentence, the advocate-general called attention to the high educational qualifications of the accused, and asked the Court to consider the harm which could be done by the writings of such a man. Gandhi replied: "As a man of responsibility, a man having received a fair share of education, having had a fair share of experience of this world, I should have known the consequence of every one of my acts." The Mahatma acknowledged that he was aware that he was playing with fire, and he assured the Court, that in the event he was set free, he would continue to do the same.[6]

In his prepared statement to the Court, Gandhi sought to justify why he had moved from a position of staunch loyalty and cooperation to one of uncompromising disaffection and noncooperation. He recalled that as he began his public life in South Africa, he was denied his rights as a man because he was an Indian, but in spite of this, he cooperated with the Government and never sought its destruction. As evidence of his support, Gandhi cited his participation in the Boers War, and the campaign to put down the "Zulu Rebellion." He also recruited other Indians to do likewise. His efforts were repeated in the First World War. He attributed his extraordinary service to his belief that India could gain a place of equality in the Empire if Indians participated in the defense of the latter. To the contrary, the British Government reacted with further acts of repression. Gandhi observed that because of the British intrusion into India, the country was more helpless than before, both politically and economically. He viewed the Government of

---

[5] Gandhi, "Shaking the Manes," in Jack, 195-196.
[6] K.P.K. Menon, 201.

British India as having been established for the purpose of exploiting the masses. The great misfortune as he perceived it, was that the Englishmen and their Indian associates believed that they were "administering one of the best systems in the world," rather than being guilty of perpetuating suffering among the masses. Noting that "affection cannot be manufactured or regulated by law." Gandhi insisted that "if one has no affection for a person or system, one should be free to give the fullest expression to his disaffection, so long as he does not contemplate, promote or incite to violence." He regarded it as a privilege to be charged with promotion of disaffection. Although the Mahatma denied having had any personal ill-will against any particular government official or the King's person, he did express a disaffection against the government because of the tremendous harm which it had perpetuated on India. For his crime, he asked the judge to inflict upon him the highest penalty possible.[7] Expressing high regard for Gandhi, the judge sentenced him to six years in prison, but because of his illness, he did not serve the full sentence.

In years that followed, Gandhi was accused by the Government of using his non-violent campaign to provoke violence. Likewise, his loyalty during the Second World War was questioned by those who felt that he would take advantage of the international crisis to drive the British from India. The Mahatma denied wanting to see the British defeated, nevertheless, he continued to insist that any role which his country should play in the war, should be conditioned upon it being an independent nation. Although, accusations of disloyalty were made against Gandhi for the remainder of his life, his immense popularity, both in and out of India, made it impossible for his opponents to discredit or destroy him.

An Uncontrolled FBI

In the effort to discredit Martin Luther King, Jr., the FBI made use of an old weapon--the accusation of Communist ties. One scholar noted that although J. Edgar Hoover had been pressured by the Attorney General to enter the struggle for racial justice, the FBI chief still had strong personal feelings concerning African-Americans. Arthur Schlessinger observed that Hoover acted as if "in compensation for the ground he had been forced to give on civil rights, he redoubled his determination to discredit the movement," and "to

[7] Menon, 202-205.

discredit the Kennedy administration too, if it persisted in its alliance with Martin Luther King," At the time Hoover launched his attack, the Bureau had on file information that indicated that during the previous forty years, the Communists had been unsuccessful in their attempt to influence African-Americans. Disregarding this information, he insisted that the Civil Rights Movement was in danger of being infiltrated.[8]

Considering it his patriotic duty to reveal this Communist threat, Hoover, in April 1962, wrote a letter to Attorney General Robert Kennedy, indicating that the Bureau had information that two of King's advisers had Communist ties. Reacting to pressure from the FBI, Robert Kennedy agreed to the tapping of the telephones of Stanley Levison, one of the accused. In the meantime, President Kennedy, having become concerned about how this accusation would affect his civil rights bill, held a Rose Garden conversation with King regarding the matter. He advised the civil rights leader that it would be in the best interest of the Movement if he would terminate his relationship with the accused. King complied by severing ties with Jack O'Dell, but hesitated in breaking relations with Levison for whom he had great respect. At the request of the latter, however, formal ties were broken.[9]

Although President Kennedy had urged the breaking of ties with Levison and O'Dell, he was willing to give the Civil Rights Movement a clean bill of health. In a press conference on July 17, 1963, the President revealed that there was no evidence that indicated that any civil rights leader was Communists or that demonstrations led by them were influenced by Communists. He noted that, in the past, it was the practice of some to attribute all of our problems to Communists, and to suggest that if the "Communist movement would only disappear," our many problems would be solved.[10]

In part, the FBI's preoccupation with destroying King had been attributed to his criticisms of the agency. The Southern Regional Council, in November 1962, issued a report which blamed the lack of respect for the FBI by African-Americans in Albany, GA on its racist attitude. In reacting to the report, King observed that a major problem was that "the agents are white Southerners who have been influenced by the mores of the community," and in order for them "to maintain their status, they have to be friendly with the local police and people who are promoting segregation." King questioned how could such an

---

[8] Schlessinger, 352-353.

[9] Schlessinger, 358.

[10] Schlessinger, 358-359.

official honestly and objectively investigate racial problems. When the assessment by King appeared in major papers, the FBI was quick to respond, noting that only one of the five man team was a Southerner. A memorandum from the assistant director in charge of the general investigation division, attributed King's statement to the influence of Communist advisors. In the meantime, an effort was made to contact King to arrange a meeting to correct the "misconception," but when the phone call was not returned, FBI officials became incensed. Assistant Director Cartha DeLoach perceived the "snub" as an indication of King's lack of interest in the true facts; instead, a desire only in using "deceit, lies and treachery as propaganda to further his own causes."[11]

Later, in assessing King's March on Washington address, an FBI official labeled it a "powerful demagogic speech," and warned that King should be considered the "most dangerous Negro... in this nation."[12] In the meantime, the FBI released a document entitled: "Communism and the Negro Movement--A Current Analysis," which concluded that the stature of King, as the "leader among leaders of the Negro movement" was growing daily and that "Communist party officials visualize the possibility of creating a situation whereby it could be said that, as the Communist party goes, so goes Martin Luther King, and so also goes the Negro movement in the United States."[13] David Garror noted that the monograph focused heavily upon the past role of Levison in the Communist Party, and his "powerful present day influence on King," while not presenting any evidence that in his relationship with King was Levison representing the Communist Party or its belief.[14]

In its effort to neutralize King as an "effective Negro leader," the Domestic Intelligence Division of the Agency discussed ways in which to develop evidence concerning the reliance of King upon the Communists for guidance and direction. According to Garror, while the pretension was the search for Communist ties, there appeared to have been an undue emphasis on the discovery of material to discredit the civil rights leader. Personal habits and financial management were included in the investigation. An official emphasized that the Bureau had already collected material that would prove King unfit to serve as a minister of the gospel because of serious weaknesses

---

[11] David J. Garrow, *The FBI and Martin Luther King, Jr.* (New York: W.W. Norton and Co., 1981), 59.
[12] Garrow, 68.
[13] Garrow, 73.
[14] Garrow, 87.

in his character. The FBI sought to gather additional information concerning his alleged use of liquor, and involvement with women.[15]

In an intra-bureau memorandum, the assistant director in charge of the Domestic Intelligence Division suggested that at the "right moment," King should be revealed as "a fraud, demagogue and moral scoundrel." The strategy was to use collected material to knock the civil rights leader from his pedestal and "reduce him completely in influence so that he will no longer be a security problem and no longer will be deceiving and misleading the Negro people." According to the memorandum, the dethroning of King would leave African-Americans without a national leader; therefore, efforts should be made to prepare the desired type to fill the leadership void. Samuel R. Pierce, Jr., who later became President Reagan's secretary of Housing and Urban Development, was suggested as a possible candidate for such a position.[16]

On January 29, 1964, Hoover testified before an executive session of the House Appropriation Subcommittee concerning the role of Communists in the Civil Rights Movement. When information relative to his testimony became public, King expressed dismay over what he considered to be Hoover's cooperation in helping "extremists smear the civil rights movement." He found it difficult to accept the word of the FBI on Communistic infiltration into the civil rights movement when it had been "so completely ineffectual in protecting the Negro from brutality in the Deep South." Later, in a television interview. King challenged those who claimed to have had information concerning Communist infiltration into the civil rights campaign to make known their names in order that they could be removed, since they were not wanted in the Movement. Simultaneously, he expressed dismay that Hoover had aided and abetted "the racists and the rightists in our nation" by accusing the Movement of having been infiltrated with Communists.[17]

King's selection as *Time*'s "Man of the Year" for 1963 angered the FBI, but it was helpless in the situation. Later, the Bureau intervened in the futile effort to prevent King from being awarded honorary degrees from Marquette University and Springfield College (Mass.), and to stop the Pope from granting him an audience. The FBI reacted to his having been selected the recipient of the Nobel Peace Prize by circulating derogatory reports to all

---

[15] Garrow, 73.
[16] Garrow, 105-106.
[17] Garrow, 114.

agents of the government which were presumed to have had an interest in King's travel abroad.[18]

At a press conference in November 1964, Hoover, in replying to a statement made by King two years earlier, referred to him as the "most notorious liar" in the United States. The latter considered the remarks of the FBI chief to have been irresponsible. King admitted that he had questioned the effectiveness of the Bureau in racial matters--especially in cases where bombing and brutalities perpetrated against African-Americans were involved--but he denied having attributed this "merely to the presence of Southerners in the FBI." He observed that no arrest was made in Albany, GA in spite of the many brutalities against blacks during the civil rights demonstration nor in regard to the murdering of the four children in Birmingham, nor the murdering of the three civil rights workers in Mississippi.[19]

In his public statement concerning Hoover, King appeared to be less restrained. He suggested that the FBI chief had "apparently faltered under the awesome burden, complexities and responsibilities of his office." In a later interview, King contended that instead of being a critic of the Bureau, he had been a mediator--seeking to encourage African-Americans to maintain faith in the FBI, in spite of what they perceived to be a lack-luster record in the civil rights field. He noted the difficulties he faced in trying to explain to African-Americans "why a plane can be bombed and its pieces scattered for miles and the crime can be solved, but they can't find out who bombed a church." King was supported in his feud with Hoover by leaders of other major civil rights organizations, who informed the President that King's criticisms of the FBI represented the views of the black community.[20]

During the latter part of 1964, the Bureau apparently made its greatest effort to destroy King by mailing to Coretta, his wife, a composite tape of his activities, which included alleged sexual misbehavior. Along with the tape was a letter which began with the salutation: "King," noting that he did not deserve being referred to as "Mr.," "Reverend," or "Dr.". In the letter, King was advised to search his heart and realize that he was a "complete fraud and a great liability to his race." He was told that although he could have been a great leader, he had become a "dissolute, abnormal moral imbecile;" thus, in

[18] Garrow.
[19] Garrow, 122-123.
[20] Garrow, 124.

the future, blacks would have to rely upon such older leaders and men of character as Roy Wilkins. King was told that he was finished, and that even his honorary degrees and Nobel Prize, which was called a "grim farce," could not save him. The letter appeared to carry the implied suggestion that the famed civil rights leaders should commit suicide within the next 34 days in order to avoid embarrassment. He was advised that the tapes would expose him as "an evil abnormal beast," and damage his ties with church organizations and other supporters. According to Garror, the letter, which gave the appearance of having been written by a dissatisfied black, was actually written and mailed by an official of the FBI.[21]

Realizing that the Bureau's hostility was damaging to the civil rights cause, James Farmer, leader of CORE, and Roy Wilkins, executive secretary of the NAACP conferred with FBI officials. King also held a conference with Hoover and his associates, and used the occasion to express his dislike for Communists, and to advise them that his criticisms of the Bureau had been taken out of context. For the most part, however, the conference was dominated by Hoover's discussion of the role of the FBI. The meeting appeared to have accomplished very little; thus, the campaign to destroy King continued. Wiretapped tapes of King's activities were offered to *Newsweek*, and several newspapers, including: the *Chicago News*, *Los Angeles Times*, *New York Times*, *Los Angeles Times* and the *Atlanta Constitution.*[22]

Likewise, through the use of wiretap, the FBI was able to learn about possible financial contributions to King, and it sought to use this information to prevent them from taking place. When it was learned that Nelson Rockefeller might contribute $250,000 to the SCLC, the Bureau sought to brief the governor on what it considered to be the immoral activities of King.[23] The FBI also tried to prevent the Ford Foundation from making a similar grant, but McGeorge Bundy rejected the offer to hear the Bureau's evidence against King. It was successful, however, in halting a King-Hoffa meeting, which might have resulted in a contribution by the Teamsters. The Bureau publicized the intended meeting by leaking the plans to the press; thus, preventing King from proceeding with a talk which was to have been secret.[24]

---

[21] Garrow, 125-126.
[22] Garrow, 129-130.
[23] Garrow, 132.
[24] Garrow, 179.

The FBI sought to conduct its campaign against King through the press, by preparing news articles that were unfavorable to him, and through the release of damaging material. According to Garror, the Bureau prepared a newspaper article which criticized King's indecisive stance in regard to "Black Power," but apparently could not find a reporter who was willing to make use of it.[25] Likewise, the FBI attempted to use an editorial from a small black newspaper that was critical of King, by sending it to a national newspaper chain, but the latter refused to use it. Bureau officials believed that, if printed, the editorial would hamper the King-Belafonte money-raising efforts, and also would "publicize King as a traitor to his country and race."[26]

After King delivered his address at Riverside Church in April 1967, both the White House and the FBI intensified their concerns over his future plans. John P. Roach, an advisor of President Johnson suggested that the address was an indication that King had thrown in his lot with the "commies". In the meantime, officials in the FBI were claiming that "King's strong criticism and condemnation of the Administration's policy on Vietnam...shows how much he has been influenced by Communist advisers." His speech was compared with the Communist position on Vietnam. A letter from Hoover's office to President Johnson's personal secretary read: "Based on King's recent activities and public utterances, it is clear that he is an instrument in the hands of subversive forces seeking to undermine our nation."[27]

In December 1967, as plans were progressing for the Poor Peoples March, an intra-bureau memorandum suggested that because King had "urged massive civil disobedience throughout the country in an effort to spur Congress into action to help the plight of the Negro," it was necessary to install devices to secure the "racial intelligence information" concerning the plan. Such intelligence, the memorandum indicated, would enable the Bureau to take necessary countermeasures to ensure the internal security of the nation. Attorney General Ramsey Clark rejected the idea, informing Hoover that there did not appear to be adequate grounds for considering the demonstrations a direct threat to the security of the United States.[28]

In March 1968, as the FBI began to move more aggressively against what it considered to be "Black Nationalist Hate Groups," a report recommended

---

[25] Garrow.
[26] Garrow, 183.
[27] Garrow, 182.
[28] Garrow, 184.

that efforts be undertaken "to prevent the rise of a 'Messiah' who could unify, and electrify, the militant black nationalist movement." It suggested that King could be a serious contender for this position "if he abandoned his supposed obedience to white, liberal doctrines," [non-violence] and embraced "black nationalism."[29] Less than a month later, King was assassinated, but his death did not end the efforts by opponents to discredit him.

THE STATE VERSUS LUTHULI

In the effort to discredit Albert Luthuli and other foes of apartheid, not only did the Government rely upon existing laws, but also drafted new ones. One of the laws that was utilized was the Suppression of Communism Act of 1950, which considered opposition to apartheid as a means of furthering Communist objectives. Acting under its provisions, the South African Government reacted to the adoption of the Freedom Charter by arresting 156 opponents of apartheid, including Albert Luthuli and charging them with treason. They were accused of "being members of a conspiracy inspired by international Communism to overthrow the South African State by violence."[30]

In prosecuting the case, the State scrutinized, closely, the history of the ANC during the 1952-1956 period, with special attention given to the Freedom Charter. Specifically, the prosecutor sought to prove that "the accused were all members of the National Liberation Movement whose speakers had propagated the Marxist-Leninist account of society and the state." A second objective was to show that the Freedom Charter was designed to bring about a Communist state, if necessary, by revolution. The defense denied the charges, noting that "it was not 156 individuals who were on trial, but the ideas that they and thousands of others in our land [South Africa] have openly espoused and expressed." When the preliminary investigation was completed in September 1957, the magistrate found that there appeared to be sufficient evidence to try the accused on the charge of high treason.[31]

By the end of 1957, the charges of high treason against Luthuli and sixty-four others were dropped. He received this news with mixed emotion,

---

[29] Garrow, 187.
[30] Benson, *South Africa: The Struggle for a Birthright*, 189.
[31] Benson, 192-193.

preferring that his fate be decided along with the others who had been accused. Luthuli insisted that although he had been cleared of the charges, his organization was still on trial; thus, throughout the ordeal, he appeared as a witness for the defense.[32]

Although Luthuli was no longer one of the accused, the prosecutor sought to prove he was aware of the movement of the ANC away from its nonviolent course. During the interrogation, he was questioned concerning the alleged interest of the organization in overthrowing the ruling class. Luthuli's response was that the ANC was not seeking to overthrow the ruling class, but to provide greater opportunities for participation of Africans in the government. He insisted that it was never the purpose of the organization "to seize power in the sense of throwing out the White Government and replacing it by a Black Government." When pressed by the prosecution as to how this goal was to be obtained, Luthuli stressed the ANC's commitment to the promotion of justice through the changing of the attitudes of the white minority. He suggested that "through sheer moral persuasion," some whites would see the justice of the cause, while some others may need more extensive reeducation, due to their ignorance of the conditions of the oppressed, or their prejudice. The chief suggested that others might be appealed to through their vested interest.[33]

During the trial, Luthuli also responded to the implied accusation that the Freedom Charter was a revolutionary document, which could not be implemented without destroying the entire political and economic structure of the present South Africa. He agreed that under the Charter, the government would be radically and fundamentally different from that of the present system, but he maintained that the demands which were made in the Freedom Charter were no different from those stated in any other bill of rights.[34]

Anticipating the attempts to destroy his organization, Luthuli launched a campaign to enlighten the government of the true role of the ANC. In a letter to Prime Minister J. G. Strijdon in early 1957, he advised him that his organization was "deeply wedded to the ideals of democracy and has at all times emphasized its firm and unshakable belief in the need for the creation of a society in South Africa based on the upholding of democratic values..." The

[32] Luthuli, *Let My People Go*, 179.

[33] "Does the ANC Advocate Violence?" in Karis and Carter, *From Protest to Challenge III*, 583.

[34] Karis and Carter, 591-592.

letter challenged those in government who had accused the ANC of being highly subversive, and fostering a "communistic-tainted African nationalism or a rabid tyrannical and narrow African nationalism." Luthuli denied that Africans were seeking to deprive whites in South Africa of their fair participation in the government, insisting that "Congress believes in a common society and holds that citizens of a country, regardless of their race or colour, have the right to full participation in the government and in the control of their future." The Chief also used the occasion to respond to a press report concerning the Government's intention of banning the African National Congress and arresting many of its leading members, Luthuli warned that such a move would "increase the dangerous gulf that exists between the Government and the African people." He suggested that rather than silencing Congress and its leadership by such means as bannings and arrests, it would be wiser for the Government to endeavor to accommodate the "progressive aspirations of the African people."[35]

As indicated, the ANC was accused of being a Communistic-tainted organization, a charge which provoked Luthuli to respond. Although admitting that there were Communists within the resistance movement with whom he had cooperated, he insisted that the primary concern of the ANC was liberation, and in that struggle it did not intend "to be sidetracked by ideological clashes and witch hunts." According to Luthuli: "We leave our differing political theories on one side until the day of liberation, and in the meantime we are cooperating in a defined area, in the cause of liberation."[36] The Chief perceived true Christianity as being able to deter Communism. He suggested that "the Christian Faith, undiluted, and other creeds which assert justice and humility, whose strength is spiritual rather than material, are strong enough to withstand any onslaught." Luthuli warned that "were Communism to triumph, it would not be so much because of the zeal of the Communists as the failure of Christians."[37]

When the Treason Trial ended on March 29, 1961--after more than four years--the ANC was vindicated. The Courts found that the African National Congress had been infiltrated by the Communist. Based upon his perception of the evidence, the Judge concluded that the ANC and other organizations

[35] Luthuli, "Letter to the Prime Minister, Mr. J. G. Strijdom, May 28, 1957, in Karis and Carter, 396-403.

[36] Luthuli, *Let My People Go*, 154.

[37] Luthuli, 155.

were "working together to replace the present form of state with a fundamentally different form of state based on the demands of the Freedom Charter," but there was no evidence indicating that the type of state envisioned was a Communist state. The victory might have been a hollow one, however, since the Government, acting through legislative and administrative means, had outlawed the ANC approximately one year prior to the end of the trial.[38]

With the ANC outlawed, Luthuli had no organization in which to be President-General. Not satisfied with having weakened him significantly, the Government utilized the Sabotage Act of 1962 to further limit his influence. Declaring Luthuli guilty of engaging in prohibited activities and espousing the cause of Communism, the Government, on May 25, 1964, imposed upon him a fourth ban. It became a serious offense for his remarks or writings to be published. Anyone who quoted Luthuli was liable to imprisonment for up to three years.[39]

Luthuli's words were more limited in South Africa than abroad. His autobiography, *Let My People Go*, which was published in 1962, although banned in South Africa, continues to tell the story of his struggle to the outside world. Likewise, his statement responding to the Rivonia Trial, in which Nelson Mandela and others had been sentenced to life imprisonment, was read before the United Nations Security Council by the representative of Morocco. Although silenced by the Government of South Africa, after death his voice has spoken even louder, especially to the rest of the world.

THE CHURCH IS ACCUSED

With all of the liberation organizations banned, the task of spearheading the anti-apartheid drive fell on the shoulders of the Church. Assuming a major role as a spokesperson for the oppressed was Bishop Desmond Tutu who, in 1978, became the general secretary of the South African Council of Churches. Inasmuch as the country had included a strong commitment to Christianity in its constitution, the Government, at times, found itself in an embarrassing position when dealing with the overt opposition of the Church to its racist policies. Not being able to check the influence of Tutu by depriving him of his passport, the Government sought other means of silencing him, including the

[38] Callan, *Albert John Luthuli and the South African Race Conflict*, 35.
[39] Benson, 66.

discrediting of the South African Council of Churches (SACC), which he headed.

Prior to Tutu assuming office as general secretary of the South African Council of Churches, the Government made clear its opposition to ties between the SACC and the World Council of Churches, which it perceived as a Communist front. Likewise, the Government condemned liberation theology, which it also equated with Communist doctrine. Inasmuch as Bishop Tutu continued to preach liberation theology, and retained ties with the World Council of Churches, it was inevitable that the Government would "crack down" on his activities--using the argument that it was fighting the spread of Communism.

In 1979, Police Minister Louis Le Grange condemned the Council--which he perceived as being led by "leftist ministers,"-- for its "propaganda actions." He denounced the SACC for its encouragement of civil disobedience, disinvestment in South Africa, and conscientious objection to military service. Likewise, he deplored its condemnation of security legislation, caring for families of political detainees, financing political trials, and "describing the government as suppressive and illegal and giving whites a 'guilty conscience.'"[40]

In response, Bishop Tutu expressed shock that a person in such a "responsible position could speak so irresponsibly." The Bishop insisted that "The SACC and the Churches reserve the right to condemn, if need be, any legislation which is abhorrent to the Christian conscience, and which represents an abrogation of the rule of law." He listed detention without trial and arbitrary banning as being in the above category.[41] Likewise, he informed the minister that "if it was a crime to provide relief for political detainees, and for providing legal defense for those involved in political trial," then the SACC "openly and proudly pleads guilty." Tutu maintained that everyone should be provided with the best defense possible; therefore, the Council should be praised rather than condemned for its role in this critical area. The Bishop reminded the Government that although the SACC had expressed criticisms of the role played by foreign investment, it had not, at that time, suggested a withdrawal of investments. He also accused the minister of gross untruth, when he stated that funds were being distributed by the Council to the

---

[40] Caryle Murphy, "S. African Bishop Takes Defiant Stance Against Rule of White Minority," *The Washington Post*, June 10, 1980.

[41] Tutu, *Crying in the Wilderness*, 50.

resistance movement. Tutu questioned why they were not being persecuted if they were doing what was obviously illegal in South Africa He challenged the ministers to stop playing God. Tutu insisted that "they are human beings who happen to be carrying out an unjust and oppressive policy with a whole range of draconian code." He reminded the Government that the SACC is a Council of Churches, and that the Church has existed for almost 2000 years. During that period tyrants and others have tried to persecute it, but they have failed. According to Tutu "the Church of God remains, an agent of justice, of peace, of love and reconciliation. If they take the SACC and the Churches on, let them just know they are taking on the Church of Jesus Christ."[42]

Lower governmental ministers were not alone in attacking the SACC, Prime Minister Pieter Botha also joined the chorus, accusing the Council of distributing more than three million dollars for the promotion of unrest within South Africa. He perceived a linkage between civil disobedience and the banned ANC. Tutu expressed disgust over such allegations, insisting that if the Government possessed evidence of such nefarious activities by the Council, why not bring charges openly in the court.[43] Following attacks upon the SACC by governmental ministers, and reports of two commissions, the Government appointed the Eloff Commission to investigate such matters as the Council's interpretation of its foreign ties and its financial records. In a report by a commission which was established to investigate the media, extensive references were made to what was perceived as Bishop Tutu's role in a "'total onslaught' against South Africa by forces ranging from the World Council of Churches to the Soviet government and the 'anti-South African establishment in the U.S.A.'" According to the report, the World Council of Churches and the South African Council of Churches "are actively engaged in violently anti-South African, left-radical liberation politics which include open support for the terror attack on South Africa--an attack they seek to sanctify by the invocation of the theology of revolutionary liberation."[44] Thus, when Tutu appeared before the Eloff Commission he was aware of the many accusations which had been made.

During his testimony before the Commission, Tutu cited both Scripture and hallowed Christian tradition and teaching to justify the role which the SACC was playing At the outset, he made clear that the Council did not owe

[42] Tutu, 50-52.
[43] Allister Sparks, "Black Cleric in S. Africa," *The Washington Post*, Sept 4, 1982.
[44] Tutu, *Hope and Suffering*, 153-154.

its loyalty to "any human authority however, prestigious or powerful, but to God and to His Son, Our Lord Jesus Christ alone, from which we obtain our mandate." He advised that "we must obey the divine imperative and word whatever the cost." The Bishop emphasized that what was on trial was not the finances or activities of the SACC; instead, its Christian faith and that of its member churches. Tutu maintained that it was their Christianity that was being scrutinized. He concluded that they were being tried for being Christian by a Government which claimed to be Christian. The Bishop insisted that "it may be that we are being told that it is an offense to be a Christian in South Africa."[45] Tutu challenged the right of any secular authority or its appointed commission to determine what is a church and what should be the nature of the Gospel of Jesus Christ. He did not consider the theological existence of the SACC as being a matter in which the Commission had a right to conduct an inquiry. Tutu argued that only member churches can do that.[46]

Bishop Tutu felt compelled to respond to the criticism that the SACC was accepting money from foreign sources. He maintained that while we may want local churches to be self-supporting, such is not the case; thus, "it is no aberration for a more affluent part of the Church to give of its wealth, of which it is only a steward on behalf of God--when one part suffers the whole suffers with it and when one part rejoices the whole rejoices with it."[47]

Also appearing before the Commission was Lieutenant General Johann Coetzee, the security police chief and close advisor to the Prime Minister, who expressed concern that the Council, under the administration of Bishop Tutu had used funds obtained from abroad to advance the cause of the ANC. He urged the Government to declare the ANC an "affected organization," which would make it illegal for it to accept foreign funds. He also recommended that limits be placed upon the Council's ability to raise funds within the country. According to the chief, such could be accomplished by "withdrawing the immunity it has from a law that requires organizations to submit their bylaws and financial statements to the Government as part of a formal application for a license to raise funds." In order to convince the Commission of the need to restrict the SACC, Coetzee showed documents from television of various activities in which the organization was involved.[48]

---

[45] Tutu, 154.
[46] Tutu, 157.
[47] Tutu.
[48] Joseph Lelyveld, "Pretoria Police Take on Church Council," *New York Times* Feb. 15, 1983.

In its report, the Eloff Commission did not recommend the banning of the SACC, since it was not a "tool of foreign manipulators." It concluded that although the money spent by the organization for aiding "the needy and deserving was meagre when compared with that used mainly for political purposes, innocent people will suffer if the SACC were to be rendered largely ineffective." The Commission was critical of the way the finances of the organization were administered, noting the fraud associated with the administration of the previous general secretary. It recommended that a law be passed "making advocacy of international disinvestment in South Africa criminally punishable as 'economic sabotage'." Likewise, Tutu was denounced for statements which he made criticizing military conscription and "lending respectability to the African National Congress."[49]

Contrary to expectations, the accusations, investigations, and threats by the Government did not deter Bishop Tutu in his campaign for a just society. He continued to insist that in carrying out the assignments of God, he had nothing to fear. Apparently, the Government also perceived a direct attack upon the Bishop as being counterproductive; therefore, it did not take extreme measures against him and the SACC, as it had done in the case of Luthuli, years earlier.

Throughout history, those who possessed economic and political powers attempted to preserve the status quo by accusing reformers of seeking to overthrow the state. With the advent of the Cold War, with its anti-Communist mania, another dimension was added. Not only were reformers accused of undermining the present system, they were also perceived as pursuing their goals in the interest of international Communism. Opponents of social reform; therefore, tried to derail the campaigns of Gandhi, King, Luthuli, and Tutu by portraying them as anti-patriotic.

[49] *Current Biography Yearbook*, 1985, 420. XI Farewell to the Prophets, but not Their Prophesies

Chapter 11

FAREWELL TO THE PROPHETS, BUT NOT THEIR PROPHESIES

> Martin had the great advantage of drawing from Gandhi's historical legacy. But Gandhi had no such body of recorded experience because the rich though hidden, heritage of nonviolent struggle had not yet been systematically documented.[1]
>
> Coretta Scott King

When Gandhi was assassinated on January 30, 1948, Prime Minister Nehru announced to the people of India that "the light had gone out of our lives and there is darkness everywhere." While it was true that their beloved Gandhi would no longer dwell among them and offer advice and consolation, the light which he had lit, never again could be extinguished. Nehru indicated that the light which had guided the Indians for years would continue to illumine the country, and "a thousand years later that light will still be seen in this country and the world will see it and it will give solace to innumerable hearts."[2]

Not only were tributes paid to Gandhi by the people of India, but by the international community, as well. Kings, prime ministers, presidents, diplomats, scholars and people from all walks of life praised his contributions. In mourning his death, Sir Stafford Cripps, who negotiated with Gandhi concerning independence for India, questioned if leaders can be found today

---

1 Gene Sharp, *Gandhi as a Political Strategist*, Boston: Porter Sargent Publishers, Inc. 1979, x

2 Jawaharlal Nehru, "The Light Has Gone Out," in *Homage to Mahatma Gandhi* (New Delhi: Ministry of Information and Broadcasting, 1948), 9-10.

"who are able to emphasize by their own life and actions the overpowering force of love in solving our difficulties." He expressed hope that we will learn that "it is idle to try and save ourselves from destruction by the use of force and that our greatest weapon of salvation is the supreme and redeeming power of love."[3]

Unlike the death of Gandhi, the passing of Luthuli in 1967 was not marked by an official period of mourning in his home country. The Government had no tribute to pay to the man whom it perceived as trying to destroy their "beloved South Africa." Restrictions, bans and other means of repression, however, could not prevent others from noting his departure. Typical of such tributes was one given by Alan Paton, a white South African who had been active in the struggle to bring about a just society. He praised the deceased for having done what other heroes have done, noting that "He stood for the rights of his people, for the rights of all people, for the rights of the dispossessed, for the rights of the poor, for the rights of the voiceless." Because of his attempt to speak for others, Paton observed, he was compelled to make a choice between "his chieftainship and his rights as a man to fight for what he thought was good." Luthuli made his choice and was willing to suffer, and even die for what he considered to be right. According to Paton, "They took away his chieftainship, but he never ceased to be the chief. They took away his temporal power, but he never ceased to have his spiritual power. They took away his freedom, but he never ceased to be free. He was indeed more free than those who had bound him."[4] Apparently other admirers of Luthuli, although less vocal, echoed the sentiments expressed so eloquently by Paton. In their silent tributes they resolved to continue the efforts of their fallen leader and thereby build a South Africa in which Luthuli will be accorded the recognition he deserves.

When Martin Luther King, Jr. was assassinated in Memphis on April 4, 1968, the United States entered a period of official mourning. President Lyndon Johnson expressed sadness over the tragedy, noting that although King had been struck down "by the violence against which he preached and worked...the cause for which he struggled has not fallen." The President advised the nation that "the voice that called for justice and brotherhood has been stilled but the quest for freedom to which he [King] gave eloquent

[3] S. Radhakrishnan, ed., *Mahatma Gandhi* (London: George Allen & Unwin Ltd., 1939), 385.
[4] Alan Paton, "In Memoriam: Albert Luthuli" *Christianity and Crisis,* XXVII, 5, Sept. 18, 1967, 206-207.

expression continues." He called upon Americans of all races, religions, and regions to unite their efforts "to deny violence its victory, and to fulfill the vision of brotherhood that gave purpose to Martin Luther King's life and works."[5]

Nearly ten years after his death, the United States recognized the achievement of King by bestowing upon him posthumously, the Presidential Medal of Freedom, the highest award given to a civilian in the United States. In making the presentation, President Carter noted King's "unswerving dedication, superb courage, sensitivity and humility and a dedication to peace."[6] The citation read, in part, "Martin Luther King, Jr. was the conscience of his generation. He gazed upon the great wall of segregation and saw that the power of love could bring it down....He made our nation stronger because he made it better. His dream sustains us yet."[7]

After a democratic government had been achieved in South Africa, and Archbishop Tutu willingly relinquished his leadership position in the struggle for racial equality, his efforts were noted by President Mandela. He praised him for his "selfless commitment to the poor, the oppressed and downtrodden." Tutu was perceived as "an effective voice of the people of South Africa when so many of their leaders were imprisoned, exiled, banned and restricted." According to Mandela:

> Desmond Tutu is esteemed the world over for his commitment to justice and peace everywhere. He is forthright in condemning corruption. As President of the All Africa Conference of Churches he missed no opportunity to speak out against human rights violations and oppressive regimes in our continent and elsewhere. The Nobel Peace Prize measures his extensive international recognition.[8]

Mandela thanked "the Archbishop for his valuable contribution to the struggle for freedom and justice."

---

[5] US President, *Public Papers of the Presidents of the United States* (Washington, DC: Office of the *Federal Register*, National Archives and Records Service, 1968-69) Lyndon B. Johnson.1968-69, I, 180-181.

[6] US Presidents, (1977), Jimmy Carter, 1977, 964.

[7] Carter.

[8] "Mandela's Speech at Thanksgiving for Tutu," 23 June, 1996, Issued by Office of the President Republic of South Africa.

Although the death of three of the prophets have been mourned, the legacies they created continue to inspire others to seek the realization of their prophecies. Illustrative of this is Gandhi's dream of a just society which not only survived him in India, but in other parts of the world as well. While many of those dreams remain unfulfilled, devoted apostles of nonviolent resistance continue to believe that they can be accomplished. This is a fitting tribute to the Mahatma, who waged his struggle for social justice, primarily, in South Africa and India, but envisioned his efforts as having universal applications. He perceived the nonviolent struggle in India as providing an excellent model for oppressed people throughout the world who were seeking to obtain liberation. Gandhi suggested that India could promote peace by resisting her exploitation by peaceful means. He maintained that if it could achieve independence by nonviolent resistance, this would be the greatest contribution any nation could make to world peace.[9]

Perhaps, nowhere was the Gandhian influence more apparent than in the United States. Even before the death of the Mahatma, African-Americans were studying his philosophy and seeking to apply it to the struggle for racial equality in this country. In order to better understand nonviolent resistance, several African-Americans visited Gandhi during the mid-thirties. Among those making the pilgrimage were the noted theologian, Howard Thurman and his wife. They appealed to the Mahatma to come to the United States and assist African-Americans in their struggle. Although sympathetic with their plight, Gandhi advised them that the message had to be made effective in India, before he could carry it abroad. He continued, "I do not say that I am defeated, but I have still to perfect myself. You may be sure that the moment I feel the call within me I shall not hesitate."[10] As they terminated their conversation, Gandhi suggested that it may be "through the Negroes that the unadulterated message of non-violence will be delivered to the world."[11]

Gandhi also received as his guest, Channing Tobias, the director of the Phelps-Stokes Fund, who expressed appreciation to the Mahatma for the impact which his non-violent campaign had made upon him. He, then, inquired as to how African-Americans struggling to obtain freedom from

---

[9] Gandhi, *Young India*, July 4, 1929, reprinted in R. K. Prabhu, *India of My Dream* (Ahmedabad: Navajivan Publishing House, 1947), 78.

[10] M. K. Gandhi, *Nonviolence in Peace and War* (Ahmedabad: Navajivan Publishing House, 1962), I, 124.

[11] Gandhi, 124.

segregation could best employ nonviolent resistance. Acknowledging that he, too, had faced similar racial discrimination in South Africa during his stay there, Gandhi endorsed nonviolence as the only feasible approach. He advised African-Americans that "with right which is on their side and the choice of non-violence as their only weapon, if they will make it such, a bright future is assured."[12]

Gandhi also received as guest, Dr. Benjamin Mays, an educator, who later became the president of Morehouse College. The latter expressed concern over the effectiveness of a minority using nonviolent resistance as a weapon against an overwhelming majority. In his reply, Gandhi insisted that "a minority can do much more in the way of non-violence than a majority." He recalled that during his stay in South Africa he had less difficulty leading his Indian minority than he did in his home country where Indians constituted the majority.[13] He hastened to say, however, that the conclusion should not be drawn that nonviolence is a weapon of the weak. During his conversation with Mays, the Mahatma sought to dispel the idea that his word was the final one in regard to nonviolence, observing that he had limitations, and that he was only "a humble seeker after truth." He noted that every experiment had extended his "faith in non-violence as the greatest force at the disposal of mankind." Gandhi suggested that "its use is not restricted to individuals merely, but it can be practised on a mass scale."[14]

The use of nonviolent resistance on a mass scale was what attracted many American civil rights leaders to Gandhian methods. Amiya Chakravarty contended that what was needed most in the struggle for racial equality in the United States was a "dynamic personality" that could clarify and vocalize "the emotion fermenting for the wanted change." During the mid-fifties, a young African-American admirer of Gandhi emerged upon the scene and was successful in using his nonviolent methods to restructure American race relations. Chakravarty noting that "it was in the person of Dr. Martin Luther King that the movement gained its greatest clarity," concluded "Through his life he was able to bring together, again and again, the different strands of

[12] Gandhi, 137.
[13] Gandhi, 141.
[14] Gandhi, 142.

protest and unite them into a single direction, to mould the many fires into a blaze aimed directly at injustice."[15]

King was very impressed with Gandhi's ability "to lift the love ethic of Jesus above mere interaction between individuals to a powerful and effective social force on a large scale."[16] As King embarked on a serious study of Gandhi's works, he was inspired to use many of his strategies in his efforts to alleviate the plight of African-Americans. He was aware, however, that because of differences in the situation, methods employed by Gandhi were not always applicable to the civil rights struggle. John Ansboro suggested that in assessing the techniques used by the two nonviolent leaders, one should understand that "Gandhi was seeking independence from an alien system," while "King's goal was the transforming of the structures of the existing system so that all citizens could experience integration within the system."[17]

Although King never had the privilege of conversing with the Mahatma, he did derive inspiration from his pilgrimage to the land of Gandhi which he undertook in 1959 in response to an invitation from the Gandhi National Memorial Fund. Upon his arrival in India, he remarked, "To other countries I may go as a tourist, but to India I come as a pilgrim. This is because India means to me Mahatma Gandhi, a truly great man of the age."[18]

While the author found no statement to support the belief that Luthuli was a student of Gandhian thought, there are strong indications that he was aware of the efforts of the nonviolent leader--especially as they related to the struggle for a just society in South Africa. It should also be remembered that Luthuli was a visitor to India in 1938, a time in which Gandhi was in the midst of his campaign for liberation of his country.

To what extent did the struggle of Luthuli influence the efforts of King, or the reverse? In a sense, the two were contemporaries and were somewhat aware of their common efforts. The repressive regime in South Africa, however, prevented Luthuli from being as well informed concerning the civil rights campaign in the United States as was King's awareness of the liberation efforts in South Africa. Unfortunately, Luthuli was under South African bans during most of the major events associated with the American Civil Rights

---

[15] Amiya Chakravarty, "Satyagraha and the Race Problem in America," in Sibnarayan Ray, *Gandhi's India and the World* (Philadelphia: Temple University Press, 1970)308.
[16] King, *Stride Toward Freedom*, 97.
[17] John Ansboro, *Martin Luther King, Jr.: The Making of a Mind* (Maryknoll, New York: Orbis Books, 1982), 134.
[18] Lewis, *King: A Biography*, 99.

Revolution; thus, was unable to receive information relative to them. King, on the other hand, maintained an interest in the various battles being waged in South Africa, and often expressed admiration for those leading the struggle. He sought to send a copy of *Strides Toward Freedom*, the book he authored, to Luthuli. In 1962, through the efforts of the American Committee on Africa, the two leaders collaborated in a joint statement condemning apartheid. Much to the dismay of their followers, both men died tragically, with the assassination of King taking place within a year of that of Luthuli.

When Desmond Tutu emerged on the scene as a leader of nonviolent resistance, the legacies of Gandhi, King, and Luthuli were there to guide him. Having grown up in South Africa, the Archbishop was quite familiar with the historic struggles that had been waged against racial injustice by Gandhi and Luthuli. Likewise, his frequent visits to the United States made him aware of the philosophy and strategies of King. On numerous occasions, he made reference to the valuable contributions, which the American civil rights leader had made to the cause of social justice. To many observers, the efforts of the Archbishop have been compared with those of King, whom he admired greatly. When Howard University awarded an honorary degree to Tutu in 1985, the citation read: "Like King, you have never softened your attacks on the government through fear for your personal safety."[19] Likewise, the *Christian Century* noted the similarities between the two leaders, but it suggested that although "US racial segregation during Martin Luther King, Jr.'s time was ugly, demeaning and oppressive," compared to South African apartheid, "it was but a troublesome wrinkle in the nation's social fabric."[20] In 1986, perceiving Tutu as following a path similar to that of the assassinated American civil rights leader, the Martin Luther King, Jr. Center for Nonviolent Social Change presented the Archbishop with the prestigious Martin Luther King Award.

With Gandhi, King and Luthuli no longer on the scene, how has history noted their achievements? As indicated earlier, official recognition has been accorded the contributions of both Gandhi and King by the observance of their birthdays as national holidays, but no such recognition was given to the contributions of Luthuli by the racist government of South Africa. The United Nations, however, has praised the efforts of the latter, regarding them as

[19] *New Direction*, (Howard University), Jan. 1985, 25.
[20] *Christian Century*, Jan. 2-9, 1983, 3

meaningful steps toward the achievement of a peaceful and just South African society. Generally, historians have credited these prophets of social justice as making valuable contributions, not only to their respective nations, but to the world at large.

In assessing these prophets, consideration must be given to the extent to which they achieved the goals they sought. During Gandhi's campaign, he sought to obtain: (1) better treatment for Indians in South Africa, (2) the independence of India, (3) harmonious relations between Hindus and Moslems, and (4) the ending of untouchability. When Gandhi left South Africa in 1914, he expressed satisfaction with the gains which had been made by Indians in their struggle for better treatment. He was less satisfied, however, with the achievement of his second objective. Even though his beloved country had gained its independence from Great Britain by the time of his death, it did not afford him the jubilation which he had anticipated. The Mahatma devoted his life to the obtaining of independence for a unified India, but such was not to be the case, inasmuch as the country achieved nationhood as two independent states--India and Pakistan. Also to Gandhi's regret, hostility between the Hindus and Moslems outlived him. Perhaps, India's effort to create a better life for the untouchables will stand out as that country's greatest tribute to the beloved Mahatma.

More than three decades after the death of King, how do we assess his accomplishments in regard to: (1) the ending of racial segregation, (2) the establishment of equal voting rights, (3) the elimination of poverty, and (4) the maintenance of world peace? In regard to the first two goals, it can be said that his campaigns were very instrumental in the adoption of laws that recognized the plights of African-Americans in such crucial fields as accommodations, employment opportunities, and voting, but in regard to the third and fourth goals, King's appeals appeared to have fallen on "deaf ears." Many of those who supported his efforts to obtain the first two goals, turned away from him when he initiated widescale campaigns against poverty and the War in Vietnam. While the Government did institute programs designed to eliminate poverty, King considered these efforts to be inadequate. In years that followed, a more conservative mood dominated American politics, with the Government being less willing to embrace programs that were designed to erase poverty from American life. During his life time, King was criticized bitterly for his opposition to the War in Vietnam, but after his death, many Americans began to adopt his view. Were King alive, he would have found comfort in this change of attitude, but more than likely he would have been dismayed over the limited strides which the country has made toward making war a thing of the past.

Like Gandhi and King, Luthuli envisioned a just society, and he dedicated his life to bringing into existence a state in which there would be a truly democratic government. As a realist, Luthuli was aware that such a society could not be brought about overnight, but he considered it to be a major task of the government to achieve such without inflicting harm on industry, commerce, farming and education. At the time of the Chief's death in 1967, South Africa was not marching in the direction of the goals which he had sought, but rather was growing more hostile to those who were waging the fight for liberation. While Luthuli did not achieve his desired goals, he could be credited with being the thorn in the side of the South African Government, which constantly made it aware of the determination of Africans to obtain their freedom, regardless of the obstacles placed in their paths.

Archbishop Tutu stated that he had assumed a prominent leadership position in the struggle against racial oppression because the legitimate African leaders were either in prison or in exile. The freeing of Nelson Mandela and the unbanning of the ANC and similar organizations made it possible for him to return to a position more consistent with his title. His real victory, however, was achieved with the inauguration of Mandela as the first president of a democratic South Africa on May 10, 1994. The prayer Tutu offered on that occasion suggested that he felt that his involvement had not been in vain. He prayed:

> Thank you, O God, for freeing our country from racism and oppression and for liberating all our people. Thank you for the courage of those who initiated change. Thank you, O God, for those who sacrificed their freedom and even their lives in the struggle for justice. Thank you for bringing those who were previously enemies around the same table to achieve a negotiated settlement...[21]

He also thanked God for those in and outside the country which contributed to the victory and he asked God's blessing on South Africa and its beautiful people.

---

[21] Tutu, *The Rainbow People of God*, 268.

Tutu's prayer also included a plea that reconciliation could be obtained. His prayer was answered, in part, when he was appointed to head the nation's Truth and Reconciliation Commission. In this new assignment he perceived himself as working as an agent of God to accomplish what he had prayed for--reconciliation. The completion of this new assignment ended a phase in which the Archbishop had played a prominent role in efforts to achieve both racial justice and reconciliation. His feeling of having planted seeds of success, perhaps, can best be expressed in words he used to end his book, *No Future Without Forgiveness:*

> Our experiment is going to succeed because God wants us to succeed, not for our glory and aggrandizement but for the sake of God's world. God wants to show that there is life after conflict and repression—that because of forgiveness there is a future.[22]

Too often Gandhi is associated only with the independence of India, and King with the successful civil rights struggle in the United States. If they are judged only by those standards, there is little doubt about their unparalleled success. Gandhi found no reason, however, to rejoice over his accomplishments since to him the important thing was not the gaining of independence for India; instead, his inability to persuade Moslems and Hindus to live together in harmony, and his failure to convince Hindus of their error in continuing to regard their brothers and sisters as untouchables.

Likewise, King refused to divorce his struggle for civil rights from the broader struggle for social justice. According to Smith and Zepp, "King's vision of the future included a society which would be free not only from the malformation of persons resulting from racial hatred but also free from the abnormality of persons resulting from economic injustice and exploitation."[23] Although King regarded justice for African-Americans as a major objective, he realized that the struggle to obtain it could not be waged in isolation. The racial plight of African-Americans, as he perceived it, was intertwined with other social and economic problems; thus, all had to be dealt with simultaneously. To him, racial injustice, poverty, and war were all threats to the well-being of the oppressed.[24]

---

[22] Tutu, *No Future Without Forgiveness*, 282.
[23] Smith and Zepps, *Search for the Beloved Community*, 122.
[24] Tutu, *Crying in the Wilderness*, 101.

Rather than judging Gandhi, King, and Luthuli on their successes and failures in the campaigns which they waged within their home countries, one should view them from a global perspective. It is from the latter that we are able to gain a better perception of their contributions. Not only have their use of nonviolent resistance contributed directly to world peace, but it also inspired others to use similar methods. Today, throughout the world, advocates of social justice continue to build upon foundations laid by Mohandas Gandhi, Martin Luther King, Jr., and Albert J. Luthuli.

Fortunately, the prophets of social justice left guidelines for future human rights leaders to follow. Not only did they leave apostles, who were willing to take up the battle, but also writings which detailed their philosophies and strategies. Among the works of Gandhi which have been frequently quoted are: *My Autobiography*, *The Story of My Experience with Truth*, *Satyagraha in South Africa*, and *Indian Home Rule***.** King also left a body of writings to guide his followers, including: *Strides Toward Freedom*, *Why We Can't Wait*, and *Where Do We Go From Here*. Although kept under close surveillance during most of his active life, Luthuli was able to describe his struggle in his autobiography, *Let My People Go*. While this book was initially banned in his homeland, it helped to enlighten the rest of the world on conditions in South Africa and on the nonviolent campaign to bring about change in South Africa.

Supplementing the works of the prophets were those written by scholars and activists associated with their various campaigns. The Indian Government published a multi-volume study of the Gandhian movement, as well as a collection of writings by Gandhi. A similar project was undertaken in regard to Martin Luther King, Jr.

The legacies of the prophets also are being kept alive by organizations and programs that are dedicated to the perpetuation of their philosophies, ideals and teachings. Outstanding among them are the Gandhi Peace Foundation of India, the Mahatma Gandhi Memorial Foundation of Washington, DC, the Lutuli Memorial Foundation of London and the Martin Luther King, Jr. Center for Nonviolent Social Change of Atlanta. The prophecies also are kept alive by scholars associated with special study programs at major universities.

In comparing the campaigns of the four advocates of social justice, several conclusions can be drawn. Firstly, recognizing that they could not use the political weapon effectively, each utilized the "appeal to conscience" both domestically and internationally. Use of this weapon on the international level was very important since the failure of the particular government to respond to the call for social justice tended to compromise that nation's standing in international affairs. While the media played an important role in internationalizing the Gandhian struggle in India, it was more effective in the King campaign in the United States. The expanding influence of television combined with the growing impact of Third World nations on the Cold War aided King greatly. Unlike Great Britain and the United States, South Africa was more repressive in regard to the media, nevertheless the conflict there was internationalized. It can also be said that the awarding of Nobel Peace Prizes to Luthuli, King and Tutu enhanced the internationalization of their causes.

Secondly, it can be concluded that nonviolent campaigns can be conducted successfully both by oppressed minorities and oppressed majorities. In the cases of Gandhi in South Africa and King in the United States campaigns were waged by minorities, but in the cases of Gandhi in India and Luthuli and Tutu in South Africa the struggles were led by groups composing the majority. In India and South Africa majorities were seeking rights denied them by their respective constitutions, but in the United States, African-Americans were seeking rights which they were entitled to under the national constitution.

Thirdly, in all cases advocates of social justice encountered strong opposition from those who controlled the social, political and economic structures of their respective nations. Likewise, in all instances governmental officials sought to derail the movements, sometimes by illegal means.

Lastly, as indicated above, advocates of nonviolence tended to benefit from the philosophies and strategies of those who proceeded them. King and Tutu benefited from the teaching and experience of Gandhi, and Tutu profited from the philosophy of Gandhi and the road paved by King. In recent years, advocates of social justice throughout the world have sought to emulate Gandhi, King, Luthuli and Tutu.

Of the four prophets, only Archbishop Desmond Tutu remains on the field of battle. Although South Africa is now under African leadership, he continues to look forward to a nation that is "more open and more just." In a general sense this was the goal which Gandhi, King, and Luthuli sought. They have now gone to join the prophets of old. Gone are these prophets, but not their prophecies. Others will arrive on the scene and accept the challenge of the Prophet Isaiah, to "cease to do evil, learn to do right, pursue justice and champion the oppressed."

INDEX

A

B

C

D

E

F

G

H

I

M

N

S

T

U

V

W

Y

Z